Nimrod Chronicles

LIFE IN NIMROD, MINNESOTA

Jerry Mevissen

North Star Press of St. Cloud, Inc.

ISBN: 0-87839-192-4

First Edition, August 2003

Printed in the United States of America by
Versa Press, Inc., East Peoria, Illinois.

Published by
North Star Press of St. Cloud, Inc.
P.O. Box 451
St. Cloud, Minnesota 56302
nspress@cloudnet.com

Dedication

To the people of Nimrod, Minnesota, for their friendship and inspiration

CONTENTS

Summer

Fall

INTRODUCTION

WHEN HENRY BUTZIN, NEIGHBOR, FRIEND, and resident woodsman, died in 2000, I wrote a eulogy with the intent of reading it at his wake or funeral. I couldn't muster the courage. Tim Bloomquist, editor of the *Review Messenger*, agreed to print it, which led to discussion of a weekly column. And so, the *Nimrod Chronicles* was born. Now, two and a half years later, there are enough Chronicles to fill a book.

Subject matter for the columns meanders from local history to current events, profiles of contemporary and historical residents, essays, and humor. My criterion is that the subject reside or occur within a five mile radius of Nimrod. That may sound like a challenge, with Nimrod having a population of seventy-five. Not so. There's material here for a dozen books, a few of which have already been written.

Rural and small-town life has been mined for literature many times. It's a tribute to its richness that there are still stories to be told. The richness comes, I think, from lives having been tested, and survived. Self-reliance is worn like an old seed-corn hat. And it makes good fodder for writers.

I thank Tim Bloomquist for the opportunity and the challenge of writing a weekly column and for the freedom of expression he granted. I thank the editorial team: Cindie Ekren, Bernice Eckenrode, and Linda Kuschel, who grappled with a stack of columns, selecting this one, tossing that one, offering revision advice, never making a bad column good, but often making a good column better. Finally, I thank my Nimrod neighbors and friends who dispelled the theory that a person must be born into a community to be a part of it.

My first column was "Requiem for Henry." Appropriately, it is the first chronicle in the book.

Jerry Mevissen, July 15, 2003

Winter

REQUIEM FOR HENRY

WE BURIED HENRY ON SATURDAY. Henry Butzin: husband, father, grandfather, brother, neighbor, friend. I fell in the last category.

I met Henry shortly after I bought land in the Nimrod area seven years ago. My wooded fifty acres hadn't been managed. The woods were mostly mature popple and jackpines, with some red and white oaks, birches and basswood, and ash closer to the river. That, and a jungle of hazelnut brush.

I asked my neighbors for recommendations for a woods clearer; the answer was unanimous—Henry.

I met Henry at the Nimrod Bar & Grill and asked if he had interest in selectively cutting my woods. Yes, he would cut, but he had one job to finish, another to start, and there was a possibility of a third. A qualified maybe. I was beginning to learn an important lesson: the future unfolds at my time, and the future unfolds at Nimrod time. They aren't always the same.

In due time, Henry's time, he appeared with his International tractor and skidder and started clearing. Henry worked slowly, methodically, carefully; sawing popples and jacks, skidding them to the landing, and cutting them in bolts.

During this time, Jeff Pederson began building the house. Henry selected choice popples for the ceiling boards. He detoured north and selected black ash for the floor. I walked through the woods with him, looking for candidate trees. A tree that looked good to me didn't always look good to Henry.

"Take a look from this side. It's got a bend twelve feet up."

PHOTO COURTESY MRS. HENRY BUTZIN

After the trees were cut, the boards sawed and kiln dried, and the lumber planed, it returned to within a few hundred yards of where it grew. Henry was the late afternoon construction foreman, stopping after work in the woods to monitor progress.

It's not a "Henry" house, but he did take pride in it. And ownership. He led visitors on tours during and after construction, providing details on the complex design and the source of the lumber. And with his characteristic grin, he would say, "I cut that myself."

He wore a copper wrist band to combat rheumatism in his shoulders. But he baffled me with the three potatoes, hard as golf balls, he carried to relieve aching knees. I can't argue with success, Henry. It worked for you. You bounced on and off the tractor like a teenager.

I got the news of Henry's death at noon on December 5. Massive heart attack, I heard, while ice fishing with his brother. It was hard to believe and impossible to accept. But Henry remains around me. The ash floor I walk on, the popple ceiling over my head, the jack pine in the fireplace. The cleared pasture, the tractor and peeler parked in the snow along the driveway.

I hardly knew you, Henry, when I looked in the casket. Your flannel shirt was bleached white. Your chore jacket tailored into a navy-blue suit. Your face shaved slick as glass. And I can't remember seeing you without a cap.

You had a habit of getting the last word, always had a final comment after the final comment. Well, Henry, this time I get the last word, nothing profound. "Goodbye, buddy. You take it easy."

And I can see that glint in your eye and the laughter in your voice. "I probably don't have much choice."

A WINTER IDYLL

NINE-FIFTEEN P.M. The sofa, the fireplace, and a CD of Julian Bream's guitar have seduced me. My sight falters, my concentration wanes. Ann Beattie, in the form of New Yorker fiction, tilts forward and falls to my lap. The phone rings.

Later, awakened, I look toward the river. I see the fire reflected in the window. No sounds, but I know from the energy of the flames that wind at chimney level is creating good draft. I check accumulated snow on the porch. Extravagant flakes fall, like a farm-sized pillow fight. I walk outside to split a log for tonight's fire, to check the livestock.

The winter setting reminds me of my grandfather. The wood fire, the snowy November night, the cattle in the barnyard. I choose a grampa chore coat, a cap with tie-down ear flaps, and chopper mitts. I forsake the battery-operated flashlight that illuminates from here to across the river for a kerosene lantern.

I strike a farmer match, depress the lever that lifts the lens and light the wick. Black smoke slithers, then tumbles out of the lantern. I trim the wick, pull on the choppers, and head for the barn.

Kelly walks before me, tail wagging, uncertain about this late night foray. The lantern, swinging beside my leg, lights only the pathway. Hay stacks, the wagon, the sleigh, everything outside a ten-foot diameter, is dark. The lantern casts grotesque shadows on the snow. I am reminded of ghosts of my childhood, the fear of imagined wolves awaiting me in Grampa's woodshed.

The cattle are in and around the barn, some contentedly chewing cud inside, some standing under the lean-to, some lying in snow under jackpines. The smell is warmth, that familiar smell of barns in winter. I hold the lantern high; distinct figures give the barn depth. Modest light illuminates texture as well as color. Rusts and russets and ochres of winter cattle coats are worthy of a Rembrandt palette. Mac Duff, herd patriarch, ambles forward. The lantern catches a golden glint in his eye.

The lantern casts eerie shadows on rough-sawn popple walls. The familiar becomes fresh, like looking at an everyday room through a mirror. Wood stanchions, standing in a row, are soldiers at parade rest. Hay forks, hanging tine-side up, are props in a Stephen King movie. The horse stall, bedded with straw, is a nativity setting.

I note the *blink, blink, blink* of the electric fencer. I depress the floating plate of the watering system until water flows. I rub a mittened hand along Mac Duff's long, wavy haired spine.

Time to return to the house. Snow continues, absorbing the lantern's meager light. The smell of wood smoke entices me back. I fall into my best grampa stride and retrace footprints that fill and fade, like memories.

THE ROAD LESS TAKEN

JACKPINES TOWER THIRTY, FORTY FEET. January wind rustles through the treetops. Below, it's cold but still. Late afternoon sun glints through spare branches and cuts shafts of light into the clearing. A team of draft horses stands tethered to a tree, their heads lowered. They shake their harnesses. Wisps of smoke rise from the bunk house chimney and shift with the wind. The ground smells of crushed pine needles and fresh sawdust. A second team of horses tramps out of the woods, lugging a few logs. The teamster snakes them up the trail, between trees, to the landing.

A scene out of the early twentieth century? Nope. It's happening today in Huntersville State Forest. Tinker Skov, Terry Pickar, and Adam Otterstetter are the three sawyers who cut timber under a permit with the DNR.

Joel Holden of the Nimrod Forestry Station explains that permits are sold for areas in the State Forest to clear dead standing trees. Permits begin in early winter at ground freezing and expire at the end of March. Typically, local folks buy permits to cut their own supply of firewood. Others, like the three above, cut and sell to the mill in Pillager, where the trees are processed into wood shavings.

The local DNR issues about a dozen permits a year. The payoff is some gain in fire prevention and the battle against insects and disease. The larger payoff is the opportunity to interact with the community.

Sawyers must protect live trees, and that's where horses excel. The space between the trees doesn't always allow for a tractor and front-end loader. Horses can squeeze through a six-foot opening.

On a typical day, the crew of three arrives at the landing with horses loaded in a livestock trailer. They start cutting about noon. In a minor bow to technology, they use chain saws instead of crosscuts. When the crew has fallen a supply of trees, Tinker and Adam drive the teams into the woods to haul out timbers. Terry keeps felling and limbing until there's a truck load of eight-foot bolts in the landing. They hand load the bolts onto the truck, and Terry heads for the mill in Pillager.

The woods around the landing are criss-crossed with groomed paths where dragged trees blend snow, bark, needles, and moss into a smooth trail. Horses plow through chest-high brush to retrieve fallen trees. Tinker lugs the evener to the trees, snaps a tow chain around them, and takes the reins. "Bell and Tricksey, gee over." The team leans into the harness, and the fallen trees drag another new trail.

Why take the trouble to log with horses? It's easier on the live trees, probably faster, but primarily, it's the fun of working in the woods where ingenuity replaces technology. "And, it gives me a chance to be with my two best friends," says Tinker. He glances at Adam and Terry, but says "Bell and Tricksey."

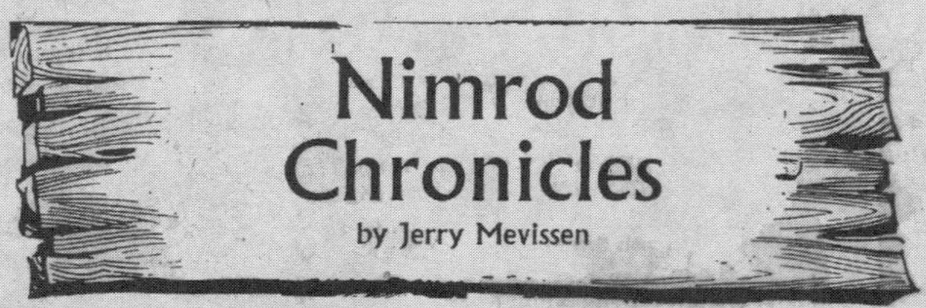

The photo pops up every now and then. In local family albums, in Nimrod history books, in the 1979 Nimrod Centennial issue of *The Review Messenger*. Hand-printed in the lower left corner is "Christmas Shopping in Nimrod in 1941."

Doesn't look like much shopping going on. Nobody carrying packages. No shopping bags straining under the bulk of bingo games, toiletry sets, banks, hand tools, mixing bowls. No tan paper bags bulging with sweater sets, dresser scarves, Big Boy flannel shirts. Wigwam wool socks, handkerchiefs. Just a farmer carrying a cream can, one handed, to or from the creamery. And a parade of parked Model Ts and Chevys, all the way from Roy and Hilma Sirois' Cafe (meals, short orders, confectionery, 3.2 beer) to the Nimrod Store, the Fairway Market.

Nimrod was a bustling town. Even then, on the decline from its glory days at the turn of the century as a half-way town, from Park Rapids north to Wadena south. But in 1941, the Cafe on the south and Fairway Market on the north looked like underworked bookends in the photo, loosely containing Stigman's Food Store, Everett Frisbie's Garage, Harry Morgan's Shoe Shop. And the Nimrod Hall, back off Main Street.

Out of sight of the camera is Alec Monty's Blacksmith Shop (general repair work and welding); Tomlinson Lumber Milling Co., with stacks of sawn lumber behind big enough to fill a baseball field; Greene's Store, Ben Larson, operator; the Nimrod Creamery, with Ervin Bohlig at the helm; the Co-op Store, Dave Chavez, manager; Kenny Blow's Service Station (Skelly gas, oils, tires, accessories); the Nimrod Feed Store, co-op owned and managed by Ernie Westra; Stan and Ed Nielsen's Garage, Nimrod's Ford Agency; and Wesley Tomlinson, dealer in used cars, trade and terms. Who did I forget?

The year, 1941. December. Big news is the bombing of Pearl Harbor and President Roosevelt's message to Congress, broadcast on the floor model Philco radio, signaling our entry into World War II. Nimrod wasn't spared the horrors of grief and separation of that. But life went on. Ginger Rogers was "Kitty Foyle" at the Cozy Theater; "the most amazing novel written by a man about a woman," according to the studio publicist. Also, a *Time Marches On* short subject. Fred Allen, eyes like two fried eggs, clowning on the radio on Wednesday night with wife Gracie.

The Nimrod Boosters, local businessmen, preparing for the big Christmas celebration on December 23, with Santa Claus. Free candy, nuts and apples to every child. Lila Perkins' store, stacked to the rafters with gift ideas. Yard goods, notions, wedgies for the ladies, oxfords for the men. Percale pillow cases, Osgosh B'gosh overalls, appliances from fans to freezers.

The Riverside Club counting the days until the Christmas meeting on Wednesday afternoon. Ann Stigman, hostess. Orange jello salad, hamburger noodle hotdish, Boston cream pie for dessert. Ladies in a tribal circle in the living room. Smaller private conversations in the kitchen. Christmas gifts exchanged. And one for your "secret pal."

Do you smell the turpentine in the jack pine smoke from the wood-stoved houses on Main Street? See the red, made-in-Japan (bad word!) candled wreaths in the window? Hear the crunch of so-clean-you-can-eat-it snow under your Red Ball overshoes?

Fast forward to 1993. August. Hot, still afternoon. Felt like somebody hit the "pause" button and calcified the town. My first view of the place I would later claim as home. A few pickups napping on the west side of Main Street. Gravel parking lot in front of the service station hosting a convention of yellow butterflies, folding their wings, open and closed, like little pages of a book. The only things moving in town.

I expect Gary Cooper, jaw jutting like a front bumper, to saunter out from behind the bus garage, trigger fingers at the ready. Desperadoes to lurk behind the Riverside Grocery, sucking on a stem of crow's-foot grass. Grace Kelly to tilt a lace curtain in the square front window of Hillig Mercantile.

Fast forward again to today. I view the town from the vantage point of the 1941 photographer. Snow-packed streets, a few buildings on the west side of Main, trucks parked in front. A man carries mail instead of a cream can.

The more things change, the more they stay the same.

NIMROD: DECEMBER 1941

THE PHOTO POPS UP EVERY NOW AND THEN. In local family albums, in Nimrod history books, in the 1979 Nimrod Centennial issue of *The Review Messenger*. Hand-printed in the lower left corner is "Christmas Shopping in Nimrod in 1941." Doesn't look like much shopping going on. Nobody carrying packages. No shopping bags straining under the bulk of bingo games, toiletry sets, or piggy banks. No brown paper bags bulging with sweater sets, dresser scarves, Big Boy flannel shirts, Wigwam wool socks, or handkerchiefs. Just a farmer carrying a cream can, one handed, to or from the creamery. And a parade of parked Model T's and Chevys, all the way from Roy and Hilma Sirois' Cafe (Meals, Short Orders, Confectionery, 3.2 Beer) to the Nimrod Store, the Fairway Market.

Nimrod was a bustling town. Not bustling as it had been in its glory days at the turn of the century when it was a half-way town, from Park Rapids to the north and Wadena to the south. But in 1941, the cafe on the south and Fairway Market on the north look like under-worked bookends in the photo, loosely containing Stigman's Food Store, Everett Frisbie's Garage, Harry Morgan's Shoe Shop. And the Nimrod Hall back off Main Street.

Out of sight of the camera is Alec Monty's Blacksmith Shop (general repair work and welding); Tomlinson Lumber Milling Co., with stacks of sawn lumber behind big enough to fill a baseball field; Greene's Store, Ben Larson, operator; The Nimrod Creamery, with Ervin Bohlig at the helm; the Co-op Store, Kenny Blow's Service Station (Skelly gas, oils, tires, accessories); the Nimrod Feed

Store, owned and managed by Ernie Westra; Stan and Ed Neilson's Garage, Nimrod's Ford Agency; and Wesley Tomlinson, dealer in used cars, trade and terms. Who did I forget?

The year, 1941. December. Big news is the bombing of Pearl Harbor and President Roosevelt's message to Congress, broadcast on the floor model Philco radio in the living room, signaling our entry into World War II. Nimrod wasn't spared the horrors of grief and separation of that. But life went on. Folks sought distraction from the war with entertainment. Ginger Rogers was "Kitty Foyle" at the Cozy Theater; "the most amazing novel written by a man about a woman," according to the studio publicist. Also, a "Time Marches On" short subject. Fred Allen, eyes like two fried eggs, clowning on the radio Wednesday night with his rival, Jack Benny.

The Nimrod Boosters, local businessmen, prepare for the big Christmas celebration on December 23, with Santa Claus. Free candy, nuts and apples to every child. Lila Perkins's store, stacked to the rafters with gift ideas. Yard goods, notions, wedgies for the ladies, oxfords for the men. Percale pillow cases, Oskosh B'gosh overalls, appliances from fans to freezers.

The Riverside Club counts the days until the Christmas meeting on Wednesday afternoon. Ann Stigman, hostess. Orange Jell-O salad, hamburger noodle hot dish, Boston cream pie for dessert. Ladies in a tribal circle in the living room. Smaller private conversations in the kitchen. Christmas gifts exchanged. And one for each person's "secret pal."

Is that a hint of turpentine in the jackpine smoke from the wood-stoved houses on Main Street? See the red chenille, made-in-Japan (bad word!) candled wreathes in the window? Hear the crunch of so-clean-you-can-eat-it snow under the Red Ball overshoes?

Fast forward to 1993. August. Hot, still afternoon. Feels like somebody hit the "pause" button and calcified Main Street. My first view of the place I would later call home. A few pickups nap on the west side of town. Gravel parking lot in front of the service station hosts a convention of yellow butterflies, folding their wings, open and close, like little pages of a book, the only thing moving in town.

I expect Gary Cooper, jaw jutting like a front bumper, to saunter out from behind the bus garage, trigger finger at the ready. I imagine desperadoes lurk behind Riverside Grocery, sucking on a stem of crows foot grass. Is that Grace Kelly tilting open a lace curtain in the square front window of Hillig Mercantile?

Fast forward again to today. I view the town from the vantage point of the 1941 photographer. Snow packed streets, a few buildings on the west side of Main, trucks parked in front. A man carries mail instead of a cream can.

The more things change, the more they stay the same.

NEITHER RAIN, NOR SLEET, NOR SNOW . . .

SEVEN A.M.. FIVE INCHES OF NEW SNOW OVERNIGHT. Wind from the north, with gusts up to twenty miles an hour and a wind chill of minus forty. School openings delayed. No travel advised. Dale Mattson trudges into the Sebeka Post Office to begin sorting mail for Rural Route Two. Neither rain, nor sleet, nor snow. . . . How does that rhyme go?

Dale has been with the USPS since December 1981 and a full-time route man since 1988. Sebeka rural routes have always been his beat, and he picked up Route two, the Nimrod route, in 1990. But another chapter of local history comes to a close. Dale announced his retirement, sometime in May or June, 2001.

I was surprised at the numbers associated with rural free delivery. Three hundred boxes on Route Two. Two thousand pieces of mail plus twenty-five packages a day. At Christmas, that grows to twenty-five hundred to three thousand letters a day, and seventy packages. One hundred and thirty-three and a half miles of driving a day, six days a week. Five days for Dale, and one for the substitute. The volume of mail has doubled during his tenure. So much for e-mail taking over the world.

Dale finishes his mail sort at 9:00 A.M. and begins delivery, east of Sebeka, north to Huntersville, east to Highway 64. He drops the Nimrod mail at the Post Office and takes a coffee break. That's where I met him.

Dale occupies a chair at the prestigious men's coffee table at the Nimrod Bar & Grill. His luck, or lack of it, at getting stuck with the tab is legendary. The camaraderie means a lot to Dale. We talked about assembling a book of Nimrod humor.

But the real humor is the spontaneous comical observation by Ray Pederson, which reminds Jerry Graba of the time that. . . . And then Jerry Schermerhorn wraps it up with a below-the-belt punch line. As they say, you had to be there.

Back to work for Dale, with more deliveries until lunch break at one-thirty and a return to Sebeka between three and three-thirty.

Rural Free Delivery began in the United States in 1896. Before that, farm families picked up mail at town post offices, while city families had it delivered to their doors. After extensive lobbying by the National Grange, rural residents in three small West Virginia towns began receiving home delivery. By 1905, there were petitions for 32,000 rural routes, which sparked a triple effect: a link between industry and commerce and their rural consumers, the development and improvement of roads, and the growth of the mail-order business. One hundred years later, it still sounds familiar.

Dale talks about trends in U.S. mail usage. We all know about the increase in third-class presorted standard (junk) mail. Dale expects the use of catalogs to double, with Internet purchasing not living up to expectations. He estimates that eighty percent of his mail is addressed with the newly assigned street numbers, instead of the old box and route numbers. Surprise! But Dale sorts his mail by name, not address.

I asked Dale about any unusual deliveries, pick-ups, or requests over twenty years of driving country roads. I had visions of peeping baby chicks in the back seat, sprouting seed potatoes arriving in spring, frozen oranges arriving in winter. Requests to pick up a dozen eggs from the grocery or drop off the kids at grammas. Nothing like that.

Dale hasn't missed a day because of weather. The big snow of November 1997 delayed him—nearly trapped him. Snow laden trees fell and blocked the road. Electric lines sagged and snapped under the added weight, sparking and popping like the Fourth of July. Dale sings the praises of the local snow removers. This coming from a man who plowed snow for two townships prior to delivering mail.

Any accidents? Just five deer in twenty years, four of them around Nimrod. And four bear sightings.

So what will Dale do after the big retirement party? He'll help son Darin in the body shop. He is committed to staying busy. Maybe we'll collaborate on the Nimrod humor book.

LYONS TOWNSHIP ANNUAL MEETING

IT'S THE SECOND TUESDAY OF MARCH, and in Lyons Township hall, the annual meeting was about to come to order. Maynard Benson was directing traffic in the parking area behind the hall, greeting neighbors outside as they negotiate what had been three-foot snow banks. Don Fredericksen was keeper of the flame and had a comfortable fire going in the wood stove. Pat Pederson sat at the table in front of the hall, a little on edge, maybe. She faced a re-election challenge as soon as the annual meeting adjourns.

It was three o'clock, and the meeting was called to order by Clerk Ray Heideman. We pledged allegiance to the flag, and fifteen people stood, a respectable attendance out of a total of ninety-six registered voters, a population of one hundred and sixty-eight. First order of business was election of a moderator, and guess who got nominated. The thinking being that, if he was busy running the meeting, he wouldn't have time to capture, record, and publish his observations in the local press. Wrong!

The meeting was scheduled for one hour, with the ballot box opening at four o'clock. Ray read the minutes of last year's meeting; a motion was made to approve, seconded, and passed. Ray read the treasurer's report. Total receipts for the year: $11,019.51; total expenditures: $13,993.07. (Think about it. We ran the township for one year for half the price of a new pickup truck!) Not to worry about deficit spending. Lyons Township had an ending balance of $73,649.80, split between an interest-bearing checking account and three certificates of deposit.

Road and bridge maintenance represented the largest element of expense: $8,916.49. Lyons Township has six and one-half miles of roads to maintain. Our $515 per mile for regular maintenance was within the range of typical township experience. Maynard gave the road report. Plans for 2001 were discussed, motion made, and passed to continue T-184 upgrading to County 26, and proceed with one mile of T-167 south of County 9.

Next item of business: set levies for taxes. Ray recommended $2,000 for general revenue, $5,000 for road and bridge, and $1,500 for fire protection. Motion made to approve, seconded, discussed, and passed.

Up to now, I didn't recall a single dissenting vote. But the next two items —approving the annual meeting and election posting places—generated enough adrenaline for Don to stop stoking the wood burner. Bottom line was that meeting notices would be advertised in the local press, and the election hours would be extended, one o'clock to eight o'clock, with the annual meeting to follow.

Maybe Ray expected some spirited debate on those issues. When he prepared the agenda, he provided a little comic relief with the next item of business: setting gopher bounties. Now, a gopher bounty, for my out-of-the-township readers, is the payment made for the front feet and tails of pocket gophers. Last year, we paid out $450 at one dollar a gopher, a four-fold increase over 1999. Not that a person could tell it from the number of gopher mounds on my patch of land.

On with the show. Bob announced a public hearing on a county zoning ordinance dealing with telecommunication towers. Then we got to "Other New Business."

There followed a lively discussion on upgrading the township hall, once a District 55 South schoolhouse. Sentiments ran deep for preserving it in its original (present) state. Sentiments ran equally deep for bringing it up to twentieth-century standards, if not twenty-first. I'm talking new siding, windows, roof shingles. I'm talking hooking up to electric power. The case was made for acknowledging the extremely limited use the hall got and the cost of amortizing minimum electric service charges over two or three meetings a year. The same could be said for upgrading the exterior. The roof was old and looked like the original cedar shingles. No doubt, the siding and windows were original too. Date of construction of the hall was anybody's guess. I'm guessing 1900 to 1905. A lot of people's grampas went to grade school there.

Maybe the building would/could get more use if it were electrified, spiffed up a bit. But it had a charm the way it was. I had photographed it from County 9 heading west. When I drive that stretch, I always notice the stair-stepping of the three roof lines: hall, entry, and pump house/wood storage shed. And I love the wood siding, can't imagine wrapping that grand old building in vinyl. That would be like dressing the Queen Mother in polyester.

Bottom line: the building would be electrified, by a vote of eight to seven; and Jim Dailey would secure bids on the external upgrading. The motion did not include acting on the bids.

It was four o'clock. No more new business. Meeting adjourned. Time for election. The ballots were blank because no one filed. Two offices are open, and the incumbents are known candidates: Pat Pederson (Roger's Pat, not Raymond's) for supervisor, and Bev Komula for treasurer. But that year, there was competition. Dick Pickar for supervisor and Denny Benson for treasurer. The candidates had to have done some effective get-out-the-vote phoning because fifty-eight people voted out of ninety-six registered voters. That compared with about twenty-five during the last township election.

The winners! Pat Pederson and Bev Komula, both with thirty-seven votes. Sounded like a coalition.

It was a good day. Democracy at such a grass-roots level, one could smell the chlorophyll. The old schoolhouse turned into a township hall. Neighbors sharing views and opinions. Majority rules. Only one problem. The cookies served with coffee after the meeting were store-bought. Next election, let's have homemade brownies and lemon bars.

LADIES OF THE ROUND TABLE

AS REPORTED IN AN EARLIER *CHRONICLE*, men and women enjoy their coffee at separate tables every morning at the R&R Bar & Grill in Nimrod. To insure their insularity, the women post a "No Men Allowed" sign on their table. What do the ladies talk about that requires such secrecy? Diets? Grandchildren? Recipes? *All My Children?* This intrepid Nimrod Chronicler broke through the barrier and came up with this report.

Just Ask: "What are your plans for the holidays?"

Mae Stennes—retired, electricity consumer, fashion plate: All the kids and grandchildren come home for Christmas. We attend the Christmas Eve service at Nimrod Lutheran and have dinner on Christmas Day. My specialty is lutefisk and lefsa. If the children eat it, they get to open their gifts. I try to introduce some culture by playing Elvis Christmas records. At night, we turn on the yard lights. The house, garage, and shed are decorated, as are the trees, shrubs, trellises, bird houses, windmill, waterfall, flag pole, and garbage can. The kids love to watch the dial spinning wildly on the electric meter.

Connie Frederickson—cashier at Ernie's Grocery, prize winning oatmeal raisin cookie baker: We start Christmas Eve with Tammy, Tom, and Kelly, and then join all the relatives at Mom's on Christmas Day. We don't do Elvis at our house; I like country, as in Vince Gill. With Tammy gone, I put up fewer Christmas decorations. But why should I? I can look out the window and see Mae Stennes's yard with more lights than Las Vegas.

Gladys Metteer—retired, community center treasurer: We have celebrated Christmas at our house since emigrating from South Dakota in 1967. Did I ever talk about that trip? Well, everyone here knows how Harold hates to ask directions. . . . But that's another story. We go to Nimrod Lutheran Church for Christmas Eve, and then we get together on Christmas, Harold and I, and our seven kids, eighteen grandkids, and eleven great-grandkids. Son Jim, bless his heart, always brings me a quart of those big, succulent oysters from Morrie's, and I make oyster stew. We snack all day and then have dinner and open gifts. Harold

always surprises us with his gift purchases. Last year he bought a pair of red nylon halters for his draft horses.

Alice Graba—retired, homemaker: We traveled to Minneapolis last weekend to spend an early Christmas with our two sons. We opened gifts after dinner. We attend the Christmas Eve service at Sebeka Methodist. I like to sit on the aisle near the door when Jack sings "Joy to the World." He may not be Elvis, but he does make a mean batch of lefsa.

Jeanette Frame—retired, election judge: We spend Christmas with our children and their families, friends, and Grandma Clara. We have a huge dinner at noon, and then we play games. The grandchildren do the decorating.

Deloris Shore—bartender, fry cook, and Nimrod traffic watcher: We spend Christmas at my mom, Marcy's, home with all my kids—Laurie, Rodney, Lyle, and Bobby and their families. This year I went overboard on Christmas gift buying due to unprecedented wins at the casino in Walker. We open our gifts on Christmas Eve, and the greatest gift of all is my family at home. That, and the cute teddy bear that a secret admirer left on my fence. (I know who you are, R____.)

Pat Pederson—horse trainer, cattleman's wife, and snowbird: We spend Christmas with our three kids: Ricky, Roxanne, and Robin, their spouses/significant others, our six grandkids, and others. On Christmas Day, the Pederson family gathers here for dinner and opening gifts. The tree this year is non-traditional. Not spruce, balsam, or scotch pine, but crocheted cotton. Doesn't need water, and doesn't shed needles. Gift buying is simple and practical. Everybody gets socks. Every year. So there! (I hope they don't read this before Christmas.)

Donna Metteer—waitress, grandma: We attend church service on Christmas Eve and then spend Christmas with all the kids and grandkids. We decorate the house from top to bottom and open gifts after supper. We are introducing a family tradition in the form of a competition to see who can make the biggest and fastest mess.

There we have it. But we still don't know what happened on *All My Children*. MERRY CHRISTMAS.

KARAOKE CHAMPIONSHIP, 2001

FLOOD LIGHTS ROTATED OUTSIDE THE BAR & GRILL Saturday night, pushing beams of light in the cloudless sky that could be seen all the way to Dad's Elwell Corner. White limos snaked to the door, unloaded celebs to the cheers, hoots, and flash cameras of velvet-roped fans along the walk, and then they circled to the rear and parked in the snow-plowed outfield. Warm-up music, stuff by Tim McGraw, Shania Twain, the Dixie Chicks, blared from a megabuck sound system parked in front of Hillig Mercantile. It was the finale to the five-week Nimrod Karaoke Contest.

All the Nimrod glitterati were there, in outfits by Carhartt, Levi Strauss, and Saddle King. It was SRO at eight o'clock, and the contest didn't begin until ten. Sure, there were warm-ups for contestants, and a final qualifying round thrown in by genial emcee, the Hitman. Gil Baker, a wild card from Georgia, and Jenny Pederson, a local birthday girl, both competed and both won.

It was the CMAs, the Grammy Awards, and Oscar night, all in one. Tension was so high, no one could have heard a fuel tanker explode. The natives deal with excitement by raising their voices to decibels usually associated with claps of thunder, a DC-10 at takeoff, or the screeching of brakes on a runaway semi.

At a table in a far corner sat an unknown, in fur cap with earflaps tied on top and a floor length mackinaw. A thin-blooded California talent scout, we surmised.

"You think about entering?" a local wag wondered, her gin-soaked eyes zooming in and out, trying to focus like a Leica lens.

"Shucks," I said. "I'd as soon bungee jump off the Oylen bridge."

After the white zins, the Miller Genuine Drafts, the Captain Morgan rum and cokes; after the crowd was charged high enough to run the bulls at Pamplona, after the smoke approached the level of a burning pile of Firestone recalls, the contest began. Contestant names were drawn randomly by our ubiquitous emcee, the Hitman.

Gil Baker, the token out-of-stater, won the luck of the first draw and did a reprise of his qualifying song, "Feel Like Makin' Love." Lyrics not by Stephen Sondheim, not even Steven Foster, maybe Steven King. Judges were hard pressed to score this guy. Especially male judges. Especially in the category of stage presence.

There followed Corrine Dailey, the daughter-half of a mother-daughter pair of contestants, who reeled off a perky, confident rendition of "My Baby Loves Me." A little bit like listening to Lisa Minelli and thinking Judy Garland.

Julie Horton, with home-field advantage, whispered through "Constant Craving," saving her warm smiles until she hung up the mike and walked through the crowd of neighbors offering high fives.

Then the birthday girl, Jennie Pederson, aglow with golden Caribbean tan and a chain to match, gyrated through a convincing "Man, I Feel Like a Woman," her fans following every turn, like kids following a candy-throwing float in the Jubilee Days parade.

The Pepsodent-smiling Hitman picked another out-of-towner (well, more of a Nimrod suburb, than out of town), Dwight Kern from Sebeka, who crooned a very respectable version of "Miss the Dance" despite the theatrics of his groupies. His mike work was good, and he sang with cowboy sincerity. Too bad we couldn't see him except when he appeared momentarily between swaying heads, fractional images like a strobe light.

Then one of two odds-on favorites, I thought. Cindy Warmbold, a local who had graced this stage many times before as lead singer for Lonesome Dove. The other half of the mother-daughter team. She sang her trademark "Black Velvet," and for the first time since two that afternoon, the place was quiet. She sang it warm, and she sang it bold. A standing ovation.

By this time, the crowd was fever pitched. Even the jack-in-the-box histrionics of the Hitman couldn't overcome the hubbub and hullabaloo. A name that sounded like Erin Bosette competed for quiet air pockets with "Cross My Heart." Lou Lambert, another local, did a relaxed and gratifying rendition of Roger Miller's "King of the Road," with the audience joining in the refrain and then the stanzas. And Rino from Park Rapids gave us a wrenching "Crying Over You."

Midnight, and time for the last contestant. The Hitman, still side-splitting and quirky, can't understand where little (size one?) Deana Skov gets her energy, her ability to belt out a song. The other half of the two odds-on favorites, I thought. She had more moves than Fran Tarkenton up there, and she had the audience eating out her little (size one?) hands when she sang "Bye Bye, Baby, Bye Bye."

Time for judges to tally scores. Time for the cunning and clever Hitman to sing one more song. Who does he remind me of? A geriatric Pinky Lee? The stakes are high. Fame for sure, and a modest fortune. Two-hundred dollars for first place, one-hundred for second, and fifty for third. The judges conclusions are final. A drum role, please.

Only one point separating first from second, and one point separating second from third. And a tie for third. Deana and Rino. Applause! A special award to Julie for attending each of the five qualifying rounds. Second place, Cindy Warmbold. First place going to an out-of-towner, Dwight Kern, proving there's nothing provincial about these Nimrod judges. Dwight grabs the mike and does a vocal victory lap.

It was fun. And I'm not a country western music fan. Back home, I slipped on some Andrea Bocelli and Kiri Te Kanawa discs. Happy to have a home town to celebrate. Happy to have talented, gutsy, fun-loving neighbors to celebrate with me.

JUST ASK

THIS ROVING REPORTER ASKS SOME FOLKS who have been around town for a while "Do you have an early memory of Nimrod?"

ALICE OEHLENSCHLAGER: "Yes, I do. I remember going to Nimrod as a girl. Dad drove a high-wheeled wagon to town hauling cream to the creamery. He'd say 'Hang on, girls,' as we drove down the steep hill and forded the Crow Wing River. Dad called it 'meandering' around the rocks and holes in the river. Tomlinsons had the creamery and lumberyard. We did our shopping at Cohrs General Store—tools, groceries, dry goods, men's overalls. The grocers always had a treat for the little kids, a paper sack with candy."

JOHN MARSHALL: "Well, there was a halfway house along the river, a hotel, half way between Hubbard and Verndale, but that was before my time. There was another halfway house further south. Back in those days, the wheat trail between Hubbard and the railroad at Verndale was a busy route. The trip with horse-drawn wagons took more than a day. Farmers or teamsters stayed overnight at Nimrod. By the time I arrived in Nimrod in 1916, at age four, the halfway house was gone.

"But I do remember celebrating the Fourth of July in Nimrod, particularly the year I was twelve. There was a foot race for boys twelve and under. I won the race, but I was bashful when the judges asked my name. A couple young men shouted, 'That's John Marshall!' My prize was seventy-five cents, a lot of money in those days. My dad had a team of horses, and we drove to Nimrod. Dad tied the team and did his shopping. Some local boys tossed a firecracker, which spooked the team. They broke away and got hung up on a pier in the river. One of the horses took a spike in the chest, but she was okay."

MARGARET HIGGS: "I was married when I came to Nimrod. Harold and I went to the movies at the town hall on Thursday nights. They were mostly cowboy movies—Gene Autry and Roy Rogers. We sat on planks on top of sawhorses. Gene Stanich ran the movies and sold the popcorn."

LORRAINE LOWEEN: "I came to Nimrod for my first teaching assignment—#21-1 in the Nimrod District. Nimrod was a busy town then, with many businesses and two or three restaurants. No saloon, though. They sold 3.2 beer in the restaurant.

"I taught grades one through seven and had ten students my first year. And I remember some of my students—Dean Estabrooks, Yalonda Raddohl, Diana Olson, and Esther Bowers. And there was Duane Sams! Duane had the tobacco habit already. I wondered how to deal with that. I told him he had to put his tobacco in my desk drawer during school hours and take it when he left after school. And no lighting up until he was off school property. He minded, and I never had a problem with him. I never had to use a ruler on the kids. They minded well because they minded at home. We were taught to visit the families of students and get to know them. That helped, knowing something of the students' home lives. But teachers lived in a glass bubble then. We had to lead exemplary lives."

CLARA FRAME: "I remember that life on the farm was hard work. Dad died in 1924. We made hay with the help of our cousins, using horses. We pitched hay onto the wagon, then pitched it off to make haystacks. We didn't have a barn with a haymow, just a low-ceiling log barn. At night, we milked by the light of kerosene lanterns. We had a Jersey bull who was ugly! He put me up a tree once, and I always took the dog with me to get the cows after that. I wasn't sorry the day he got shipped!

My cousin, Ted Rice, had a buggy and plug horse that his sister, Stella Pickar, and I used to haul five-gallon cream cans to the creamery. We got a check for the cream and bought groceries. My sister Ann and I took eight-quart baskets of eggs to Bill Niska's grocery."

AUDREY PICKAR: "I arrived in the Nimrod area in 1928 and went to Nimrod School #3. My teacher was Virginia Kleen. We had a play day in Nimrod at the end of the school year. All four Nimrod schools participated in a day of races, games, and pot luck dinners. We won ribbons for the games. For the ball game, we played with sticks for a bat, and a ball made of twine with a denim cover.

"The first person we met in Nimrod was Kenny Blow, who lived in Canada at the same time as my dad. In fact, they played together. Kenny owned a garage and pumped gas."

LUCILLE SWANSON: "Mother was born in Wadena, and we came to Nimrod in 1932. We settled near the John Marshall place. I was seven when we moved here from the Iron Range. It was pouring rain. Everything got soaked. We were hauling furniture in my uncle's open cattle truck. Mother was most upset about her piano getting wet. But she rubbed it down, and it was okay.

"Alice Oehlenschlager was my eighth-grade teacher at #55 North. I had a bicycle, a girl's Schwinn bike, red and white. I think every kid in school learned to ride bicycle on that bike. We rode during recess and lunch hour. I'm surprised it survived as well as it did."

MARCY SHORE: "We moved to Nimrod after Glen and I got married, about 1950. Oh, my land! Nimrod was a busy place then. Two cafes, two grocery stores, two garages, a creamery, a feed store, a car dealer, a lumber yard, and the Alliance church. I remember Saturday at the creamery there was a drawing for all the farmers who came to town. They drew names for butter and other prizes. I could watch the cars coming down the road heading into town. Isabelle Swenson was my neighbor, a farmer's wife. I remember her walking to town in a dress and white, cut sandals. Later, we worked together at Badoura Nursery in Akeley for thirty-one years.

"Glen was in the Army when I was pregnant with Elsie. He had a furlough before she was born, and I asked him to buy something for the baby. He bought a blanket, pink and blue, from Lila Perkins' store. Elsie still has the blanket, and it's in good condition. Elsie was fourteen months old before she saw her dad. It took a long time for her to get comfortable with him.

"We boarded Floella Lemon at our house. Floella was a Nimrod school teacher. Room and board amounted to fifteen dollars a month. She was a wonderful lady. She took care of baby Kenny.

"I've been in this house for forty-nine years, and I intend to stay as long as I can. I have my two daughters close by to look out for me."

ELAINE SCHERMERHORN: "I was born between Nimrod and Huntersville in 1931. My folks had a dairy farm, and I remember the trips to town on Saturday, delivering cream to the creamery. We got a nickel to spend for our treats.

"I remember the Nimrod and Huntersville dances every Saturday night. The dances at Nimrod were in the town hall. The music was live, and I was single. We had a ball! That's where I learned to dance. Smokey and Mary, a husband and wife team of KWAD Wadena radio fame, provided the music. They played the accordion, guitar, violin, and drums. The girls swooned over the violin. The crowds were unbelievable! There was no food served at the hall, so at intermission, we went to Edna Schermerhorn's restaurant. It was great fun."

LILA PERKINS: "When we arrived in 1946, Nimrod was a booming town. Pal, my husband, and I were uncertain as to what to do. Pal had just got out of the Army. The store was for sale, so we bought it from John Hepola. We named it Perkins General Store. We lived behind the store in an apartment. We also operated the post office, and Ann Stigman got her start in the USPS there.

"We stocked clothing, shoes, groceries, meat, hardware—a real general store. We had two kids when we bought the store, and my third child, Connie (Pickar), was born at the store. All the people in town were our age, and we were one big family."

ANN STIGMAN: "I first saw Nimrod when I was about thirteen or fourteen. We heard that there was a Fourth of July celebration, so my dad drove us in his old Model T. We came up on the worst sandy road to get to Nimrod. And, lo and behold, no celebration!

"Dad bought us ice cream cones, and we headed for home. I never, ever thought I would be living here for over sixty-seven years. My thoughts of Nimrod were that it was the worst place in the country. But now, I wouldn't want to be anywhere else but Nimrod, my home sweet home."

We LO
You!
Jeff

JOHN MARSHALL: ORIGINAL NIMROD CHRONICLER

JOHN E. MARSHALL WAS NINETY YEARS OLD LAST JULY FOURTH. Stereotypical images of a ninety-year-old man come to mind: frail, dependent, unreasonable. Prepare yourself for a new image. John still splits his firewood, cares for a small herd of Herefords and his Belgian mare, and hunted deer last season. His dependency, if he has any, is the one we all have—social. But in day-to-day living, John is on his own, with companionship of faithful dog Spook and weekend check-ins from the family. Regarding reason, John is a treasure of memories and stories that he's eager to share.

Time out for a short confession. I thought, after seeing the title for these columns—"Nimrod Chronicles"—that John had already chronicled Nimrod history. I have his book, *Tales from a Crow Wing Native*. And I later learned that sister Alice Oehlenschlager wrote the Nimrod news for the *Review Messenger* some years back. But, whereas *Tales* tends to be a series of essays with a family backdrop of eighty years' residence, lovingly told in rich, precise detail, "Chronicles" tends to have tongue planted firmly in cheek and are reflections of the new kid on the block.

We talked about his memories of life on and around the Crow Wing River. John included a tribute to the river called "Ode to a Queen" in his book. I thought of using that as a point of departure and asked for stories based on the river. His comments sounded familiar. Later, I discovered that his memory of ricing on the river is chronicled in the essay "Opening Day." How about something more seasonal? What are his memories of the ice breakup in the spring? My notes duplicate his essay "Ice Jam." Any memories of hunting or fishing on the river? Again, my notes are an outline for his essay "Trapping Adventure."

So, I'm left with my own observations of this seasoned farmer, hunter, woodsman, author, family historian. The link between us is draft horses. I needed runners for a sleigh. John was suggested as a source. He not only made a gift of the steel runners, but also provided the oak to rebuild them.

John is down to one Belgian mare now, Betsy, and Betsy has an easy life. Easier than John's. John shoveled a path to the corral after last weekend's snow dump, and he hand-feeds small round bales (baled himself, of course) daily. His wood pile, split and stacked, is enviable. The house is clean; the dishes are done.

Books are spaced here and there. A journal lies on the table. He talks of another writing project—a romance. The story, his mother and father's courtship and marriage, is prompted by a letter his father wrote when John was at Ag School in St. Paul. He talks of his father, Milo's, first impression of his mother, Marie. She is remembered as the blue-eyed girl picking hazelnuts. John warmly remembers his wife, Paulyne, and includes her in many of his stories. Seems that long-term commitment and affection are in the Marshall genes.

John apologizes for his handwriting, but he doesn't use it as an excuse for not proceeding with the romance story. He eschews the modern contrivances—typewriters, word processors, tape recorders. We share respect for the written word: "written," as in hand-written.

The day of my visit was warm. The high afternoon sun beckoned us outside. Snow melted off roofs. Melted snow accumulated in tire ruts. Earth, exposed by shoveling and plowing, lay warming in the sun and hinted at spring. We walked the shoveled path to the corral, Spook leading, John proceeding cautiously. John introduced me to the livestock. They reflect their owner's disposition—quiet, gentle, content.

We talk about the qualities that we share: our love for this part of the country, our spiritual connection to the river, the importance of family and friends, our affinity for draft horses, our common bond as writers. Then he pays the ultimate compliment: "You know, you and I are alike in a lot of ways."

I'll try to live up to that, John.

STRIPES AND SOLIDS

SEVEN O'CLOCK, WEDNESDAY NIGHT. Nimrod in mid-winter. Cold hawk is flying in. Full moon a'rising. Snow crunches as I walk, my back hunched a bit, hands in pockets. The neighborhood hatches are battened down, right? Wrong. It's pool league night at the R&R.

Nimrod fields three pool teams of four players each. That's one sixth of our population. Don't think we don't take the game seriously.

The three teams are R&R #1, R&R #3, and the GB Empire. R&R #1 and #3 played host on Wednesday night to a couple Huntersville teams. GB Empire played at Huntersville. Jumping to the bottom line, the two local teams taught their opponents a lesson in humility. The away team settled for a tie.

R&R #1 team members are David Pederson, Kevin Milbradt, Rick Pederson, and Mark Schermerhorn. These guys look sharp in their short-sleeved, royal blue, collared T-shirts. Mark looks like he's been pumping iron, until I realize it's his long underwear rolled up under his sleeves. There's a coin toss to determine who breaks. Huntersville calls the coin and leans into the break. The Huntersville guy, unlucky in love, eyes the formation, says "This is for you, babe," and smashes balls like he's avenging fifteen years of bad feelings. Dave Pederson is up, holds his cue like it's the arm of a princess, taps the cue ball, kisses the four ball. Plunk.

Meanwhile, at table two, R&R #3 team members are awaiting the arrival of their Huntersville opponents. If they are thirty minutes late, the home team can declare a bye. They arrive at 7:29. R&R #3 team members are Danny Gilster,

Coleman Rydie, Harvey Horton, and Cindy Warmbold. They've loosened up with an intramural game and are ready to roll. Danny breaks, sinks the nine ball. Runs off two more balls. Huntersville is up, leans over the table, shivers, studies it forever. We wonder if this is strategy or whether he forgot if he is stripes or solids.

Back at table one, Kevin is faced with a "Donny leave," patented by Donny Borg. In golf, this is called an "impossible lie." Donny had the knack of parking the cue ball tight against the rail, behind the eight ball, or buried among the stripes (if the opponents were solids). He's working second shift now, so he's not a league player this year. But his name is invoked often.

Why is pool the big attraction? From players I talked to—Cindy, Rich, and Todd Grotberg—it's a chance to break away for an evening of fun. A chance to add some spice to a winter schedule. I notice the teams are quiet during the game, allowing the player to concentrate on his shot. A good shot gets "attaboys" all around, from team members and opponents.

How does Cindy like being the only female on the Nimrod teams? Actually, she's not. Ruth Stahl is a substitute player for R&R #3. The last two years, Nimrod fielded an all-female team. "We were good," Cindy says. "It was fun to see an all-guy team lose when they thought they had an easy night."

The pool league has a mid-season tournament, and a final tournament in March. The final tournament is paired with a banquet, where trophies and a jacket are awarded. This league isn't about trophies, though. It's about having a good time. The game hasn't changed much in fifty years, although I note on the Internet that CueSight is offering a laser-sighted pool cue set for an after-Christmas sale price of $119.00. Or, how about a bank shot mirror? Really!

I hear on Thursday that the GB Empire team—Todd Grotberg, Mike Roberts, Clint Childers, and Brant Rhul—played to a six-six tie against Huntersville #1. The teams play twelve games a night, eight singles and four doubles. The game is straight eight.

Pool has gotten a bum rap from contemporary culture. The Music Man comes to mind. "We got trouble right here in River City. That game with the fifteen numbered balls is the devil's tool." Well, my friends, we got Good Times, right here in Nimrod City. And that starts with G, and it rhymes with P, and that stands for pool.

HOUSE OF CHRISTMAS LIGHTS

TRAFFIC ON ACORN STREET PICKS UP THIS TIME OF YEAR. Vehicles exit Main Street and drive slowly east to the house of Christmas lights. Maybe they turn into the circular drive. Maybe they go to the end of the block, wonder how to get back to Main Street, and hook a "U" turn. It's worth the trip. The Stennes house wins "best decorated" prize (if there is one) year after year.

Mae and Harris Stennes moved in from the farm north of town in December 1983. With all their newly found spare time, they began outdoor decorating at Christmas in 1984. Harris died in 2000. We all wondered if Mae would keep up the tradition, alone. Mae wondered too. And as the days ticked off before Christmas, she found herself rummaging through a garage full of boxes of decorations. She finally gave in, and for the last two years, she has decorated the house, lawn, garage, clothes poles, flag pole, dog house, wishing well, trellis, sidewalk, driveway—by herself, with an assist from family and friends.

How many decorations are lighting up Mae's neighborhood? "About half," says Mae. "My half. The half that isn't up is Harris'."

What started as a modest outdoor decoration program grew year after year, as lights, plastic snowmen, Santas, stars, toy soldiers, bells, and balls were attached to anything that would support them. This year the bird house was spared its decoration. The last time Mae decorated it, the step ladder swirled around the slick anti-squirrel post, and Mae landed in a snow bank.

Don't expect to see Santa's sleigh on the Stennes roof. Mae doesn't do ladders anymore.

Of course, such a display attracts mischief makers, but losses have been minimal. Santa and a snowman were kidnapped one year. Santa appeared briefly at various spots along Highway 227 but never made it home. Mr. Snowman met his demise on Main Street.

Inside the Stennes house is another Christmas decorating extravaganza. Mae's Christmas village must have a larger population than Nimrod's seventy-five. That, plus the usual Christmas tree, wreathes, garlands, poinsettia swags, angels, and window decals. And, on a good day, a plate of fruit cake and a pot of coffee.

Do all those lights impact her electric bill? "Yes," says Mae. "The electric bill makes a definite jump in December." Maybe Todd Wadena Electric Co-op should honor her as consumer of the month.

Mae's house is sandwiched between Pedersons, Rathckes, and Anne Stigman, who have a front-row seat for viewing and listening to the Christmas carol music box. "All good neighbors," says Mae. "Someone to count on."

Without snow this season, we need all the stimulants we can muster to get us in a holiday mood. According to the Lonnie Lilly at the DNR, we have had snow every Christmas since 1989. Some years as low as three inches. Last year, we had thirteen inches. So, for all those driving the kids or grandkids around town, take a detour down Acorn Street to see the house of Christmas lights. If viewers are luckier than I am, Mae won't pull the plug while they're admiring the view.

HAPPY HOLIDAYS

THE GIRLS OF WINTER; THE BOYS OF SUMMER

"B - 10."
"I - 25."
"N - 40."
"G - 55."

CHARLIE TUORILA IS THE CALLER. Forty sets of eyes scan about two hundred cards, like gold miners panning for nuggets. Marcy Shore needs O - 71 to win.

"O - 70," calls Charlie.

"Oh, something else," grumbles Marcy.

"BINGO!" shouts a dowager from table one.

It's the neighborhood bingo binge, each Sunday afternoon, January through March, at the Community Center. Proceeds go to a revered local institution, the Nimrod Gnats baseball team. Charlie calls one, coaches the other.

Bingo hasn't escaped the technology revolution. I picked my cards and looked for the box of corn kernels to place on the called numbers. No luck. Now we have little sliding windows. And no longer is it just five across, up or down, or diagonal. I heard many variations during my hour. Postage stamp, four corners, six pack, picture frame, and the letter N. I suppose there could be letters A through Z.

They play sixteen games, with a pot of fifteen dollars per game, twenty dollars if the winner scores with ten or less numbers called. But usually the num-

ber calling goes on and on. Everyone at our table needs only one number to win. Tension mounts. It's so quiet, a person could hear coffee cool. This can't continue. Charlie keeps calling.

"I - 16." The interval between his call and our expectation of a shout is like the time between a bolt of lightning and a clap of thunder. Everyone knows it's coming.

"BINGO!" The hall erupts. One "YES!" Thirty-nine "Just about had it."

And so it goes, until four o'clock. Average take per Sunday is between one and two hundred dollars.

The Nimrod Gnats, beneficiaries of the local largesse, are one of four baseball teams in the South Division of the Lakes and Pines League. They competed in the state tournament in 1998. And they competed in the regionals in 1999 and 2000.

There are expenses associated with funding a baseball team, according to Charlie. Uniforms, balls and bats, insurance, and umpires. Bingo is one source of revenue. There was also an auction last fall. The Gnats make some bucks sponsoring the softball tournament during Jubilee Days. That, plus passing a collection plate at home games.

The team has done well, not only in providing summer weekend excitement, but in the area of capital improvements. The ball field, completed in 1998, is a monument to a grand tradition of baseball in Nimrod. There is talk of a donation for a lighted field. Can a domed stadium be far behind?

And how is the 2001 season shaping up? "We have most of the same team returning," says Charlie, "and a couple new prospects." I hear optimism in his voice.

So when our team jogs onto the state tournament field this summer, we can feel good about our meager contribution in January that helped them get there. And wave our GO GNATS pennants accordingly.

CHARLIE'S ANGELS

'TIS THE SEASON FOR ANGELS. "Cherubim and seraphim, in unceasing chorus praising." Nimrod has its own angelic order—Charlie's Angels. Not the old television show variety. But these angels are also involved in the criminal justice system. Charlie, in this case, is Charlie Tuorila. His angels are convicts who work off part of their jail time or pay off fines in the Sentencing-to-Serve (STS) program. The program is administered by Todd Wadena Community Correction under the auspices of the Probation Department.

Charlie begins his twelfth year in the STS program in 2002. His project area is all of Wadena and Todd Counties, ninety plus miles north to south. Watching Charlie manage the Nimrod Gnats baseball team and sitting across the kitchen table from him, anyone can see he is the perfect man for the job: a commanding presence, an authoritative voice, a sensitive demeanor. That, plus a ready smile. He enjoys his work.

Clients that take advantage of the STS program are from the State of Minnesota, Todd and Wadena Counties, and townships and cities within those counties. The state, by funding half the program, gets one third of the STS projects. Two state agencies that benefit, according to Charlie, are the DNR and the Community Action Council. The CAC manages state housing projects and keeps five crews busy building houses, Charlie's Angels among them. The work is general construction, starting with pouring foundations and laying blocks, up through finish carpentry. "Everything except plumbing and electrical wiring," says Charlie. "We leave that to the professionals."

Work for townships includes roadside brush cleaning. For Wadena County, park maintenance. For the cities, clean up and maintenance of public facilities. The STS crews just finished painting the DAC building in Sebeka. For Nimrod, they have constructed bleachers at the park, painted the Community Center building, landscaped the ball field, and built the fence around the West Lyons cemetery.

Terry Simon, Division of Wildlife, DNR Brainerd office, considers this a good program. The STS crews do wildlife management tasks, like clearing parking areas and boundary lines, trail maintenance, gate construction—many of the manual labor tasks that are essential to good park management but take time and funds to get done. Terry's area covers over 5,000 acres in Wadena County, and includes thirteen wildlife areas. One of the spring projects is to build and erect fifty to one hundred wood duck houses. "The Sentencing-to-Serve people have done a great job for us over the past ten years," says Terry.

Charlie is the only full-time work supervisor for the STS program. Three others work part time. A crew typically includes both men and women. Offenses that result in convictions and sentencing are seventy-five percent DUI and drug related, says Charlie. Convicted workers deduct five dollars an hour from their fines for field work, or deduct one day off their sentences for every three eight-hour days worked. Most workers are in the twenty to thirty years old age group, but range from pre-teens to seventy-five-year olds. "These people are happy to work," says Charlie. "It's a chance to get out of jail and to work off their fines."

I asked the obvious question—How many escapes in eleven years of supervising these crews? "Only three," says Charlie. "The last one was in Staples where I supervised sixteen people at four job sites." Obviously these people are carefully screened for trustworthiness. The sentencing judge and jail administrator determine that.

Wayne Wendel is the Director of the Sentencing-to-Serve program and a probation officer in Long Prairie. He says the program has been in place for eleven years, and Charlie was and is their first full-time crew supervisor. Wayne also directs three part-time adult programs and the juvenile program. Juveniles, twelve to eighteen, stack firewood and shovel snow this time of year, and rake and do park maintenance summer and fall. Glenn Motzko, of Oylen fame and the one-man Wadena County Parks Department, gets a big assist from the juvenile crews in removing park garbage every Monday during park use months.

"Some communities donate money and equipment," says Wayne. "With a limited budget, everything helps."

I asked Wayne about the selection of candidates for the STS program. He calls the program a trust situation. The workers have plenty of opportunities to split. But they realize it's a good program for them. They not only get out of jail and reduce their fines, but they also learn new skills and develop good working habits. "We appreciate the work Charlie has done," Wayne says.

What's in store for 2002? "A full schedule," says Charlie. There is a city office addition to finish in Staples. Two or three houses to tear down in Long Prairie. Sidewalks and ramps to construct at the DAC in Browerville. A forty-by-sixty pole building to erect for the Staples Maintenance Department, which includes three to four hundred yards of concrete. That, plus continued road brushing and park and wildlife maintenance.

The Sentencing-to-Serve program works on several levels. Besides the obvious one of participants getting the opportunity to get out of jail, work off their sentences, do something constructive, the rate of destructive behavior diminishes after these people have spent time cleaning up a park or other public facility. Some have learned construction trades and taken jobs in their new fields.

The Sentence-to-Serve program works on the community level, with projects getting done that would have to compete for scarce time and funds. The program works on a personal level too, giving the participants increased self-esteem, a sense of accomplishment. As Charlie says, "A chance to look back after a day's work and see something there that wasn't there this morning." Good work, Charlie.

CHOCOLATE-COVERED CHERRIES

IT'S CHRISTMAS TIME, the time of year that we resurrect memories of childhood, sugar coat them, and pass them on as family lore. I have a memory of Christ's birthday that begins on another December birthday, mine, on December 12. It was 1941, and I was nine years old. Life was meager in rural Elk River. We fed and milked cows morning and night. We walked one mile to school. We were on relief. The Chevy was on blocks for the winter. We toted water, hand pumped, in milk cans on a sled from the well by the barn, and we lugged chunks of oak and elm for the wood box. Five kids slept upstairs in an undivided, un-insulated bedroom. It was, as they say, The Good Old Days.

The Japanese had bombed Pearl Harbor a few days earlier. The only Pearl I knew was Pearl Schenk, my second grade teacher. I felt sorry for this Pearl Harbor lady, but I couldn't understand why her being bombed was cause for us to enter World War II.

Those were the days before television, before computers, calculators, the Women's Rights Movement, tubeless tires, the innerspring mattress, microwave ovens, home thermostats, and Pac Man. We had recently witnessed the advent of electricity on the farm.

But, life was good. I had three older sisters: Delores, the sweet one; Lil, the outspoken one; and Rose Mary, the managerial (I wanted to say bossy) one. Phil was (is) five years younger than I, the first darling of our new blended family. Jim was even younger, and Frank still slept between Mother and Dad in the downstairs bedroom.

On December 12, the mailman delivered a brown paper package addressed to me from Aunt Minnie. When supper was finished and the dishes washed, Delores carried the candled birthday cake into the living room where the family gathered to listen to Lux Radio Theater. Cherry-red patches glowed in the wood stove. Mittens lay underneath, drying stiff as kitchen linoleum. Diapers hung from clothes lines nailed to the wall, their moisture coating the windows with hoarfrost as thick as Grandpa's glasses.

It was time to open the gifts. Not considering consequences, I opened Aunt Minnie's package, surrounded by my family. They waited like timber wolves encircling a stranded fawn, yellow eyes leering, white teeth gleaming, pink tongues salivating. But I digress.

A box of chocolate covered cherries! I tore through the cellophane (also recently invented) and stared at a picture of dark chocolate balls with creamy vanilla filling around a succulent red cherry. I wanted this moment to last forever.

"Aren't you going to pass them around?" Mother asked.

I opened the box and counted the cherries. Eight. I counted my family circle. Eight. Should I be generous and show some early Christmas spirit? Or should I be assertive (Rose Mary would say piggy) and acknowledge that this gift was mine on my special day? I looked around the room, spotted a weak spot between Jim and baby Frank, and did an end run up the stairs.

I made the mistake, maybe thirty years later, of relating this story to my sons, Mark and Greg. They found it hilarious, if not incredible. No television! Get real! But they picked up on the chocolate covered cherries. And for Christmas that year, I got another box of, guess what! By thirty-nine, however, I had lost my taste for Brach's chocolate, sweet vanilla filling, and maraschino cherries, which they well knew. But it was a clever gift. So clever, in fact, that I saved the box, unopened, and gave it back to them the next Christmas.

We rotated the cherries year after year, spending hours and big bucks on clever packaging disguises. And I expect to get a box again this year, probably in the glove compartment of my real Christmas gift, a Lexus LS 430.

That's how family traditions are born. A simple act of kindness, or stinginess, as Rose Mary would say.

DAUGHTER OF THE CIVIL WAR

WHAT STARTED OUT AS A STORY about the daughter of a civil war veteran took a turn as I talked to Stella Pickar. Stella, born in 1910 to Ernestine (Madlung) and George Washington Rice II, is very much a Daughter of the Civil War, but she has led and continues to lead a full life in her own right.

George Washington Rice II served as an enlisted man in Company F of the Eighth Regiment Minnesota Volunteer Infantry. He was mustered into federal service at Ft. Snelling in November 1862. To save readers a trip to the Civil War website, confederate troops attacked Fort Sumter in April 1861. To quote William H Houlton: "The Eighth Regiment was organized under the 600,000 call, during the darkest days of the Rebellion. In August 1862, McClellan had been beaten before Richmond, and Lee threatened Washington. The Union cause was desperate."

Enter the men from Minnesota! Farmers and lumberjacks, strong in survival skills, experts in the use of firearms, and hunters from the time they were old enough to carry a gun.

Coincidental with the onset of the Civil War were the clashes between American Indians and white settlers. At the time of enlistment, the Eighth Regiment expected to go south, but instead they were diverted to the most exposed points of the frontier, guarding white settlements and earning themselves the title Indian Regiment.

The Eighth Regiment concluded their frontier guard duties in September 1864, returned to Ft. Snelling, and headed south in October. It fought in the battle of Murfreesboro (Tennessee) and fortified its reputation as the best drilled and most reliable regiment in the command.

In November 1864, General Sherman began his march to the sea; in December, Sherman occupied Savannah, Georgia; and in April 1865, General Robert E. Lee surrendered to General Ulysses S. Grant. In July 1865, Company F returned to Ft. Snelling, and George Washington Rice was honorably discharged.

There followed brief careers in race horses and real estate before moving to the homestead in Orton Township in 1905 with his wife Ernestine. (Ernestine's sister is Frieda Madlung, mother of Clara Frame, proving once again the prudence of talking well about your neighbor, because they're all related up here.) The marriage produced five children, the youngest, Stella, born in 1910. George Washington Rice died in December 1917 and is buried in Lyons Cemetery. Ernestine, his second wife and thirty-seven years younger, died in 1957. Youngest daughter, Stella, is very much alive and lives near the old homestead east of Nimrod. Another survivor in the mold of her Civil War father.

Somehow, this woman had evaded me for seven years. I'm always on the lookout for older folks who don't act their age. And I mean that in the best sense.

Walking into her house, I enter a room that is the production area for a variety of crafts: wood, plaster, plastic resins. Wood-cut silhouettes hang from the walls. Further inside the house is the finishing room, stocked with works in progress and paints of many kinds and colors. She talks of gifts for the grandchildren, garage and craft sales. She complains about losing her steady hand, but the intricate cuts on her scroll saw belie that.

She talks with an energy that feels like she will be around for a while. She mentions an oral history project that was sidetracked after a son's death. A great-grandson, wise beyond his years, she hopes, will carry family history forward.

Daylight fades. Chickadees distract us at the feeder outside the kitchen window. A young doe feeds in the backyard. Two hours after I arrive, I go into overload.

I'm going back. I want to hear the Civil War stories. And maybe we'll walk through the Lyons Cemetery and look at family headstones. But only after son Skip Pickar plows the cemetery road.

DEAR NIMROD CHRONICLER:

ONE OF THE REASONS that the *Review Messenger* has less distribution than, say, *The New York Times*, is that there's no "Dear Abby" column. But, gentle reader, we can rectify that, right?

After posting small, obscure notices advertising such a service at the bar & grill, the service station, and the community center, I was flooded with responses. Herewith, a few:

Dear Nimrod Chronicler,

Why am I having so much trouble finding Mr. Wonderful? I've looked at the casino in Walker; I've searched the singles dance in Wadena; I've gone to every church supper within a fifty-mile radius. Nothing.

Signed, Ready to Join the Convent

Dear Ready to Join . . .

At the risk of sounding like a country western tune, you're looking in all the wrong places. True love, like happiness, is found in your own backyard. Raise your sights a couple notches, and check out Nimrod. We have more eligible bachelors than legendary Herman, Minnesota. However, to appeal to a Nimrod man, you must project domesticity, love of outdoors, and zest for life.

Offer to clean his house (for minimum wage). Plan to spend four hours; for the first three, put a pot roast in the oven; for the last hour, bake a chocolate cake. Do one task in each room. Wash dishes in the kitchen, clean the bathroom sink, make the bed. Stack the newspapers and magazines in the living room. DO NOT THROW ANYTHING AWAY! The pot roast and chocolate cake should have him one-third hooked.

Appeal to his love of outdoors by fitting yourself in a pair of insulated coveralls from Fleet Farm. Pick up a three-horse power ice auger, a Clam 6800 portable fish house, an infrared underwater camera. Know the difference between a tip-up and an Ugly Stik. Toss out phrases like "jigging a foot off bottom." You're two-thirds there.

Demonstrate *joie de vivre* (and this is so obvious) by riding your Harley wherever you go. Ice fishing on Saturday, bingo on Sunday, house cleaning on Monday. You'll hook Mr. Wonderful before you hook a three-pound walleye.

And let me know when you're available for house cleaning.

Dear Nimrod Chronicler,

Help! I'm ready to quit college. People ask me where I'm from. When I answer "Nimrod," they get hysterical. "Nimrod? There is such a town? Har, har, har."

Desperate at UMD

Dear Desperate,

I hear you. Tell them about the biblical derivation of the name, and they still laugh. Here's what you do. Get a selection of University of Nimrod sweats and T-shirts. Wear them everywhere. To class, to games, to dates, to coffee. Borrow the Nimrod Jubilee street banner and hang it from the second floor windows of your dorm. Call your campus radio station nightly and request dedications to the "hottie" from Nimrod. Attach your license plate, proclaiming "Nimrod, Minnesota, population, whatever." Just like a cuss word, the name loses its power after it's repeated a few hundred times. Hang in there. Don't cop out and say you're from Oylen.

Dear Nimrod Chronicler,

I can't seem to find Ms. Wonderful. I'm a Plain Joe kind of guy. Love pot roast and chocolate cake. My idea of fun is an afternoon of ice fishing and a ride on my Harley. Any ideas?

Signed, Lonesome in Lyons Township

Dear Lonesome,
How would you like all that, plus a clean house?

NIMROD NEWS

Mr. and Mrs. Dean Estabrooks of north Nimrod attended the Valley City Winter Show, along with other members of the Mid-Minnesota Beef Growers Association. Dean took a day off from tractor repair and wore his Alaska red suspenders instead of the John Deere pair. Nothing runs like a Deere?

Mr. and Mrs. Jeff Pederson and family made a weekend visit to Park Rapids. Son Jordan was less than enthusiastic. "I hope they have a vegetarian restaurant," he said.

Kevin "Henry" Milbradt was spotted at a Brainerd shopping mall by talent scouts for Minnesota's Coen brothers, who made the movie *Fargo*. Henry was encouraged to enter the Tom Selleck Look-Alike Contest.

Keith Frame, auto mechanic at Nimrod Service, was interviewed and photographed for *Chevy Times* while changing oil on a 250,000-mile Chevrolet pickup truck. When asked for his opinion on Chevrolet versus Ford, Keith answered with his characteristic enthusiasm, "Whatever."

Delores Shore and Cindy and Dan Warmbold made a trip to Northern Lights casino in Walker. Delores won forty-five dollars on the quarter slots. Cindy won one-hundred dollars in the Video Poker Tournament. Dan paid for the gas.

Mr. and Mrs. Glenn Pederson of Oylen returned from a month's vacation in Mesa, Arizona. Their pickup truck was loaded with oranges and grapefruit for their many friends and neighbors. Thank you, Glenn and Brenda.

The Sunday bingo games, sponsored by the Nimrod Gnats baseball team, continues to draw huge crowds. Recent local winners of fifteen-dollar jackpots include Adeline Avelsgard, Marty Horton, and Bob Wagner. Bob returned his prize to the Gnats. Atta boy, Bob.

Clara Frame, one of Nimrod's active octogenarians, was the sole occupant of the women's table at the R&R coffee klatch after the big snow dump Monday morning. "Don't know about this younger generation," quipped Clara.

Speaking of the coffee klatch, Jerry Schermerhorn, a regular at the men's table, announced his retirement from the board of directors at the West Central Telephone Association. Jerry has served for over three decades. Early photos show him with hair.

Ann Stigman, Nimrod's postal clerk, was honored by the United States Postal Service for ten consecutive years of post office operation without a single fatal outbreak of "post office rage." Ann received a certificate and a packet of USPS stationery.

Bob Hames was one of several Nimrod neighbors who cooperated in a day of pig butchering. Bob has promised some sausage to his neighbors.

Mildred Bickford, Lorraine Loween, and Lila Perkins were luncheon guests of Connie Frederickson. Connie served a chicken salad with green grapes, taken from a recipe in the March issue of *Farm Journal*. Lunch was followed by a few hands of Hearts.

Jerry Mevissen, a local farmer, was taken into custody on charges of misrepresentation of facts, maligning character, and cross-country skiing on public lands without a license. Sentencing will be in May at Wadena Seventh District Court.

ANN STIGMAN, POSTAL CLERK

SMALL TOWNS LOVE GOSSIP. Well, I have a tidbit to add. Part confession, part declaration. I admire Ann Stigman.

For those who have been in town for less than ten minutes, Ann is the Nimrod postal clerk. She declines "postmistress" even though she's head honcho in the eighteen-by-eighteen-foot building on Main Street.

Ann is (dare I reveal her age?) eighty-eight and has been sorting mail and selling stamps since 1967. To give that a historical perspective, Lyndon B. Johnson was president then; the Vietnam War was morphing into a major conflict; and a three-cent stamp cost a nickel.

Ann arrived in Nimrod in 1934, newly married to Jack Stigman, himself a legend, I'm told. Fun loving. A good neighbor. The true Nimrod cut. Through the years, they operated a cafe and country store, brought four children into the world, and suffered fear and loneliness in World War II when Jack served overseas in the U.S. Navy.

In time, they sold the store, and Ann became a full-time mother. From some of the legends I've heard, the four kids—Al, Dick, Jeanette, and Dave—could hardly be classified as reclusive. Sociability was inherited from both mom and dad.

Ann's postal career began in 1967. First she was a part-time clerk when the post office was the back room of Lila Perkins' store in Nimrod. When that building burned, the postal function moved down the street to a former filling station, remodeled to a shoe shop, and later enjoying its third life as a municipal building, which it is today.

Ann recalls the primitive heating systems in the building, beginning with a portable oil space heater. As the price of postage rose, she graduated to a used trailer heater, which was still operating (occasionally) when I arrived in 1993. Then a year or so ago, with a three-cent stamp now costing thirty-four cents, she finally merited a thermostatically controlled oil space heater. Must have been a long wait, considering that she has a son in the fuel oil business.

"Good morning, good looking," I say as I enter the post office. "How you doing today?"

Her eyes sparkle. "Oh, pretty good for an old lady," she says, understatement being a characteristic of the natives.

We talk of common things: temperature and snow depth, birds at the feeder, family visits. I take inspiration from her and other seniors in the neighborhood past the age where contributions to society are expected. Yet Ann—and the others—still clerk, and cook, and keep the gardens neat and the grass cut.

Word-weary folks from the coffee klatch next door wander over at ten o'clock to pick up mail and get a free smile, part of the daily routine in Nimrod. Ann opens the building six days a week at nine and keeps it open until noon.

I wonder about the future of the Nimrod Post Office, and so does Ann. She has an annual goal for stamp sales: ten thousand dollars for 1998, rising to fifteen thousand dollars in 1999. The office is classified as a Rural Station, which sounds like a candidate for being a victim of an efficiency reorganization.

So why does an eighty-eight-year-old woman who has led a full life still open the post office daily? Why not crochet afghans for her nineteen grandchildren and her thirty-three (with one more on the way) great-grandchildren? Habit, she says. That, and her love of people and her need to stay in touch. I also believe that she knows that, with her behind the counter, the post office in Nimrod will stay open, irrespective of stamp sale quotas.

THE RETURN OF "JUST ASK"

ABOUT A MONTH AGO, I asked some Nimrod seniors for an early memory of Nimrod. What were they doing, and what was happening in the town. Now it's time to turn the tables and ask some high school students from Nimrod for a prediction of what they will be doing ten years from now, and what the town will look like.

KATIE BECKER (high school junior, Nimrod Princess 2001, focused). "I'll stay in the Nimrod area. After graduation, I plan to go to Bemidji State and major in Social Work and probably work in a school around here. I think Nimrod will grow—a lot!"

STEVE FUNK (high school freshman, baseball, outdoor guy, extrovert). "I don't think Nimrod will grow beyond 100, but the area around Nimrod will. I like to hunt and fish, so I'll look for a career in forestry or conservation. I plan to continue with the Nimrod Gnats. They are the magnet that pulls people to town."

BETH KUSCHEL (high school senior, Nimrod Royalty 200, confident). "I'll stay in Nimrod, too, because of the people. I'm connected to Nimrod. My fantasy is to open a Bed and Breakfast, the Triple B (Beth's B&B), and serve the canoe and snowmobile trade and visitors for Jubilee Days. My reality is to attend Brainerd Central Lakes for two years of general education, leading to primary grade teaching. I expect Nimrod to have a population of 100 in ten years, but I'd like to see it still be the small town it is today."

VENESSA MARTHALER (high school freshman, farmer's daughter, determined). "I plan to live in the country, but *not* on a farm. I'm thinking about a career in home interior design, but I don't think that would play in Nimrod. As for the town, I see the gas station adding a convenience store, the Bar & Grill staying the same, Hillig Mercantile expanding, and maybe a new cafe."

NICK METTEER (high school senior, trumpeter, basketball, competent). "I see Nimrod growing slowly to about 100 people. People who leave tend to return. Opportunities are limited for young people. My family is what will keep me here. I have two terrific grandpas who are great storytellers (Harold Metteer and Clarence Tappe). I'm keeping my options open for next year, probably a business college with an accounting major. I'd like to play college sports, maybe continue in music."

TAMMY MOENCH (high school senior, engaged, grocery clerk, confident, assured). "I expect Nimrod to grow to about 100 people, too, in ten years. Maybe a few more buildings, maybe a bigger grocery store. But probably not any more opportunities. It would be great to have something for young people, like a roller rink. There's a lot of interest in that now, but would it be able to attract enough people? After graduation, I plan to move to Wadena, and attend Tech School this fall, training to be an administrative assistant. Then maybe move back to the Nimrod area in five or six years. My family and friends here are the big attraction."

BETHANY PEDERSON (high school freshman, rodeo queen, ambitious). "I probably won't be living in Nimrod. Maybe a Twin Cities suburb, maybe a closer town like Wadena. I'd like the benefits of living in the country, with less of the work. I can make that happen because, today, I plan to train to be a dentist. And what do I predict for Nimrod? A population of 100. Young people who leave tend to come home. I like Nimrod, but there's not much for us to do."

BRYAN PEDERSON (high school senior, cattle baron, NG, basketball, ace drummer). "I'm going to let the U.S. Army finance my first house and pay for my education. That will be at Bemidji State where I'll major in secondary education. I want to be a math teacher in a large school, toward the Twin Cities metro area. And the school will have a modern gym and a winning basketball team. Nimrod in ten years? About 100 people, about the same as today."

DAVIS WHITAKER (high school senior, U.S. Army enlistee, optimistic). "I plan to attend North Dakota State College in Wahpetan and train to be an electrician. Then, I'll work in the Twin Cities area. But first, I have my Army service. I've had my physical exam, and I report for basic training in August. I see Nimrod staying the same as it is today."

So, there it is, folks. A town of 100 in 2012. The same folks hanging around the post office. The same guys at the coffee table at the R&R, telling the same lies, retelling the same old jokes, still trying to get them right. I can handle that!

NIMROD GOTHIC

IT'S FIVE O'CLOCK IN THE MORNING, a full two hours before daylight on this brass monkey cold January morning. Moon is full, and it lights the path to work, which isn't a great distance. Just from the house to the barn. Of course, when starting before daybreak, quitting time is before dark, right? Wrong! Welcome to the world of dairy farming.

Glenda and Harold Gilster and son David farm 320 acres north of town on the Huntersville Road, with an assist from second son Danny. This is the family farm people have read and heard about for the past twenty-five years. The one that is an endangered species. Farming: the only business that buys at retail and sells at wholesale. The business with the highest capitalization and cost of entry, and the lowest rate of return. The industry comprised of sole proprietors who resist collective bargaining and, literally, take what's offered to them.

Having said that, the Gilsters lead the good life. Modest but comfortable. Hard working but rewarding. Victims of the vagaries of the market but independent in their day-to-day operation.

Alfred and Evelyn Gilster, Harold's parents, settled here in 1930 and raised three kids: Doreen, Harold, and Larry. The original red frame barn, built in 1945, still stands. Harold doubled the milking capacity to fifty-four tie stalls in 1990. He and David milk fifty-two Holsteins twice a day, 365 days a year. No paid holidays, no two-week vacations, no sick leave.

Dairying is an interesting business, not subject to the published laws of supply and demand. For example, the price of dairy cows is on the rise, with replacement heifers bringing around $1,700. So the price of milk should be on the rise too, right? Wrong again! Milk currently brings $13.50 cwt for grade A. The American Dairy Association touts the success of its clever "Got milk?" ad campaign, and milk consumption has increased nationally. But, as has been stated a million times before, higher prices as a result of increased demand haven't trickled down to the producer. Au contraire! If the creameries pay only $13.50 cwt, then the farmers' response is to increase the size of the herd and produce more to make up the difference. Up goes supply, down go prices. And that probably won't change.

The Gilster herd produces 3,100 pounds of milk a day, and the milk truck arrives daily to haul it to the creamery in Fergus Falls. Other local dairy farmers are members of other dairy associations and ship to other locations. The Fergus Falls truck driver is seventy miles from home here in Nimrod. And his market extends west into South Dakota.

The Gilsters feed their herd 4,800 pounds of feed per day, a mixture of alfalfa, silage, and a commercial feed blend of cotton seed, cracked corn, soybeans, salt, and minerals. Add to that thirty to forty gallons of water per cow, and the cows are ingesting about 8,000 pounds of food and drink per day. If they produce 3,100 pounds of milk, everyone knows where the rest is headed. The tractor and manure spreader are parked inside, under the barn cleaner ramp. Cleaning the barn is a matter of flicking an electrical switch. Whatever happened to the wheelbarrow, the manure fork, and the slippery plank from the double doors to the top of the frozen manure pile?

Tom Hovde, Wadena County Extension Editor, reported in his column in this newspaper last month that dairy farms in Wadena County decreased from 440 in 1983, to 231 in 1989, to 150 in 1995, to 97 on January 1, 2001. Hardly a growth industry. Tom assessed the rationale behind the decline as economic. Today's farmers are retiring, and young farmers have trouble securing financing. Add to that the cost of land, a dairy herd, a fleet of tractors, barn and outbuildings, and all the ancillary equipment and supplies to make a farm productive, and it adds up to big bucks.

I wonder how many farmers are in it for the money. I wonder if there isn't gratification that comes from a healthy herd producing a healthy product. Gratification from setting one's own goals, and one's own schedule for achieving them. Appreciation for the rhythm of life on the farm. The seasons—planting, cultivating, harvesting. The cycles—milking, drying up, calving. The daily tangible results—a new calf, first cutting of alfalfa baled and stored, 3,100 pounds of milk today.

Will the Gilster farm continue to be a family farm? Glenda and Harold hope that David continues. David talks of keeping his options open, but my guess is that he will continue the tradition. That may mean convincing true love Karlene to make the move from Fargo.

There's a sign at Gilster's driveway off Huntersville Road that reads "Dead End." That end is anything but dead now. Hopefully, there's another generation of life, one more family in this family farm.

LEATHER AND LACE

"IN THE BLUE CORNER. From Nimrod, Minnesota. Weighing 125 pounds. LACEY KUSCHEL." She trots to the center of the ring, gives a boxer's high five to her opponent, returns to her corner. She dances, rotates her shoulders, shadow boxes. Lacey is scheduled for the ninth bout in an eleven-bout Golden Gloves boxing card at the Wadena Armory. She awaits the bell.

Without her blue leather gloves, no one would take Lacey for a boxer. Attractive, petite, soft spoken, she's more like the girl next door. She started boxing at Sebeka High School and has been at it for four years. But there's a competitive streak in her. After the match on Saturday, she rode in a barrels competition on Sunday. Monday she returned to her regular schedule as student at Brainerd Central Lakes College, where she is in the second year of a horticulture curriculum.

The bell gongs. Lacey springs out of the blue corner. Her opponent, Dannette Stamer from Grand Forks, meets her half way. Punches fly, right now! Forget any thoughts about the female as shrinking violet. These ladies are covering the ring, deflecting a punch here, landing one there. They have not fought each other before, but the "let's get acquainted" interlude is brief. Lacey is an unleashed tiger, a model of kinetic energy.

Lacey's stringent training schedule has her lifting weights three times a week, running three miles three times a week, and sparring in a routine devised by her coach, Kolyn Crawford of Pine River. Her diet is light on sweets, heavy on protein. And she gets all the sleep she can.

Back in the ring, Lacey vibrates across the floor, her eyes glued to her opponent. They exchange punches. Air hisses out of flattened gloves. Lights are intense, white hot above the ring. The ring smells like sweat, popcorn. The crowd cheers, hoots, hollers, whistles, stomps. It's like standing between two roaring freight trains. The bell rings. End of Round One.

When she boxes, Lacey goes into an automatic mode. Her motions are intuitive. Her training tells her what to do; her opponent tells her when to do it. How does she activate the adrenaline? "I think about winning," she says. Good! Is winning everything? Does she give herself credit for a good fight? "I get frustrated if I lose." Does the crowd make a difference? "Definitely!" she says. "I get pumped up by the roar."

Round Two. Lacey rebounds into the ring, with fresh strategy from coach Kolyn. The two boxers are well matched. Both are energetic, aggressive, intent. They cover the ring, trade punches, duck, dodge, reach. A round that lasts minutes seems like hours. The fact that these are females in the ring is quickly lost. This is not a powder puff derby. Their techniques, strategy, and energy rival those of their male counterparts. The bell rings. End of Round Two.

Golden Gloves originated in 1923 when Arch Ward, sports editor for a Chicago newspaper, organized an amateur boxing tournament to assist young boxers and promote amateur competition. The list of Golden Gloves alumni is impressive. Joe Louis was Golden Gloves champion in 1934. Sugar Ray Leonard, Muhammad Ali, Leon Spinks, and Evander Holyfield all started their boxing careers in the Golden Gloves. Today, 22,000 male and female athletes, ages eight to thirty-three, participate in the boxing program across the United States.

Round Three. Last chance to score a decisive victory. Last chance to implement the strategy. Last chance to make all that training pay off. But first, one must last. Is it the physical activity or the emotional pressure that's most draining? The boxers work the ring, trading controlled, calculated punches. Someone yells, "Give her the old one, two, three!" Lacey follows her opponent, watches for the opening, deflects a punch, dodges a swing. Finally the bell. The end of Round Three. The end of the match.

Lacey has a boxing heritage. Dad, Lonnie, was a boxer in high school. Her brother boxed for three years in elementary school. Mother, Betsy, confines her ring activities to the corral. She manages the family beef cattle operation north of town. Lacey is her part-time wrangler.

The referee picks up the decisions of the judges. Each boxer walks to the center of the ring, one arm held by the referee. The announcer reports the decision. "The winner, in the red corner . . ." and raises Dannette's arm. The hometown crowd is non-partisan, gives Dannette hearty applause. And the applause goes to Lacey too for a good fight. If she needs consolation, she can stick around and watch boyfriend, Dan Soukup, teach some humility to his opponent from Leach Lake in the main event.

TWIN CELEBRATIONS

WE'RE COMING UP ON THE SECOND ANNIVERSARY of the Nimrod Chronicles. The first was prompted by a eulogy I wrote for Henry Butzin in December 2000, but didn't have the strength to present at his review or funeral. Now, about a hundred columns later, the Chronicles have a life of their own. Readers provide ideas; the locals fill in the details. I record, put my spin on it and sign my name. Every week, it is printed in 3,700 copies of this newspaper.

The Chronicles have been my key into many homes. We've talked about careers, hobbies, family history, births, weddings, and deaths. We've talked about town events, entertainment, sports, and government. We've dipped into history to keep colorful local lore alive. We've mined the memories of our elders to preserve in print the glory of Nimrod past. And we've spotlighted the young people, the next generation, who are our insurance that local traditions and values will survive.

I've been asked what I'll do when I run out of subject matter. That isn't likely. I have a portfolio of articles to be written: the ladies' coffee table at the R&R Bar & Grill; the turn-of-the-century Johnson house recently sold by the Wetzels; the CCC camp at Frame's Landing; the glory days of lumbering on the Crow Wing River; another Welcome Wagon story introducing new neighbors to Nimrod (and not snubbing Patty Frame this time); the wire grass farm north of town; the Great Fire of 1976; the memories of Clara Frame; the endurance of Elsie Riley; the energy and charm of Ann Stigman.

All that, plus the regularly scheduled events—Nimrod Gnats baseball, karaoke championships, Jubilee Days, deer hunting, pool tournaments, and fishing season opener.

I've been mildly criticized for my constant mention of the R&R Bar & Grill, more often by people who don't understand the nature of a village pub. And a pub it is, derived from "public house," a place where the community congregates. The crowded parking spaces every morning in front of the R&R are testimony to the congeniality of the townspeople. It must seem incongruous to a stranger driving through town, first seeing a "Population 75" sign and then seeing half that many cars at morning coffee or at spaghetti dinner benefits for the Do-Gooders or Nimrod Gnats.

The second anniversary is that of my birth on December 12, 1932, seventy years ago, to save the arithmetic. And a good year it has been, with promise of 2003 being better. Some highlights from 2002: a divorce decree, which took my life off "hold" and gave me permission to plan a future; creative writing class at the Loft in Minneapolis; caring for the homestead on the river and acting as steward for land and livestock; photography class at North Central College; real estate appraising a couple days a week; stage debut with the Wadena Mad Hatters in *Arsenic and Old Lace* (my first and last stage appearance); watching five grandkids grow; photo/writing exhibit at Tri-County Hospital; two articles published in *Lakes Alive* magazine, and short stories published in *The Talking Stick* and *realgoodwords*; and the health, energy, and wherewithal to enjoy all these.

Some projected highlights for 2003: the new and improved photo/writing exhibit moves to New York Mills Regional Cultural Center in January for a two-month stint; several capital improvement projects around the farm—sidewalk, greenhouse, and shed, reappear after I lost momentum in August 2000; discussions with a book publisher for a collection of columns, *The Best of the Nimrod Chronicles*, with publication targeted for Jubilee Days 2003; and the five-year interval birthday party. It doesn't seem five years ago since 140 of us celebrated my sixty-fifth birthday in the garage, a tent, and a partially constructed house. Watch for an announcement in July.

So, life is good! Next to my health, friends are my greatest asset. Thanks for welcoming me into your lives.

THE LESSONS OF WAR

"Progress toward our objectives has been rapid and dramatic."

General Tommy Franks, U.S. Commander of the Attack on Iraq.

"As time goes by, they will lose more. We will make it as painful as we can."

Saddam Hussein, President of Iraq.

Christian Science Monitor, March 24, 2003

THIS MORNING, THE SKY OVER MY COUNTRY is clean blue. Geese honk up river. Finches twitter in the jackpines. Crows caw in the pasture. Two calves butt heads in the corral. That's the extent of aggression here.

Half way around the planet, it's night. Missiles whistle and bombs thud. The land reeks of burning oil, smoking factories, and the acrid odor of gun fire. This is war.

Nimrod veterans know the truth of war—the gut feelings of fear and frustration, separation and seclusion. They know the reality of war—death and destruction, renewal and restoration. To a man, the veterans with whom I spoke support President Bush and the troops. And, to a man, they support the dissenters and peace activists, which is to say, they support democracy and the freedoms inherent in it.

Harold Metteer enlisted in the army in August 1942, nine months after the United States entered World War II, the "Great War." He took basic training at Ft. Leonard Wood, Missouri, and Breckinridge, Kentucky, and was assigned to the Twenty-Seventh Evacuation Hospital. After months of frustrating stateside delays, he shipped to North Africa in April 1944. The Twenty-Seventh set up a hospital in Maddaloni, Italy, and, later, five more hospitals in France. In 1944, Harold saw the reality of war when Maddaloni Hospital treated 2,900 American and Allied Forces patients. Germany surrendered in May 1945.

"This war doesn't remind me of my war," says Harold. "We didn't know where we were going or what was going on until we got orders. And neither did the rest of the world. I think the media gets carried away. He quotes a reporter's question to a family of an early war victim. "How to you feel about the loss of your brother?"

Harold and others in the European theater didn't have CNN and imbedded reporters. They had Axis Sally's radio reports on troop movements, ship positions, and Allied casualties. And they had the sanitized news of the *Stars and Stripes*.

Jerry Graba returned from the harvest fields of North Dakota in the fall of his twenty-second year. He beat the Army draft by enlisting in the Air Force in November 1950 during the Korean War, the "Forgotten War." His dream was to be assigned to an aircraft crew, and he trained as gunner, mechanic, and radio operator. After basic training at Lackland Air Force Base, Texas, and radio school at Keesler Air Force Base, Mississippi, he was among the eight percent selected to serve on aircraft. He reported to Randall Air Force Base, Texas, and was assigned as radio operator on a B-29.

Jerry served under a commander who resisted shipping out to Korea, in spite of a gung-ho crew who craved action. The commander prevailed, and Jerry found himself flying high radar tracks out of Warner Robbins Air Force Base, Georgia. They flew from Nashville up the East Coast to Canada, and from Wilmington, Delaware, along the Canadian border to allow ground units to test accuracy of radar systems.

Time was running out to serve overseas. Jerry returned to Nashville to train on the C-119 Flying Boxcar, a two-engine transport prop job with a reputation for reliability. In February 1953, he flew to Tokyo with twenty-five F-94 pilots, all recently created second lieutenants. From there, he rode the train to the southern tip of Japan and was assigned to a C-119 that flew aircraft engines and replacement parts to Air Force bases in Seoul and Chunchon.

"We had many nations fighting with us," says Jerry. "English and Australian. We knew the U.S. was carrying the load, but other nations were there. It was an international effort, more so than we're seeing today. The wars are hard to compare. Whatever prevailed in Korea isn't present in Iraq."

Jerry talks on the emphasis he felt as appearing helpful—wearing away Korean resentment, and soft-selling democracy. "Maybe the lesson of war was to teach freedom, dignity, and quality of life." He got a taste of the horror of war when they hauled cadavers on trips back to the base.

Glenn Pederson was drafted into the U.S. Army at age nineteen during the Vietnam War, judged the "Lost War" by those who didn't fight it. The U.S. supplied combat troops to Vietnam from 1965 to January 1973, when a cease fire agreement was signed. Later in 1973, the U.S. removed its last combat troops. The Communists launched a second offensive against South Vietnam, and, on April 30, 1975, Saigon fell to the Communists, giving them control of South Vietnam.

Glenn served on a four-deuce mortar weapon system, one man of a three-man crew—sighter, loader, and holder. He served in Vietnam between November 1968 and November 1969 near Pleiku, halfway up from Saigon to the DMZ.

He arrived in Vietnam assigned to Bravo Company, an Infantry outfit, and was transferred to Echo Company, a reconnaissance and mortar squad. He saw combat in a far different environment that that shown in Iraq. Instead of a hundred miles of desert, Vietnam was jungles and mountains. Vietcong could be a mile away or a hundred yards away. Small mortars whistled as they approached, giving the GI's seconds to take cover. The threat was not chemical or biological warfare. It was mines and booby traps—bamboo covered excavations hiding spears.

He recalls the wounded Vietcong prisoners dropped by helicopter onto their one-hundred-square-yard camp. One wounded soldier stands out—his foot nearly detached, bullet holes through his side and upper leg. He sat in a crouched position, staring, showing no emotion or pain. Glenn got a sense of the tenacity of this enemy.

"Nobody likes war," Glenn says. "But sometimes it has to happen. When you're in service, you're a believer. You carry out your orders. You don't question them. It the right thing to do."

Glenn feels compassion for the soldiers, especially the new ones, the FNG's. "They're scared and don't know what to expect. The old-timers go for the glory. The new guys have to learn in a hurry. Or die."

Bryan Pederson took ten weeks of basic training in the National Guard at Fort Jackson, South Carolina, between his junior and senior high school years. Bryan was eighteen, and the year was 2001, before the September 11 terrorist attacks, before the Afghanistan incursion, and before the Iraq War. Bryan is a freshman at Bemidji State and isn't nervous about shipping out.

"I don't think it will happen." he says. "Of the seventy-five in our Company, only thirty have finished training and are eligible." Bryan is among the thirty.

Four National Guard companies comprise a battalion. Domestic duty includes flood relief, airport security, and natural disasters. Bryan is assigned to Alpha Company Apache, First Battalion, with a rank of Specialist and MOS of fuel truck driver. "I don't think about my shipping out," he adds, "but when I saw GI's pulling their gas masks on, that got my attention. I know how hard it is to breathe through those things."

How does Bryan's training differ from what he sees on the tube? "In basic training, there was constant yelling. In Iraq, officers and non-coms speak in calm tones," he says.

Harold Metteer, World War II veteran, sees a radical change in President Bush's demeanor, from dictatorial to a cooled-off stance. He sees a similar change in Secretary of State Colin Powell—from forceful at the UN, bullying countries to join the fight, to a conciliatory tone inviting dialog. He faults General Tommy Franks for giving out too much information at the front lines.

Jerry Graba, Korean Vet, says history will tell if it's President Bush's war. "He may come out of this smelling like a rose, like FDR in World War II," says Jerry. He faults the President for reducing revenue sources and pursuing the tax cut. He regrets the seventy-five billion dollars estimated expenditure for the Iraq War, and speculates on the impact of that kind of money on job creation.

Glenn Pederson, Vietnam veteran, says it's easy for the big guys in Washington to watch the grunts in Iraq. "But I gotta believe in our president and our country. That we're doing the right thing. And the right thing is getting rid of Saddam Hussein."

Bryan Pederson, National Guard, saw some early fumbling in Washington—overconfidence, maybe, that we would be in Baghdad quickly and easily. "But I stand behind what they're doing. I support it. I'm glad we're there."

All four support the right to demonstrate against the war, even if they don't share the convictions of the demonstrators. Metteer regrets that professionals often organize and march in demonstrations. "Those people are doing what they have to do," says Glenn Pederson. "It's a guaranteed right," adds Graba. "We'd be a better country if people spoke their minds. Full discussion of all functions of government is essential to a democracy, regardless of your level of information." Bryan Pederson saw protesters on campus carrying signs saying "Send Bush to Iraq." Now he sees flags and signs saying "Support Our Troops."

OPEN LETTER TO THE SNOWBIRDS

WE GET YOUR CARDS AND LETTERS where you boast of seventy-degree temperatures, lush lawns, and shirtsleeve sunshiny mornings. For a moment or two, we envy your afternoons beside the pool, your outdoor flea markets, your bike rides around the town square. We have second thoughts about staying in Minnesota when you describe hamburgers sizzling on the grill, the kiss of a nine-iron on a golf ball, the dazzling panorama of a desert sunset.

But don't feel sorry for us.

This is life in the slow lane. The only traffic jams we experience are uptown at coffee time, or at the birdfeeder when chickadees are everywhere, and a flock of finches fly in. The occasional traffic noise we hear is a pair of snowmobiles high-tailing it down the river to Wahoo Valley.

It's forty-three degrees today, one week before January 15, the mid-point of winter. Melting snow drips lazily off the porch roof. The yard is patchy brown and white. Girl squirrels chase boy squirrels up and down the stark white oaks.

Cattle lie in loose hay beside bale feeders. Chickens wander to the house and work the ground beneath the birdfeeders. Horses doze in full sun. Their coats shine and feel warm against my cheek.

Crows squabble in the pasture over important matters. A lone crow circles the barn in an easy glide and returns to the foray. A pileated woodpecker beats out a staccato rhythm and squawks something about territorial rights.

The afternoon sun highlights the edges of white birch. Stubborn rusty leaves of red oaks cling to pencil-thin branches. Tall jackpines sway to an easy northwest wind. The snow in the yard is the stuff of snowmen.

We're enjoying our January thaw without having endured our January deep freeze.

The light blanket of snow muffles faraway noise. A truck hauling pulpwood heads west on the gravel and downshifts at the Nimrod tar. The sounds are so clear, it seems to be passing through the yard.

Kelly (the collie) and I walk to the mailbox. She sniffs a deer trail and follows it down a fence line. Snow has melted on protected patches of driveway, and the gravel is wet and muddy. Jackpine needles litter the snowy areas and look like footprints of dancing crows. I crush some Norway Pine needles in my fingers and smell the North Country.

The sky is cloudless—a pale pastel blue. A contrail high above bisects the sky and points to Park Rapids.

The afternoon sun glistens across a field of cut cornstalks, transforming it to a textured carpet of snow white and gold. In the background, silver popple pose in stark contrast against a woods of dark pines.

But, enough of this. It must be time for your afternoon happy hour at the poolside bar of Exotic Estates. I can see that sunset. We're having our own dramatic sunsets this month. Last night, the sky glowed maroon and red and rose and pink, with horizontal stripes of blues. The colors hung in the sky for what seemed like hours, then darkened to auburn, faded, and disappeared.

And, while you're sitting there idly comparing tans and discussing flea market finds, I have a few tasks to finish. Haul in a wheelbarrow of firewood for the night. Fill the birdfeeders. Take the sheets and pillowcases off the clothesline and bring the smells of this beautiful Minnesota January to bed.

'TIS THE SEASON

THE MEETING WAS CALLED TO ORDER at 2:00 P.M., one hour after the Golden Age Club met on Sunday, December 2nd at the Nimrod Seniors Center. One hour to place gifts under the Christmas tree, arrange the potluck dinner offerings, exchange pleasantries. President Marcy Shore led the group in a prayer of thanksgiving, and the group formed a line for the meal.

It's easy to guess the menu—three hot dishes, five Jell-O salads, a Tupperware container full of sandwiches, four kinds of cookies. Tasty stuff, and enough for seconds. We have good cooks up here. There are two dining tables: a Nimrod table and a Sebeka table. All women. Dinner is over, and dishes are whisked away, washed, and dried by the Nimrod ladies.

Mildred Bickford explains that this is strictly a social club. No projects, no causes, no agenda. Just an excuse to spiff up and get together five times a year, around holidays, alternating between Nimrod and Sebeka. This summer the club also took in a performance at the Wood Tick Theater in Akeley. Membership is in the low twenties, and attendance is usually about fifteen. Qualifications for membership? Female and at an age that you're willing to call golden. The group has been meeting for about fifteen years.

Dishes are done, and President Shore raps an imaginary gavel to call the meeting to order. Strictly Roberts Rules of Order here. The roll call is taken: Lila Savela, Claresse Widell, Ruby Schulz, Marcy Shore, Mildred Bickford, Violet and Marilyn Lapinoja, Grace Fredericksen, Violette (love the spelling!) Smith, Amber

Bengtson, Myrtle Jenkins, Florence Lewis, and May Berg. Myrtle reads the secretary's and treasurer's reports. Motions are made to approve, second, all in favor say "aye." Old business is dealt with, then new, and the meeting is adjourned.

Time to draw for door prizes, and Violette gets lucky. Prez Shore asks for jokes, songs, recipes, bible quotes, gardening tips, anything. Hearing none, she tells a joke herself. (Note to editor: "The Jackpine Barbs" column comes in handy here.) About now, I note some shuffling, an air of unrest, sleeves sweeping imaginary crumbs off the holiday print tablecloths. "Shall we play Bingo?" asks the Prez. And in a chorus worthy of the Mormon Tabernacle Choir, they sing a mighty "YES!"

Grace Frederickson steps up to the number tumbler and calls like a practiced barker. The ladies concentrate on the cards like they're taking state board exams. Speech is silver; silence, golden. As in Golden Age. Each player has brought two gifts, and when they're won, it's time for coffee and cookies again, and Christmas gift distribution.

The Golden Age Club is one of many groups for seniors, and others, to join in Nimrod. The Nimrod Seniors Club hosts its Christmas party next week. Then there are the Nimrod Boosters, the Nimrod Do-Gooders, Lutheran church groups, Riders of the Crow Wing, pool tournaments, the mighty Nimrod Gnats, and on and on. It's a joiner's paradise.

It's good to see seniors circulate. That may be why we have people living into their golden years up here. The next meeting is a Valentine's Day party in Sebeka. Let's see. How about a heart-shaped mold with strawberry Jell-O and a few sliced bananas?

BREAKING THE BACK OF WINTER

THE WAY I SEE IT, we're on the down side of winter. The second half of January is usually no worse than the first half. February is much like December. And March resembles November, except for its promise. If winter's second half is as easygoing as its first, we live charmed lives.

Notice how trees are black silhouettes against a steel-blue sky at 7:00 A.M., the steel-blue giving way to a crack of light on the east horizon. An hour later, puff clouds are rosy cheeks on the golden face of dawn. And notice how daylight lingers longer in the afternoon, still light enough for chores at 5:30 when the wind dies. And light enough to gather an armful of firewood by starlight.

I look across the front yard and see brown. Pockets of oak leaves in the hollows, matted grass remnants, sunflower seed husks below the bird feeder. Beyond that, the river is frozen gray this year, not white with full snow cover. I count on one hand the number of snowmobile tracks that round the bend.

Have I heard the chickadees? Not the chirp-chirp song but their summer song, the one that mimics a cardinal. Chubby gray squirrels monopolize the feeder, including three blacks this year. Strangely though, the tenacious little red squirrels are at the top of the food chain. Suet from Pederson's Home Butcher Shop bolsters the protein count for nuthatches and blue jays. Flocks of goldfinches chat in high register. The redpolls opt to visit Bob Hames, who is more generous with thistle seed.

The deer are out of their winter digs, making a nuisance of themselves on the road and in the drive. Another easy winter. Another high birth rate next spring. Another heavy population next hunting season. And, yes, that roadkill on Highway 2 east of Dad's Elwell corner was a skunk who decided hibernation time was over.

I walk in the woods, where four or five inches of snow remain, pure and untouched except for mice tracks from fallen log to fallen log. A red oak leaf is embossed in snow crust. Bits of bark scatter from a limb gnawed clean by rodents.

The livestock eat less, not having to compensate for the loss of body heat to extreme cold. Less, that is, unless Dean Estabrooks delivers upland hay with snatches of alfalfa and clover. Green, good smelling stuff, tasty enough for me to sample.

The woodpile dwindles. Despite the temperate weather, I'll need more than I have. But the tractor is working like a . . . well, it's working like a tractor. The chain saws are both operational. I consider myself blessed if I hit the "off" button before the chain saw malfunctions and stops of its own accord. And the woods are full of new windfalls.

The Scottish Highland cows are known to calve in January. They're big, round, stuffed with babies. Normally they're docile, approachable, pettable. But on a warm day when I feed rolled corn in the pasture, they run, jump, twist, kick like they're auditioning for cheerleaders. Nimrod Nat, my coming one stud colt, taunts the mini mare, rears in front of mother, settles on nosing a blue plastic feed dish around the corral.

So, what can we say about the second half of January? The Christmas decorations are down and packed away. The first seed catalogs arrived. The IRS and the tax man mailed us notices. All the mechanical systems—pickup truck, livestock watering system, furnace, have checked out and proven operational at minus twenty degrees. What else can happen?

Well, we can get our January freeze after the January thaw. February can be nasty. And March, we all know, is the month of heaviest snow. But the back of winter is broken. Step outside at noon. Feel the sun's warmth. Smell earth thawing on the south side of the foundation. Listen to chickadees. Watch squirrels chasing up and down trees in their courtship ritual. Taste air blowing from the south, warm air, spring-tasting air. Sure, we'll have a blizzard by the time this is printed. But hope springs eternal in the human breast. And spring springs eternal too.

COUNTRY SCHOOL

LONG TERM MEMORY IS A GIFT. Not only does it allow us to recall details, like what we wore, what we ate, what we said after fifty years of dormancy, but it also provides an editing function. Seems we remember the pleasant stuff. Sorrow and suffering are relegated to a lesser degree of recollection.

So it is with Alice Marshall Oehlenschlager, Nimrod octogenarian and former country-school teacher. In typical Marshall family tradition, Alice has chronicled her experiences, including a fine article in an August 1985 issue of this paper, reporting the reunion of former District 55 teachers and students at the Nimrod Hall. But her story is instructive, interesting, and, at times, inspirational, and deserves retelling.

Alice taught at several schools, most in Wadena County, beginning in 1933. She earned her Rural Teacher Certificate in Staples. Training was in Lincoln Elementary School, observing and studying the first year, and practice teaching the second. She recalls the non-academic advise of her teacher, Mrs. Williams. "Watch out for the big boys! They're almost as old as you." (Alice was nineteen.) "Don't ever keep one of them after school alone." Seems Mrs. Williams knew what she was talking about. When Alice arrived at District 31 North, five of the "big boys" were taller than she.

Alice's stories could go on for days. But there are two that caught me. The first is her experience at the Isabella Lumber Camp school in 1947. Alice had four kids, including baby Carolyn. Husband, Archie, was off to the high seas as a merchant mariner. Kenny Tomlinson, Nimrod lumber baron, hired Alice to teach at the lumber camp. She recalls the environment as one big, happy family. Many of the loggers and their families were Nimrod people. Kenny built houses sided with slab wood, insulated with sawdust. Alice recalls the houses as warm, comfortable.

The school house was its own building. Supplies were provided by the Two Harbors School District, whose superintendent visited the school to audit quality of education and to deliver text books and supplies.

Wives of loggers tended Alice's babies while she taught grades one through eight. She feared for her students' safety in that wild environment. Wild, as in wolves, bears, blizzards. But she recalls that the kids were well behaved, eager to learn, closely connected through camp life.

The other memory that sounds like a period piece involves celebrations that centered around the school, like the basket social. The stated intent was to raise money for Christmas gifts for the students. But there's a strong undercurrent of sociability. Imagine the young ladies of the neighborhood preparing a basket, a shoe box, maybe, covered with colorful crepe, decorated with ribbons and flowers, and lined with an embroidered dish towel. For the picnic lunch, roast-beef sandwiches on homemade bread, wedges of chocolate cake, apples from the orchard, a Ball fruit jar of lemonade. Chores were done for the night. The estimable couples congregated at the school. One of the gentlemen volunteered to be auctioneer. The smart boys had done their marketing research and knew which basket came with which girl. The bidding started. Five dollars. Seven-fifty. Ten.

As a point of reference, the teacher's salary was probably fifty dollars a month. Bids rose to twenty dollars for the privilege of having a picnic supper with the basket provider. The "school marm" had a position of esteem in the community. Her basket brought twenty-one dollars. I suspect there was more than fund raising involved.

Then, there are the stories of Play Day, about this time of year, when one country school hosted the visit of one or more other country schools. There were contests, races, soft ball games. Parents, all farmers, took a day out of spring field work and joined the kids for a day of fun.

The Last Day Picnic had the same spirit, the same family participation, but it involved only one school. Kids got their report cards, found out if they passed or flunked. They ran races, did broad jumps, played softball. Mothers brought hot dishes for a potluck lunch. Dads uncovered ice from under sawdust, chipped it into the ice cream maker, and cranked out homemade ice cream.

And the evening Christmas program, where kids drew names for gifts, decorated the building in red and green crepe paper streamers, thumb-tacked colored pictures to the walls, sang carols, nervously recited their pieces for doting moms and dads, hammed their way through skits and dialogues, unwrapped the gift from the teacher, and walked out with a small brown bag with an apple, ribbon candy, and a half-dozen peanuts.

Johnny Lyman, one of Alice's students and now her neighbor, remembers all this and more. Interesting that his memories are also non-academic. Flooding striped gophers out of gopher holes; pulling the bell rope so hard that the bell stopped, upside down, in the belfry. Lucille Olson Swanson bringing her new girl's bike to school and letting other students learn to ride, trying hard to miss the pump handle.

Alice recalls that her students fared well, as well or better than the town school students, when they entered high school. First graders had listened to eighth graders recite out of *Prose and Poetry*. Eighth graders pulled snowsuits and overshoes on first graders for the mile-long walk home in a snow storm. Both taught interdependence, resulted in synergy.

It's a temptation to get sentimental about the good old days of the one-room country school. That's the beauty of long-term memory.

FRAMEWORK

THE CROW WING RIVER MEANDERS THROUGH NIMROD, casual and dependably constant, at a relaxing rate of four miles an hour, rising and falling with the seasons. It flows under the bridge north of town, past the homesites of Nimrod in a regular, predictable pattern, as it has flowed for years. Much the same can be said for Nimrod City Council—casual, constant, predictable. Now, one of the councilmen, Jerry Frame, is about to retire after serving for sixteen years.

Jerry was appointed to the Council by then-Mayor Larry Gilster in 1986 to replace departing Dave Chavez. Jerry was elected in 1990 for a four-year term, and has been reelected ever since. The history of the Council is surprisingly brief. As recorded by Barb Chapman in "History of Nimrod," published in Sebeka's centennial book, *Pages of Time*, a special election was held on August 28, 1946, to choose the village officers. Ernie Westra was elected mayor; Jack Stigman, Kenny Blow, and Pal Perkins, trustees; Ed Nielsen, clerk; Stan Nielsen, treasurer; Laurie Frame, constable; and William Carpenter, justice of the peace.

Jerry and wife, Jeanette, returned to Nimrod in 1970 from Minneapolis after a five-year stint in the U.S. Navy. Jerry opened Jerry's Service, a gas station and garage in the former Stigman & Frame Garage. In 1972, he moved the operation to his new garage across the street at the present site of GB's Auto Glass & Service.

Nimrod has a history of automobile sales and service businesses. Jerry counts an off-brand gas station at the site of the post office/city hall; the Bickford

& Kadow Standard Station at the site of the bus garage; Frisbie's Garage, with the hand-pumped, gravity-fed gas pumps; and his Skelly station.

Jerry's boyhood was spent in Nimrod at the site of his mother's current homestead across the river. Clara Frame remembers her son as a well-behaved lad who had a good time on the river, summer and winter, with neighborhood friends—Ed Nielsenn's son and daughter, Gene and Loretta, who lived at the present Lorraine Loween homesite; Ruby Carpenter, who lived at the Mae Stennes homesite; and the six kids of Wesley Tomlinson, who lived where Jerry and Jeanette now live. "Bus driver Mr. Bergen had to remove Jerry Brownell and Jerry from the school bus now and again," says Mother Clara. "They were too big for him to handle. But they would catch a ride and beat the bus home."

Jerry attended grade school at District 21-3, north of town, for grades one through six, and caught the bus in Nimrod for transport to Sebeka for grades seven through twelve. He graduated from high school on June 5 and enlisted in the U.S. Navy on July 18. Boot camp was at Great Lakes, Illinois, and first duty assignment was Orange, Texas, commissioning the eighty-foot mine sweeper, *U.S.S. Instill.* Jerry served on that ship, sweeping the Atlantic coast, without incident. In 1953, he returned to Orange, Texas, to de-commission the *U.S.S. Instill.*

Traditions run deep in the Frame family. In addition to Dad, Laurie, and son, Jerry, serving on the first and current slate of city offices, both served in the U.S. Navy. Mother, Clara, son, Jerry, and grandson Keith all live on the banks of the Crow Wing River. Laurie was co-owner of Stigman & Frame's Garage. Jerry owned and operated Jerry's Service for twenty-three years. Son Keith is a mechanic for the current business, GB's Auto Glass & Service. And grandson Dylan pumps gas at the station on weekends.

So, life goes on, at the station and at City Council. No big bumps in either one. The biggest item in the city budget is garbage removal at about $5,000 a year. Jerry felt it was time to retire when he had to rely on phone calls from Clerk Margaret Rathcke at 5:30 every second Monday of the month to remind him of the meeting. Any council votes in sixteen years that kept him awake nights? None, says Jerry. Council members respect each other, and their visions for Nimrod coincide. That vision is likely to continue with Council-elect Jeanne Tellock.

Thanks, Jerry, for sixteen years of service. And Nimrod, like Old Man River, just keeps rolling along.

FINN-ESSE

Vosta alkaga pieni vai oppia hyvinkin tekeen.

THE AROMA OF COFFEE GREETED ME AT THE DOOR. A wood fire burned in the stove with body-hugging heat that mocked the bleak, cold January afternoon. Cups waited at the table beside a stack of photographs. The room was warm, neat, and decorated with memories. Elsie Liimatta offered me a chair and poured coffee. A couple hours later, I walked out the door, steeped in tales of Finnish family life and tradition and aware of more multi-colored threads that make up the rich Nimrod tapestry.

Elsie was born on October 27, 1919, the third of four children of Hilda and John Ojala (both emigrants from Finland) on a farm in McKinley Township, Cass County. In July 1928, John resisted a property tax hike on the Cass County homestead and moved the family to a 160-acre farm in Huntersville Township, purchased from John Bell, an absentee owner from Kansas. Today, Elsie lives a stone's throw from the family farm.

She attended school at District 59 East, a two-mile hike from home. She recalls teachers Lillian Benhardus, Leo Vermilia, and Mrs. Dissmore, and thanks Mr. Vermilia for encouraging girls to play ball, a boys' sport, during lunch hour. Holding her own among men folk was to benefit her later.

When Elsie finished school, she did what the other girls did—worked for neighbors doing housework. At eighteen, she made the break to Minneapolis and was hired by the Stillman family (of Stillman Grocery fame) as a nursemaid for the four kids. She remembers her wages—$8.50 a week, plus room and board.

Elsie met Fritz Liimatta back home when she was twenty and he was twenty-three. The following year, 1940, Fritz enlisted in the Army for a one-year term. When the United States entered World War II, Fritz's enlistment was extended until the war ended in 1945. While Fritz served in Australia, Elsie and a girlfriend hopped a Greyhound to California where Elsie worked as a welder on a Victory ship. She recalls lugging welding equipment deep into the bowels of the ship, not exactly woman's work, especially not for a 115-pound woman.

When Elsie and Fritz reunited after his Army discharge, they eloped to Park Rapids on April 26, 1946. For one reason or another, they kept the marriage secret, and each returned to his home. Elsie remembers breaking the news to her mother after two weeks of silence at Fritz's urgings, kissing her mother good-bye, and moving into the home of Fritz's dad.

They worked together at the family farm, Elsie in the hayfield loading eight hundred bales of hay in one day. When fieldwork was done in the fall, they headed for Duluth to find work for the winter. There was nothing, so they returned to Huntersville where Fritz worked with John and Axel Ojala, father-in-law and brother-in-law, in the sawmill. Fritz was sawyer, Elsie was slab boy.

There followed the purchase of the 160-acre farm, a stint in Ag school for Fritz, employment in the copper mines of Montana, a trip to the Iron Range, where Fritz, at thirty-five, was declared too old for employment.

Meanwhile, three Liimatta children were born, and after an eleven-year hiatus, the fourth and final child, Joni, arrived. Joni is an RN at Fergus Falls State Hospital now. She thanks her mother for support and caring for her son Shannon during nurses' training.

Joni remembers Mother as being open to change, not locked in the past. She acknowledges the difficulty of raising a child by older parents, but she always felt her parents' respect for a kid's point of view.

At age twelve, Joni wanted a horse. She recalls Dad Fritz hitting the auction circuit, working hard to find a horse of good breeding. They finally found one, and Elsie recalls that the horse responded well to Joni, but not necessarily to Fritz. "It's the best thing they ever did for me," says Joni. "It got me out of the house, away from television."

Fritz's asthma forced him out of the dairy business, but they still kept animals. Elsie recalls the Great Fire of 1976, where fireballs jumped the road and burned around the homestead but spared the house. The barn and the year's harvest of hay were destroyed, the cows were scorched and had to be shipped, four pigs burned, but the horses survived. Fire burned around a field gas barrel, threatening whatever wasn't already burning. Fritz's asthma kept him from fighting the fire.

"One thing I remember," says Joni. "Mom and Dad were always together. It was a fifty-fifty marriage. Because of Dad's health, Mother helped with the farm work, and Dad was not above sweeping the floor and helping with dishes at the end of the day."

Joni's son Shannon remembers life with Grandma, and he would ask when they were going home long after they had moved into a home of their own. Joni considers the Huntersville area her home too, and dreams of returning someday. Returning to the Saturday night sauna, the aroma of *pullaa* baking, the tradition of Joulupukki, the Finnish Santa Claus. Retelling the stories of her youth—the horse, the fire, the peeping tom who ran for his life when she brandished a single-shot .22 at her mother's urging.

Elsie will be there. Independent, self-reliant, a twinkle in her eyes. "You'll laugh at this," she says as she starts another story. And she's right. She's got a million of them.

Oma tupa, oma lupa.

WINTER OF OUR DISCONTENT

TO BELIEVE THE CALENDAR, SPRING will spring in two weeks. About time! This winter will be remembered as the year that tested our mettle. We dealt with minimal snow and its consequence—frozen septic systems. Archie Lake of Lake's Service estimates that up to one-half of local private systems have frozen drain fields. Archie and crew could steam drain pipes and pump septic tanks on a twenty-four/seven basis. With ground frost from six to sixteen feet deep, this problem won't be solved until the Fourth of July. When they service your system, treat them right. You may need them back. Archie talks of retirement this year. What a flaming finish!

On a grander scale of discontent is the impending war with Iraq. Muscles flex and sabers rattle in the preface phase. Threats follow demands; an invasion force follows threats. War, or some hybrid form of confrontation, feels inevitable. In the meantime, families are separated, lives are disrupted, and the economy is on hold. Today, the stock market hit a ten-year low.

We lack definition of the enemy—someone large enough to rally against. We lack definition of our leadership—someone large enough to rally behind. Will the hallmarks of this "war" be the euphemistically labeled Homeland Security Act, with its urgings of sheet plastic and duct tape for every home, and the pronouncement of color coded alerts on Islamic holidays? Will thinking men like Secretary of State Colin Powell follow lemming-like over the cliff of civil discourse and diplomacy into the abyss of an estimated twenty- to fifty-billion-dollar bloodbath? And when it's over (whatever that means), where will we be? How have we dealt with terrorism? North Korea? Our reputation with our allies? Our own apathy? Have we looked at the root causes of why countries hate us and terrorists give their lives to destroy us and the symbols we value?

We are not ready for war. I say that having lived through World War II, served (stateside) in the Korean War, and worked in the military-industrial complex in the Vietnam and Cold Wars. Militarily we may be ready, but the home front is far from mobilized. Imagine the current response to a gasoline rationing program of a few gallons a week. No new car production? Electricity blackouts? Tokens for meat and sugar? War bond drives?

Since I have no family members whose lives are threatened or disrupted, the war feels far away. It's not on my mind. The Crow Wing River valley feels safe. I tire of hearing repeated phrases of "axis of evil" and "weapons of mass destruction." I cringe when I hear of military intelligence but am offered drawings instead of photographs.

And yet, an undercurrent of optimism plays like and old familiar song in the back of my mind. It begins each morning with early light—a hint of pink sky at 6:00 A.M. It continues with the trill of chickadees, the sparkle of snow melting to icicles, the afternoon sun pouring through south windows. Can the distraction of chemical and biological warfare and the spectre of human suffering be artifacts of winter? Can it soon be spring?

Spring

APRIL IN NIMROD

April is the cruelest month, breeding
Lilacs out of the dead land, mixing
Memory and desire, stirring
dull roots with spring rain.

SO SAYS T.S. ELIOT IN HIS POEM "THE WASTE LAND." Last night, five inches of snow fell; this morning the temperature hovers around the freezing mark. Spruce branches, lawn furniture, and board fences are graced with a lavish coat of white frosting. Chickadees and nuthatches work the bird feeder. The sun is a pale white disc in a gray sky. This is April. This is cruel?

The team of Belgians lean their magnificent heads on the gate, awaiting morning grain. Scottish Highland cattle hobble from the barn to the hay feeder, looking like they're in the tenth month of a nine-month pregnancy. Chickens roost on the barn rafters, sleeping late on this snowy morning.

Kelly the collie and I walk up the lane to where the Crow Wing bends around the point and flows east, then south. There's open water on the far side. A pair of Canadian geese swim to the opposite shore, out of range of my telephoto lens. Another pair swims toward them. They discuss territorial rights in honks and squawks, and the second pair swims downstream. A third pair flies overhead. A small flock of golden eyes flies upstream.

Back in the woods, jackrabbit tracks crisscross the fresh snow. I wonder what they find to eat, then realize that they inhabited this land long before my kind arrived. A vole burrows a tunnel to his grassy breakfast. No deer tracks here by the river. The deer are aware of unstable ice.

A breeze blows in from the north. Chunks of snow tumble from branches. Pines bend and sway. I hear a groan. One jackpine wails and moans with each gust of wind. Why this one tree? My imagination kicks in. A noble creature was buried decades, centuries ago. His bones are tangled in the roots, his spirit sapped by the tree's appetite for growth. He calls, cries with the bending of the branches. There's a story there.

Back home, I see no lilacs breeding out of the dead land. These lilacs are still in cold storage. They will wait for another kind of April precipitation. Here in north central Minnesota, April showers arrive in May, May flowers in June, and Juneberries in July. That works for me.

But April does mix memory and desire. I tromp through the snowy yard, tracing the path I have taken many times behind a lawn mower. I stop at the perennial garden and wonder what dull roots—peonies, irises, daylilies, are stirring.

In the house, the fire is warm and inviting, and there's one more cup of coffee in the pot. I'm content to work at home today and forsake the drive on slick roads. My half-sorted stack of income tax receipts commands my attention. The calendar reminds me that I'm down to days before April 15. On the window sill, seed packages promise tasty vegetables and showy blooms once planted in peat starter pots.

For now, I see five inches of new snow, slowing the arrival of spring. But, as Noah said from the bow of the ark, "Lord knows, we can use the water."

CATTLE WORKING DAY

It's dawn on the River Ranch, north of town on Saturday, Memorial Day weekend. Pickup trucks tugging livestock trailers snake up County 14, hang a right on the gravel, and park in a misty hayfield. Cowboys lead saddled horses out of trailers, snap on a pair of salty chaps, and ride in silence to the corral. Early sun tips popples and jackpines along the river and brightens a cloudless sky. Deana and Tinker Skov greet friends and neighbors, tend a small fire for branding irons, and make one final inspection of gates, fences, and pens. It's cattle working day on the River Ranch.

Before the day is over, one hundred cow-calf pairs will be wormed, vaccinated, and ear-tag checked. One hundred calves will be branded and dehorned, and bull calves will be implanted and castrated. It's an important day. The health of the herd, and the profitability of the enterprise, depend on each task being done. The measure of the day is that the tasks be done safely, quickly, thoroughly.

By eight o'clock, livestock are rounded up from the river bottom, driven to corrals, and separated—cows, calves, and bulls. Cows are worked first, migrating through a maze of pens toward a chute where they are poured and vaccinated, and into a head chute where they are branded, if they are new acquisitions.

We count fifteen cowboys, plus Tinker and Deana, working the cattle. Kevin Veronen, a sawyer from Huntersville, is foreman for the day. Kelly Dudley pours the delouser. Miles and Levi Kuschel vaccinate. Les Bell operates the head chute. Jim Leader and Steve Volmer move cattle from pen to pen. The rest, including three Kuschel families, drive and direct, coax and cajole anxious bovine mothers through the process.

It's dry. Hoof traffic stirs up dust in the pen. Wood smoke wafts from the fire. Tinker brands a cow, and the air smells acrid from singeing hair. And through it all, the bellowing of cows, the bawling of calves is deafening, persistent, plaintive.

Deana and Tinker ranch on 260 acres north of town. It's the original homestead of Tinker's grandparents, Pat and Mimi O'Neil. Grandma O'Neil still lives on the premises. Tinker rents another 500 acres for pasture within a thirty-mile radius. He buys all his hay for winter feeding. Not enough time to put up hay, he says.

Cattle working day began in 1990, Tinker and Deana's first year on the River Ranch. That year, they had five Hereford cows, makeshift pens and chutes, and an urge to go traditional with their cattle care. The number of cattle grew, and so has the number of friends who swap labor, hire on for the day, or show up as hangers-on. The crew worked Roy Bell's cattle in Leader the week before. They would move to Linda and Tom Kuschel's herd on Monday.

The ritual has some of the earmarks of old-fashioned silo filling or threshing days. Neighbors gather together at one farm for one day, do their job, and move on to the next farm. Unlike the old rituals, however, women are no longer relegated to the kitchen. They're more likely driving cattle or pushing Lepto through a needle.

It's lunchtime now, and the crew takes a break. Some years, Kim Harrington, a carpenter from Effie but a cowboy today, entertains the gang with his guitar after lunch. Not this year. The cows were worked this morning. Time to work the calves. Time for cousins Miles and Levi Kuschel to demonstrate roping skills. Time for Adam Ottenstetter and Brandon Canoy to demonstrate doggin'. The calves are roped, one at a time, and dogged to the ground for vaccination and dehorning, if little nubs are showing. Bull calves are castrated, and growth hormone implanted. The whole operation takes seconds. Then the calf is released into the pasture to reunite with mother. The calves have remarkable recuperative power. The trauma is over as soon as mother cow finds baby. And then it's lunchtime for the calf.

Are all these cowboys, and all these labor-intensive procedures necessary? Probably not. Is there a more efficient method to accomplish the same ends? Maybe. Do the old-fashioned methods work? Yes. Tinker monitors his herd health statistics in pocket-sized notebooks that fill a shelf next to his desk, the dining room table. He records birthday, weight, ear tag number, mother, and sire. He selects bulls based on genetic traits that he would like to introduce or sustain. He shops for bulls from Iowa to Canada to Montana. He works with the Hereford Association to develop herd reporting statistics.

But does it work? The results speak for themselves. Weaning weights are impressive. And last year, he lost only one calf after vaccination; this winter/spring, he lost one calf in a sub-zero delivery, during the time it took for a coffee break.

There's another element to the operation that deserves mention. It's tradition. Tinker looks, talks, and walks like a cowboy. He's got the boots, bandanna, and belt buckle. And the beaver Stetson. He practices daily contact with his livestock, moving his horse in, out, and around the herd so that the cattle recognize his voice and trust him. Deana is with him all the way. She tells of how a cow with a new calf threatened her. And how Tinker took her back into the pasture and confronted the cow with a bellow as loud as hers. No more intimidation.

Son Logan, age seven, is a likely candidate to continue the tradition. I see him perched in the saddle under Dad's old Stetson, picking a sliver out of his finger with a kid-sized Leatherman. He's got the lingo. We just have to slow him down a notch. Teach him to even out the jerks, ride a tad slower, drawl his vowels. We don't want to disturb the herd, his legacy, that we see from the kitchen window, grazing on spring pasture, contented calves at side.

THE LONG GREEN LINE

IT'S SPRING. BUMBLE BEES BUZZ from blossom to blossom. Mourning doves bill and coo from the telephone line. A doe pokes her head out of the woods and proceeds across the drive, followed by her toddling fawn. The heart goes pitter-patter. But it's not the heart. It's Maynard Benson, downstream, firing up his latest acquisition, a vintage 1951 John Deere Model MT.

Or, if it's not the tractor heard, it's Maynard's heart going put-put-put in perfect two-cylinder rhythm.

Maynard bought his first tractor in his late teen years—a 1935 Regular Farmall, for thirty-five dollars. He traded that for a 1939 Oliver 70. His passion for tractors ignited when he traded a Bonneville Triumph motorcycle for a John Deere B. His first collectible tractor was another John Deere B that he bought from Elmer Dahlvang in the mid-1960s. Today, forty years later, he has a collection of almost a hundred tractors. It's impossible to count the number, since the tractors are in so many locations and so many stages of repair.

These tractors arrive in various conditions. Maynard has a shop to disassemble, repair, tune, clean, sand, and repaint any variety of John Deere tractor. Or plow, cultivator, baler, or blade. The finished product doesn't go on display. It goes to work. With the number of tractors Maynard has, he can dedicate a machine to plow, disc, drag, plant, fertilize, cultivate, and harvest. In fact, he can have a dedicated machine for each field, for each day of the week.

Maynard doesn't call his work restoration. He calls it resurrection—bringing the machine back to life. He is not a slave to authenticity, like using nothing but John Deere nuts and bolts. His approach is more pragmatic. If he wants a single-wheel front end, that's what he builds. This year, he will use his John Deeres to cut, rake and bale hay for his Holstein herd. Other years, he has planted corn. He keeps a blade on one John Deere to scrape the barnyard and plow the drive.

If Maynard could have only one tractor to farm with, it would be his 730 two-cylinder diesel. That model has an eighteen-gallon gas tank and uses only five quarts of fuel an hour. His favorite collectible is a 1939 model BO, a low profile machine for working orchards.

Maynard is a member of the local Two Cylinder Club, a group of about twelve John Deere aficionados who meet informally to swap stories and parts. They don't do shows or parades. The value of their John Deeres is utility, not aesthetics.

A tour around Maynard's farmstead reveals more John Deere models than I knew existed. Like three John Deere model D's, one a gift from wife Marjorie for Father's Day. Her Model D belonged to her dad, who farmed with it in the Brookings, South Dakota, area. It is one of the few tractors from outside Wadena County. Most of Maynard's collection were bought from local farmers, and they still carry the owners' names, like the Schermerhorn A, the Dahlvang B, the Leonard 70.

Maynard grew up on the family farm on County 9, which abuts his property and where he pastures his heifers. He recalls the sawmill on the farm, powered by a John Deere A. During his life, Maynard has been a logger, sawyer, ricer, dairy farmer, a beef cattle rancher, and is now back to dairy cattle. He recently finished a spring job at Badoura Nursery, where he drove, what else? A John Deere. He also serves on the Lyons Township board.

For readers with an historical bent, Deere and Company was founded in 1837 as a one-man blacksmith shop. John Deere developed the first commercially successful, self-scouring plow, coincidental with pioneer settlement and agricultural development of Midwest USA. The first John Deere tractor appeared after the company bought Waterloo Gasoline Traction Engine Company in 1918. The rest, as they say, is history. John Deere owners define brand loyalty.

JOHN DEERE

Maynard's passion for John Deeres may be a genetic flaw. Son Mark shows some of the symptoms, and has the start of his own collection. He and Maynard don't have to worry about running out of tractors to collect. According to the John Deere website, there are currently sixty-four models of two-wheel drive tractors, fourteen models of four-wheel drive, and seventeen models of track tractors.

So, a tip of the green hat to a local farmer during Ag Appreciation Days. You'll never run out of projects, Maynard. Not in this lifetime. And may you and all of us always respond to the music of a farm boy's ears—the *put-put-put* of your resurrected John Deeres.

NATURAL HIGH

At about 11:30 a.m. on Friday, April 4, deputies from the Wadena County Sheriff's Department, West Central Drug Task Force, and Bureau of Criminal Apprehension descended on Nimrod and executed search warrants at two residences.

From a story in the Sebeka Review Messenger:

At about 11:30 a.m. on Friday, April 11, one week later, a second wave descends. Migratory birds and waterfowl, rabbits and chipmunks, fish and amphibians, beetles and mosquitoes, bluegrass and pussy willows, all invade the Crow Wing River valley and shock the quiet hamlet of Nimrod with the arrival of Spring!

A pair of trumpeter swans with an escort flotilla of Canadian geese case a quiet river bay, inspecting nest sites. Along the driveway, sandhill cranes pose among corn stalks, then stagger, squawk, and lift in low altitude flight. Robins flutter in small flocks, reluctant to settle in for the summer.

Catkins on popple trees hang like fuzzy caterpillars and drop to form a carpet of white shag. Sap runs from a fracture in maple bark. Sunlit Pussy Willows on swampy roadside brush urge passersby to touch their fur to their cheek. Grass sprouts green on the shed's south side. Squint across the corral's close-cropped cover and see green.

The river is low this spring, only inches deep ten feet from shore. A perch darts around a rock. A crayfish backpedals behind a deadfall. A frog surfaces, then burrows in mud.

Squirrels chase with abandon, hopping from branch to perilous branch, like drunken sailors. Rabbits are mottled white and brown, transitioning from winter to summer coats. Chipmunks tempt destiny with gutsy forays to the dog dish.

I walk barefooted and feel grass between my toes. The sun warms humus underfoot and releases an intoxicating musky aroma. I taste sap dripping from a maple tree into a bottle, just a hint of maple flavor. A high breeze hums through jackpine treetops. The sun lowers and sprinkles diamonds on the river. Sheets and pillowcases billow from the clothesline, absorb sunshine and smell of spring.

At night, Canadian geese party downriver and disturb the peace with raucous honking. A warm breeze flutters the flag. A partridge drums the rhythm of a John Deere tractor,

A mourning dove calls from across the river. Another answers from the woods, repeating a mournful, melancholy mantra. Their haunting refrains contradict the season's joy with an undercurrent of grief. We need a fix. And spring gives us that.

POMP AND CIRCUMSTANCE

WHAT A TREAT! A COMMENCEMENT exercise without challenges to the graduating class from a guest speaker of an older generation. A speaker, and a generation, who failed to meet those same challenges. A commencement exercise without advice from a regional politician on dedication and perseverance and ethics. A commencement exercise without platitudes of "*This is not the end, this is the beginning*" from some local do-gooder. The Sebeka High School commencement was of the grads, by the grads, for the grads.

The tenor for the evening was set early with a rousing processional by Mr. K and the high school and junior high bands. Superintendent Paul Lehmkuhl offered a perfunctory welcome, and Board Chairma'am Connie Pickar introduced the honor students. Then the class took over. Kassi Hinders, Jeff Kern, and Cassi Siltala reflected on the past, present, and future. Lots of inside stuff, over my head, but striking resonant chords with the graduating class. Lots of emotional stuff, offered with tear-choked sincerity. Lots of humor, laced with gravity. Class President Laurel Heino rounded out the speeches with the traditional "Let's go out there and change the world." I half-expected Amy Ratcliff to grab the mike and give us one last tongue lashing for the failure of the school bond referendum.

An historical note: Chairman Connie Pickar awarded a diploma to her granddaughter Alicia Steinke. In the audience was Lila Perkins, Connie's mother and Alicia's great-grandmother. Lila, proprietor of Perkins' General Store in Nimrod way back when, was the first woman to serve on the Sebeka School

BOY'S
BASKETBALL
GIRL'S
SOFTBALL

Board, and she served from 1961 to 1967. During her tenure, she awarded a diploma to her daughter Connie. So, Alicia, it looks like you have a tradition to uphold.

A high spot in the evening was the tribute of senior band members to Mr. K. It was a jazzed-up version of "Cecilia," a song they had learned in their early band years. Then Mr. K grabbed the baton and led the junior high and high school bands through "Reflections," aptly named and beautifully played. The round of hugs for Mr. K from the seniors spoke volumes about their relationship.

Then, last weekend was party time. Graduation parties aren't for graduates, but for the moms and dads, aunts and uncles, neighbors and friends. Occasionally a group of students comes into view, but they have thirty-eight parties to cover, and they can't stay long. And how many ways are there to make potato salad? At least six, from my taste trials here in Nimrod. No complaints. The food was good, the weather accommodating, the conversation fun.

So, does the Nimrod Chronicler have any advice for graduating seniors? None. A big round of applause for honor students and scholarship winners. And a few observations. The seniors conducted themselves in exemplary fashion on graduation night. I expected a gym full of high-flying mortarboards after they received their diplomas. But they played by the rules and contained themselves. They have an interesting summer ahead—finding a job, training in the military, getting ready for college. I admire their resolve and confidence.

Well, maybe I do have one piece of advice. Go get 'em!

GOING, GOING, GONE

TEN O'CLOCK SATURDAY MORNING, June 2, and traffic out of Nimrod heads north and west on County Tar #26, follows the Mid-American Auction Company signs. At the Pulju farm six miles north of town, it turns into a hay field converted to a parking lot.

"Get your numbers at the trailer," comes from the loudspeaker, "Coffee and doughnuts in the shed." The amplified voice startles, out of context with the idyllic country setting, on one of those rare June days that poets write about. Neighbors spot neighbors, stop to chat. Items to be auctioned, mostly farm machinery, wait in four rows south of the buildings. Tractors stand in formation in front of the barn. Bib overall guys pick though piles of scrap iron, rotate belts and chains, kick tires.

"The sale will be starting in a few minutes," announces auctioneer Al Wessel. "The Pulju family is well respected in these parts, and we're privileged that they selected us to handle their auction. Terms are cash today. Everything is sold 'as is.'" He introduces Carolyn Pulju and Donny Borg, hired man for almost twenty years. He climbs on a flat bed wagon, adjusts his microphone, and the sale is underway.

The Pulju farm was therapy for Marv. During the week, he was Dakota County assessor and lived with Carolyn in Hastings, Minnesota. On weekends, he relaxed by working the 1,800 acres that the Puljus owned in partnership with Nick Watz. That changed when Marv was diagnosed with prostate cancer in 1997. He died in December 2000.

Al Wessel breezes through the wagonload of small tools and equipment and heads for palletized piles of parts from farm machinery, parts from bale feeders, parts from pumps, hydraulic systems, shop tools. Not much small talk, just get the bidding started, keep it moving. If a person wants it, speak up, or it will be sold. "Sold," he says. "This one's going to New York. New York Mills, that is."

Carolyn Pulju, family matriarch, stands in front of the shed-*cum*-lunch room, greeting family, friends, neighbors. Her mood is buoyant, cheerful, realistic. She has walked the rows of Marv's memories, cried her tears, and moved on. All four sons and daughters and their spouses are here. And all nine grandkids. The ladies of Menahga's United Methodist Church are on hand to shore her up, and to serve barbecue hamburgers, a hundred pans of bars, and coffee. Pastor Loren Ferch keeps a pastoral eye alert.

Al Wessel taps a couple school desks "from the little old school house down the road, over the hill. 'Abraham Lincoln' scratched on this one," he lies with a grin. The bidding is on, it's over. "Okay, boys. How about this genuine, cast-iron, claw-foot bathtub? Ten bucks, do I hear twenty? Thirty? Forty? Fifty? Sixty? Seventy? Sold! That man knows a genuine artifact. Thank you, boys." Donny Williams from Leader buys a sixteen-foot Howard Rotovator for $300; buys another twelve-foot cannibalized model for seventy. "One part would cost you that much!" Al is selling.

Carolyn walks through the auction crowd, heads back to the lunch shed, escapes to the house with her family. She introduces partner, Nick, and greets his wife, Ginny. Marv and Carolyn made a farewell trip to Finland with Nick and Ginny in 1999. The trip was a lifetime highlight for them. Carolyn mimics Marv's Finnish dialect. Her memories are happy.

Colonel Al continues his lyric chanting, keeps the pace up, milks each item for its best reasonable bid. Over four hundred bidding numbers have been issued. Buyers and on-lookers stand in a circle, chuckle at the small talk, lean back and latch thumbs inside their bibs. Al picks up a sixteen-inch emasculator/castrating instrument. "Some of you farmers with young daughters might want to hang this on your mail box," Al jokes. The crowd glances nervously at Pastor Loren. Loren laughs. Everyone laughs.

The old farm machinery sells fast, and some of it stays in the area. Doug and Betty Albeck, two miles north, are proud owners of a vintage threshing machine. Carolyn's sister Kathy and brother-in-law J.P. Arretche, three miles west, pick up the combine.

It's nearly three o'clock, and the last items to sell are the four International diesel tractors. Loaded pickup trucks snake out of the hayfield. Plates and pans are empty of bars and brownies. The last tractor sells. Going. Going. Gone.

But the farm, split by the partners, stays in the family. Son Dave and wife, Brook, will live next door and operate the former Schumacher landscape business. Son Dan and wife, Brenda, delay their return to Sandstone to clean up loose ends, keep an eye on Mom. Sunday morning, daughter Jan and husband Gene deliver a Holstein calf to the family farm for the grandkids to tend and to keep tradition alive. And Christopher, son of daughter Karen and husband George, will fix everything, Gramma, with the crescent wrench he bought at Grampa's auction.

ASK NOT WHAT YOUR COUNTRY CAN DO FOR YOU . . .

WHAT IF SOMEONE WANTS TO BURN off the back meadow? Or needs a permit to burn a brush pile? Or, what if there's a package of hot dogs on hand, can someone burn down the granary and call it a recreational fire? Who is the person to call? The Township Fire Wardens, that's who. And how are they compensated for their services? An all-you-can-eat dinner once a year, plus framed certificates and plaques awarded at five-year increments. Monday night was the annual dinner meeting.

Joel Holden, Nimrod DNR Forester, was host again this year, looking as comfortable as Billy Crystal emceeing the Oscar awards. The program was brief —part information, part entertainment, but mostly neighbors greeting neighbors. And dinner. This year, as in previous years, the program was held at the Nimrod Lutheran Church. Dinner was tastily prepared and graciously served by the Mary Martha Guild.

The Nimrod DNR station has sixty-six Township Fire Wardens assigned throughout Wadena County, and Ansel and Poplar Townships of Cass County. Periods of service span from a few years to forty-six years. Irene Pederson of Oylen, and Rose and Cliff Gronlund of Sebeka, share the distinction of forty-six years of service.

The Township Fire Warden program has been around for a long time, according to Joel. The Minnesota Division of Forestry was established in 1911. Programs like the Burning Permit Program typically result from major forest fires, like the Hinckley, Minnesota, fire.

Township Fire Warden is the major volunteer program for the local DNR station. But they also participate in other conservation programs, like the outreach program at local schools. The emphasis is on fire prevention, and Joel showed a short video popular with the kids. After the video, who should appear but Smokey the Bear, a.k.a. Steve Schwab.

Both Menahga and Sebeka Public Schools have school forests. There is a forty-acre tract of old growth forest north of town, and an eighty-acre forest management tract southeast of town. Activities in the school forests fall under the tutelage of Charlie Funk. In addition to forest-as-classroom aspects, there is a hands-on opportunity to plant, clear and harvest timber products.

The DNR also supplies seedlings for Wadena County public and private school students to plant for Arbor Day, around the end of April.

Back to Monday night's meeting, Joel reported on the thirty-five area fires in 2001 (most of which were of human origin) and the controlled burning. The

2002 season is off to an auspicious start, with the dry, snowless period in January—an ideal head-start for meadow burning.

So, once again, it's time to honor those who have gathered years of service. Tonight's top honors go to two couples with forty years of service: Stella and Morris Kuschel, beef ranchers in Ansel Township; and Lucille and Walt Sowers, retired farmers in Poplar Township. Top award of the night for forty-five years of service goes to Alma and Viljo Katainen, formerly farmers in Huntersville Township, nursery workers at Badoura, and now residents of Menahga.

Sounds to me like it's all about volunteering for public service. Now that President Bush has assigned goals for all of us, I'm proud to say that Nimrod is ahead of the game again. Exhibit A is our Nimrod Do-Gooders, who garnered national attention in last summer's *American Profile* magazine for their public service in Nimrod's parks, ball diamond, and beaches. Then there are the Nimrod Boosters, who work Jubilee Days, the Easter Egg Hunt, and the Christmas Party. Equally commendable is the work of the Township Fire Wardens. Like an army, the fire wardens work best on full stomachs. So a round of applause, please, for another group of volunteers—the Mary Martha Guild of Nimrod Lutheran for a delicious roast pork dinner. One suggestion. Next year, schedule the dinner so that Lorraine Loween is available to bake her blueberry cheesecake bars for dessert.

RIDERS OF THE CROW WING

IT'S SUNDAY OF MEMORIAL DAY WEEKEND, and people start looking for something to do. They've already canoed the Crow Wing River. They've gone horseback riding. Hiked the wooded trails, smelled the lilacs, listened to the warblers, swatted a few mosquitoes. They're ready to be entertained for a change. The options are a horse show at noon, a Nimrod Gnats baseball game at two, and a potluck barbecue following the game. Let's start with the horse show.

The Riders of the Crow Wing sponsor the Spring Open Horse Show at the Nimrod Horse Arena, just south of the town's central business district. The show starts at noon. Pickup trucks line the south end of the arena and spill into the east parking lot. After a week of rain, the field is soggy, but playable. Contestants test the arena, test their horses, test themselves. Sally Sandberg announces the grand march, and the contestants fall into formation at the north gate. Bethany Pederson leads, carrying the American flag. Contestants file into the arena, circle and return, and stand facing the judging stand. Sally recites the Pledge of Allegiance, the riders file out, and the games begin.

The games are open to members and non-members. Nimrod is well represented, with Fran Kueker as judge, contestants, Bethany, Jane Melby and kids Colten and Kayla, Rachael Richards, and maybe more. The Shequen and Skeesickof families drove up from Staples and Motley; the Sazama family from Perham; and the Hageny family from Wisconsin.

The games start with the open hang man, an entertaining, if not sadistic, event where one rider jumps from a horse, clings to a rope for hours (it must seem), and waits for rider number two to circle a barrel and return for the rescue. Aside from stretched arms and threshing legs, almost everyone made it back. This event is not ballet, but it's a great show starter and got belly laughs from the bleachers.

Then came the candy bar race, where kids eight and under raced to the end of the ring, grabbed a candy bar from club Pres Bill Case, and returned. Who can resist these kids who not only know the rules but enjoy the competition?

There were barrel races, separated by age category. And open jumping figure eight, and poles, and pennant races, and open keyhole, and so on. Fran and Mary Malone kept score, Missy Wattenhofer and Deb McDonald manned the gates, Cathy Munson sold hot dogs. And a host of others righted fallen barrels, set up the next events.

The Riders of the Crow Wing Saddle Club is a non-profit club, and show production costs are offset by money raised at the show. Club members sell raffle tickets for a saddle bag stuffed with $100, a four-man tent, and a pair of quad chairs. Shows cost between $300 and $500 to produce. There are no entry fees, just a modest admission fee. Ribbons are awarded for first through fifth place, and high point trophies are awarded in three categories: peewee, junior and senior. Winners Sunday were Dylan Shequen of Staples, peewee; Jacque Peterson of Staples, junior; and Jane Melby of Nimrod (toward Backus), senior.

Proceeds from the show also pay for ground and building maintenance. Last year, the club constructed a round pen on the grounds; this year, they plan to purchase their own electronic timer. I'm wondering if anyone has a PA system to donate. It would have been great to see those contestants ride in the ring to The Star Spangled Banner. Or to hear The Oak Ridge Boys romping it up for the barrel races.

The next open amateur show is August 4, and the fall show is September 1, during Nimrod's Jubilee Days. The driving show is scheduled for September 29. Locals may remember, that's where Harold Metteer hit the big time last year as trophy winner. Will he repeat?

In the meantime, the club holds riding lessons weekly and sponsors equine health and fitness clinics annually. And it's all done with volunteer labor. So mark your calendar for August 4. There are national champions on hand to amaze you, future champions to inspire you, and a lot of sporty amateurs to entertain you.

EIGHT SECONDS

Well, it's bulls and blood, it's the dust and mud,
It's the roar of a Sunday crowd.
It's the white in his knuckles, the gold in the buckle
He'll win the next go 'round.

"GOOD AFTERNOON, LADIES AND GENTLEMEN. From the Runestone Arena, here in Alexandria, Minnesota, welcome to the final day of the National Professional Rodeo Association rodeo weekend. Our sponsors today are Coor's Beer, the official beer of the NPRA; Hubbard Mills, maker of Crystalix livestock nutritional supplement; Cenex Farmers Union. . . ."

The audience settles into bleachers. Horseback riders with flags circle the ring as each sponsor is announced. Vendors work the aisles hawking pop and popcorn.

"There are problems we have as a nation. But this is the greatest country in the world! America is the place where a child can have a dream, and work to make that dream come true! So let's turn our eyes to the red, white, and blue, ladies and gentlemen, and pledge allegiance to the flag."

Cowboys doff hats. PA system blares a musical pledge.

"America is the land of four great freedoms—freedom of speech, freedom of press, freedom of worship, and freedom from fear, and these freedoms are cherished by this great nation. And now, our National Anthem, in honor of those men and women who gave their lives that this great nation may live."

Right hands over hearts. Eyes on the flag, high in the center of the arena.

"Ladies and gentlemen, it's good to be alive in America! Are you ready to rodeo?"

Thunderous applause.

Bareback riding leads off the afternoon in the west end of the arena. Eight young men, all from Minnesota and North Dakota, dirty up in "the most athletic event in all of rodeo." Eight seconds to glory. And pay dirt.

Attention shifts to the east end of the arena for a timed event, calf roping. Travis Durphy, Savannah, Missouri, wins handily with an 8.75-second run. Tyson Durphy, brother or cousin, goes home with only a round of applause, but he inspires the announcer: "The sun was shining. The clouds rolled in. The rain began to fall."

Then a specialty act. Clown stomps out carrying a plastic milk crate and broken landing net.

"This here's a b'ar trap."

"That's a bear trap?"

"Yup. This is my b'ar trap. And I'm gonna catch me a b'ar."

"You're gonna catch a bear with that?"

"Yessir. I'm gonna catch me a b'ar."

And so on. The four-year olds loved it.

Back to the east end of the arena for another timed event, steer wrestling. Beau Wisness, Keene, North Dakota, catapults through the starting rope, glides off his horse, slides an arm around the steer's horn and knuckles his nose, digs in his heels, stops him in his tracks. All that in 3.99 seconds.

"ARE YOU HAVING A GOOD TIME?" yells the announcer.

On the west end, bulls rattle through loading chutes into catch pens. Sixteen-hundred to two-thousand pounders. Mixed breeds, most with Brahma showing. Great names like Tornado, Widow Maker, Homicide, Double Trouble, Wild Child, Rampage, Yellow Jacket.

Bull riders assemble at the door with duffel bags. They talk, stretch, don chaps. They down a Coke, tape arms, rub glycerin and resin into gloves, kill time.

"You get into any trouble last night?" one cowboy asks.

"Hell, I'm too old to get in trouble anymore."

The cowboys are more like team members than competitors. They *are* the team; the bulls are competitors. Bull ropes slide and cowbells clank out of duffel bags. Bulls shuttle into chutes. Livestock handlers walk the pen rails like gandy dancers. Six bulls quake and lurch in six chutes, and six bull riders look down, calibrate their ticket to glory, or something worse.

Barrel racers, the only distaff event of the day, finish their competition. Julie Voigt tips a barrel on the first turn.

"The only thing she's taking back to Beulah, North Dakota, is the hand your going to give her."

The volume knob on the PA system is cranked far right. The announcer yells over the adrenaline-provoking music. "ARE YOU READY FOR SOME BULL RIDING?" The crowd responds.

The final event of the day. The Big Event. Twenty-three riders, some in their teens, a couple in their late thirties, from Minnesota, Wisconsin, the Dakotas. Troy Meech, Nimrod, Minnesota, rides twelfth. Troy draws bull #505, Funeral Wagon. Troy is the cowboy to beat. Came in second at Friday night's Bull-A-Rama.

Funeral Wagon is in the chute. Troy sizes him up from above. Muscles flow up his back like foothills below mountainous shoulders. Troy lowers the bull rope. A cowboy snags it under the bull and hands the loose end to Troy. He cinches it tight, loosens it, adjusts the knot. Cinches it tight, loosens it, adjusts it again. Funeral Wagon waits, docile. Troy raises his chaps, lowers himself over the bull for a trial seat.

Eleven riders ahead of Troy. No time to watch them flying free before the eight-second buzzer. One after another. No time. Announcer's words blur in echoes. Funeral Wagon tires of life in the chute, struggles, bounds, rattles the platform. He smells bad, like musk and wet barnyard. He raises his head. Tips of horns are blunted to the size of half dollars. Eyes are yellow, determined. He sniffs, snorts.

Bull rider number eleven at the ready. Troy is number twelve. Troy stands, pulls right glove tight, grabs railing, limbers arms and legs. Pulls hat down tight, slaps his thighs. Hard. Cowboy pulls the flank rope tight on the bull. Slaps Troy on the shoulder. Again. Hard. "Go get 'em, Troy!" Troy eases down on the bull. One ton of kinetic energy waits for release.

Rider eleven bucks off. Eleven riders; eleven no times.

"Gate four. From Nimrod, Minnesota. Troy Meech. Placed in the top fifteen in the PRCA in 1993, 1994, and 1997. Riding Funeral Wagon. Troy holds second place after Friday night's ride. Can he hold his position, ladies and gentlemen?"

The PA system blares loud. Bass line like an amplified runaway heart. Crowd is yelling, stomping, inciting an eight-second ride.

Troy is on the bull, legs high. Slips his gloved hand through the braided loop of the bull rope, wraps the tail of the rope once. Cowboy pushes the head of the bull toward the gate with his boot. Troy braces, clenches, stares at the bull's shoulder, snaps a quick nod.

The gate swings wide. Troy pushes off with his free arm, waves it high. Funeral Wagon drops in the front end, kicks in the back, changes direction, rolls his body. Troy leans over his hand, stays with him. Funeral Wagon rises, kicks his hind feet to the side, lands hard. Troy stays on. Funeral Wagon kicks up, walks on his front feet, scoots, kicks, skips. Troy stays with him. Eight kicks, eight seconds. Buzzer sounds. Troy steps off, left leg high over right hand, pumps a free arm, looks over the side as the bull rises, and flies into the air. Lands on his feet. Doesn't even lose his hat. The first rider (and the only rider of the day) to go the distance. He grabs his bull rope out of the mud and heads for the chute. Funeral Wagon heads for the pickup pen. Crowd is wild.

Eleven more bull riders mount, buck off before the buzzer. Last of the bulls heads for the pickup pen. Troy walks off with the purse.

"And that's our rodeo for today, ladies and gentlemen. I want to thank our sponsors, and the Douglas County Sheriff's posse, and our cowboys and cowgirls, and our wonderful audience. And thank God for the U.S. of A."

It's boots and chaps, it's cowboy hats, it's spurs and latigo.
It's the ropes and the reins, and the joy and the pain.
And they call the thing rodeo.

IN GRACE AND STYLE

IT'S 1909. PRESIDENT THEODORE ROOSEVELT has finished his second term of office and is succeeded by William Taft. Ty Cobb is playing outfield for the Detroit Tigers. It's still five years before Archduke Francis Ferdinand is assassinated, sowing the seeds of World War I. And on a small farm, one-half mile off the Huntersville Road in Nimrod, Minnesota, a daughter, Ruth, is born to Eliza and Frank Frisbie. That was ninety-two years ago, and today, Ruth is still alive and well, thank you.

Eliza and Frank Frisbie farmed four miles north of town and raised five kids: Kenneth, Richard, Ruth, Hilda, and Everett. Ruth recalls the water situation on the farm. They lowered a bucket down an open well for house water. Of course, there wasn't enough water for the livestock, so Ruth and her siblings drove horses and cows a half mile to the river, her first memory of the Crow Wing. Later, during World War I, dad, Frank, and brothers Kenneth and Richard worked the corn-picking crews in Iowa. Frank was too old for the draft; Kenneth was too young. Eliza and the younger kids cared for a reduced herd of livestock—one cow and a team of horses. Ruth recalls leading the team to the river, arms stretched from the uneven gait of the horses.

Eliza Frisbie died in 1936, and Frank moved to Nimrod and opened a garage, selling gasoline and repairing Model T's. Frank and kids Everett and Hilda lived in an apartment behind the garage. When Frank died a year later, Ruth's younger brother Everett continued the garage business. Ruth recalls

Everett building an amplifier from radio parts and playing his guitar in the garage at night. Neighbors down river heard the refrain.

Ruth recalls her school years, all eight grades in District 21-2, a mile and a quarter from home. And she recalls her teachers—Hilda Jensen, Josephine Bailey, Cora Graba (mother of Nimroders Jack and Jerry), Louise Weiman, and Anne Howard. Interesting that Ruth's children and grandchildren also attended District 21-2. Ruth recalls a horse harness tug that teachers kept on hand for unruly kids, the tug supplied by Edgar Tappe's grandfather. The teachers used the tug as a whip too, Ruth recalls. Daughter Lillie agrees.

Ruth also recalls the good times—the Box Social at Thanksgiving. Girls fried chicken, made sandwiches, baked cakes for a lunch and packaged it in a shoe box decorated with ribbons and posies. Boys bid on the lunches at auction, and proceeds financed the Christmas party. Some lunches fetched a whopping ten dollars, if some boy was bent on having lunch with some girl. "I always baked a cake for mine," says Ruth.

The little one-room country school was also the scene of a student dance, held in the winter. Live music, of course, with Frank Frisbie at the organ, organs being a standard fixture in country schools. Vocals by the Andrew Sisters. Not Maxine, Patty, and LaVerne, but Ione, Mabel, and Doris. Did boys actually dance with girls? "Sure," says Ruth. "I remember dancing the waltz with my neighbor, Hugh Dexter."

And there were the picnics on the last day of school with tables loaded with food. For dessert, homemade ice cream. Tubs of the stuff.

Ruth recalls the legend of the Nimrod Hotel, on the west bank of the river, north of the present bridge. Adjoining the hotel, a livery stable, catering to the horse-drawn grain hauling traffic, from Hubbard to the railroad in Verndale. A two-day trip, with an overnight stay and change of horses in Nimrod.

She recalls the four-mile trip from the homeplace to Nimrod by horse and buggy, but infrequently. Mother churned butter and collected eggs, which Father sold to the grocery store in exchange for staples—flour, sugar, coffee. "The store-keeper always threw in a bag of candy for the kids," Ruth remembers.

She recalls later that brother Kenneth rode a horse to Grabas to buy eggs. He carried a pail and his mother's admonition: "For heaven's sake, don't kick the horse in the ribs or he'll throw you and the eggs." (You know the rest of the story.)

Another scene from this Early Life on the Prairie saga has brother Dick and Ruth high on the roof of the barn. Dick has the big buggy umbrella opened and is prepared to test his parachuting skills, with an assist from his sister. Fortunately, Father appears in time. No jump. No broken bones. And probably, no supper.

Ruth recalls Fourth of July celebrations in Nimrod. This is in the early 1920s, before the hall was built. Neighbors constructed a big platform out of planed lumber for a dance floor. They made a sun shade roof of jackpine boughs. Again, live music, this time featuring a violin, the Dexter boys Leon and Hugh on mouth organs, and Ace Shaw on the sax. No parade yet, no fireworks. Just a picnic with blankets spread about uptown, family picnics, and music and dancing.

It goes on and on. One memory trips over another two. Ruth tosses them out as if they happened yesterday. She sits in her chair, with ex-tomcat Mischief in her lap, surrounded by her cardinal bird collections—sun catchers, plaques, figurines, photos, paintings, cross-stitching, salt and pepper shakers. She has the company of daughter June and another daughter, Lillie, who lives a couple blocks south.

Ruth has seen another President Roosevelt serve four terms, seen Ty Cobb's baseball records blasted out of the park, and survived a second World War. She lives comfortably in her own home in Menahga, a testament to the simple virtues of self reliance, intellectual curiosity, and perseverance.

(Note to myself: Stay in touch with this lady. Call her in a month to find if the photograph album with all the old pictures of Nimrod is returned. Maybe bring a tape recorder next time. Or a camcorder. These stories are worth preserving.)

MEN'S COFFEE TABLE

ADULT EDUCATION IS ALIVE AND WELL IN NIMROD. Each morning, Monday through Saturday, "school" is conducted at the R&R Bar & Grill, beginning at eight-thirty and lasting for about an hour.

That's the good news. The bad news is that school is segregated, by sex. The men meet at the back of the room, the women at the front. Political correctness in the form of mixed tables is scheduled for introduction sometime this millennium.

School subjects (at least at the men's table) are either Current Events: Will incoming President Bush be as entertaining as outgoing President Clinton? Will Governor Jesse Ventura's extracurricular activities land him in more hot water? Or Social Studies: Who's doing what to whom around town?

This ritual at the bar and grill is at least ten years old, beginning in the Harvey Horton ownership years. Members come and go over time—some to Texas for the winter, some to jobs that preclude such perks, some to the great hereafter. There are no memorial chairs for the departed.

When I first noted this ritual, I figured that a person had to be born into the circle. Something like the House of Windsor. It's not assigned seating, although the men tend to sit in the same chairs day after day. But there's always room for one more, especially if he looks like an easy touch.

"Pull up a chair," Raymond Pederson said, to my surprise, a couple years ago. I felt like I had arrived. Like the day my dad handed me the reins to the draft horse team and gave me my own wagon of grain shocks to drive to the threshing rig.

Deloris Shore and Donna Metteer keep the coffee cups full. Somebody has a doughnut; another one has a cinnamon roll. The banter shifts into high gear.

Harold Metteer talks about harnessing his team for a winter workout. Jerry Schermerhorn reports on turkey behavior. We assume he's talking about the feathered kind. Jerry Graba (or is it Jack?) is reminded of a joke. Raymond complains about cattle prices. Bill Weisbrod nods in agreement. Dave Tullis tells the story of the six black cats. The hour slips by easily.

Time to square up. But not a simple check for each coffee drinker. Not a total check divided by the number of coffee drinkers. Out comes the dice cup. I'm not a dice player, and I guess it shows. The process of elimination is complicated and highly energized. The dice cup goes around and around. Snake eyes and

ducks and boxcars appear and disappear at the speed of light. Horses are on men, instead of men on horses. I'm impressed with the physical agility and mathematical instinct of these folks.

They shake for coffee. The number of shakes is a permutation of the number of coffee drinkers, with one man eliminated per round. They shake for donuts and rolls. The dice cup tumbles like it's possessed. Then they shake for the tip. The noise level is getting uncomfortable. There's a side bet going on as to whether Dale Mattson will get stuck again.

The early winners, eliminated in the shake for the tip, stand and begin breathing normally. I don't pretend to know the rules; I keep shaking until someone grabs the cup.

It's finally over. Thirty minutes for coffee, and thirty minutes to determine who pays. I decide I won't do this again. I love the camaraderie, but this is too complicated for a business major. Besides, Raymond says I shake the dice funny.

CHAMPIONS OF JESUS

NINE A.M. ON ANY WEEKDAY MORNING of the week of June 4, and thirty-five kids sit, stand, or crouch in the front three pews of Nimrod Lutheran Church. Amanda Metteer, seated at the organ, hits the opening bar, and, on cue, children sing hymns that are older than all of us. "Jesus Loves Me." "The B-I-B-L-E." "Do You Know Who Died For Me?" It's time for annual Vacation Bible School.

In keeping with Nimrod tradition of stretching beyond its boundaries, VBS attracts kids from Sebeka, Menahga, Pine River, Verndale. The curriculum is relaxed, fun, with "The Message" subliminal. The lesson each day reflects a virtue: walking with God, speaking the faith, forgiveness, kneeling in prayer. The lesson is played out in readings, scripture, hymns, even crafts. The kids are attentive and respectful, although the energy level at the pre-school table reaches pandemonium.

The lesson for me is the involvement of young local talent in the program. Sarah Funk, eighteen and a recent graduate of Sebeka High School, is an instructor. Her brother Steve, fourteen, is everyone's assistant and King of the Puppets. Tera Grewing, Nick Metteer, and Katie Aho are attendants.

Sarah shoehorns Sunday school instruction in her action-packed, year-around schedule, and VBS instruction in her June schedule. Aside from her recent graduation as a National Honor Society student, she completes her reign as Miss Sebeka on Friday night. She pitched ten innings of softball at the Section A title game, where she was named "All Conference," and she is preparing for an administrative assistant curriculum at Central Lakes College in September. In her spare time, she canoes and fishes the Crow Wing River, plays tenor sax, and tends her two registered Black Angus cow/calf pairs.

And how does Steve survive in the shadow of an over-achieving older sister? Very well, thank you. Steve just graduated from eighth grade, looks forward to the non-academic side of high school—baseball, student council, a band trip to Disneyland, an FFA convention in Louisville, Kentucky. That, plus tending farm

chores for the family's herd of Angus, playing Babe Ruth baseball, and baseball with the Nimrod Gnats.

Sarah has taught VBS for three years and considers this year's class her best. That reflects the quality of her students and her own maturity. She teaches first and second grade. Nine kids registered for the class. In other years, she felt like a baby sitter. This year, the kids were excited about being in class. They memorized their verses, volunteered to read, jostled to sit by teacher during prayer time. Younger brother Paul, one of her students, was her pinch hitter, stepping in without notice to fill a gap.

Steve's big moment each day is the puppet show. From his casual observation of the classes, he digests the gist of the lesson of the day and presents it in puppet format at the close of class. Four hand puppets—an elephant, walrus, lamb, and lion, become prophets and disciples, preaching the good news to kids in kid format. A winning combination!

Steve, recently confirmed, has been asked to teach Sunday school, an offer he is considering. Sarah is thankful she waited a couple years between confirmation and teaching—time to mature in her faith, gain confidence in her teaching and outgrow her students. Steve, the practical one, wonders how he would get to class with no driver's license. Sarah, the pragmatic one, knows that any of a dozen people would give him a lift.

Sarah and Steve chuckle about incidents this year: Logan Skov losing his tooth on Friday and the dedication of his classmates to find the tooth, which they did. Bailey Meech, age four, misinterpreting the offering basket, and helping himself to a dollar.

They reflect on the changes in class behavior—how the kids played softball, softball, softball when Sarah and Steve were VBS students, and now, hanging out is the thing, inside or outside.

The VBS week came to a close on Sunday with a student-led service. Thirty-five students saw one of their lessons, Speaking the Faith, in action. And they saw it from Sarah and Steve, not much older than they. Kids themselves who could have been living up to their stereotypes: sleeping in, playing video games, glued to the net or the phone. Sarah said she teaches VBS because she hopes to make a difference in at least one life. Well, Sarah, you've already done that. And I expect you will continue to make a difference in many more.

THE BRIDGES OF WADENA COUNTY

IN APRIL 1940, A NEW BRIDGE was commissioned on State Aid Road 2 (now CSAH 18) in Orton Township north of Nimrod. It had a split-stone masonry headwall, and a graceful arch under which flowed Big Swamp Creek on its journey from Badoura to the Crow Wing River. In April 2003, the bridge is slated for demolition. Goodbye to another local landmark.

The Big Swamp Creek bridge was one of five bridges built and ten bridges reconstructed by the Works Project Administration (WPA) in Wadena County. WPA is also responsible for several other county projects—326 miles of roads, three public buildings including the Red Eye Township school in 1936, a park in Wadena, plus water conservation dams, ditches, culverts, riprap, and fences.

The WPA was established in 1935 by executive order of President Franklin D. Roosevelt as the Works Progress Administration, renamed Works Project Administration in 1939. It was created in a time of widespread unemployment to put men to work on useful construction projects. Nationwide during its life, WPA workers built 116,000 buildings, 78,000 bridges, 651,000 miles of roads, and improved 800 airports. At its peak, WPA employed 3,500,000 men; total appropriations amounted to almost $11,000,000.

Jerry and Jack Graba remember when the bridge was constructed. Big Swamp Creek meanders through their family farm and crosses Highway 18 in front of their homestead. Dad Cliff Graba was a dairy farmer and worked on the bridge as a teamster with draft horses Bob and Barney.

The Big Swamp Creek bridge story begins in July 1935 with a letter from Harvey Dartt, Wadena County Engineer, to Lyle Culvert and Pipe Company in Minneapolis, requesting a rough sketch of a completed multi-plate bridge. Construction was delayed until January 1940, when it was designated Project no 7270 and construction began, with Alfred Muskala as foreman.

Jerry and Jack recall some of the workers on the project—Albert Nelson, a county employee and equipment operator; Buck Frier, a stonemason who hand split the rock that forms the headwall; Gregor Reul, a local farmer who fired the stove in the construction tent to keep concrete from freezing overnight; Alonzo Woodbridge, William Nohrenberg, and Cliff Graba, who drove teams of horses; Albert Nelson, Roy Thorson, John Montgomery, and Edwin Bimberg, who drove trucks; and DeWitt Downer, Ray Cattrell, and Oscar Skaar, who manned shovels.

The result is a beautiful stone arch, eighteen feet across at water level with stone riprap seven feet out on each bank. Railings are concrete. From the highway, the bridge is inconspicuous.

In 1973, a Physical Inspection Rating reported "No visible signs of fatigue or deterioration noted." In 1974, Swamp Creek rampaged and undermined bridge abutments, washed out the fill and collapsed the asphalt roadway. The bridge may have suffered structural damage. Today there are cracks in the headwall and mortar. The bridge has been on the deficiency list for years.

The new bridge is a pipe design, essentially two fifteen-foot culverts embedded in concrete. It is one of two bridges slated to be replaced in April/May 2003, according to Bill Ness, Wadena County Engineer. Demolition and construction are expected to reroute Highway 18 travelers for only thirty days.

Projected cost is $191,000, of which the majority is provided by the state's bridge bonding program. By contrast, Monthly Job Reports for the stone arch bridge for January through May 1940, detail $4,155 for labor, and $1,215 for materials and supplies. The foreman from Lyle Culvert was paid fifty cents an hour; laborers were paid twenty-five cents. Even at those rates, Minnesota WPA workers were among the highest paid in the nation. The average monthly earnings for the fourteen-state Region 4, which included Minnesota, were $47.86. For Minnesota, the average was $56.64.

MNDOT estimates traffic on CSAH 18 at 387 vehicles a day. That's an average figure, taking account of a slow day like today, or a busy day like opening weekend of deer hunting, Huntersville Trail Ride weekends, or the trove of Nimrod Gnats baseball fans heading north to see their team drub the Huntersville Horseflies.

Take a drive up and see an example of the fine craft of split stone masonry, back when craftsmanship was a hallmark of public works.

LAND SAKES!

A SMALL CROWD GATHERED at Walter Warner's auction Sunday. A few neighbors. A few onlookers. A few buyers. Walter was selling his 160-acre farm, six miles east of Nimrod, in three parcels—the house, outbuildings, and ten aces; seventy adjoining acres; and eighty acres across Cass County tar #20. No tractors, cattle, or machinery; no wagon loads of tools, equipment, or supplies; no furniture, antiques, or knickknacks. Just three items to auction. How long can that take?

Fifteen minutes is the answer. And if people forgot that Sunday was the first day of daylight savings time and didn't set their clock ahead, they missed the action. At one o'clock, Col. Al Wessel of Mid-American Auctions gave the invocation. He explained the terms of the sale and threw in some color. "If you live within a hundred miles of here, you know Walter. If you live within three hundred miles, you've heard of him."

Col. Al started the bidding. Within five minutes, Parcel One sold—the house and ten acres—for $48,000. On to Parcel Two, the adjoining seventy acres. The bidding was brisk. "You owned it for a little while," Col. Al told one bidder, "but not long enough to claim depreciation." In five minutes, the seventy acres sold for $725 an acre.

The last parcel to be auctioned was the eighty acres across the highway. With a bid at $400 an acre, Col. Al proclaimed, "That's about the price of a new pickup truck." In five minutes, the eighty acres sold for $450 an acre. That a grand total of $134,750, or $842 an acre.

What's happening to local land values? Harvey Chermak, Wadena County Assessor, recalls that when he hired on in 1988, hunting land sold for $100 to $150 an acre, and tillable land sold for $200 to $300 an acre. Now, hunting land sells for more than tillable land. Hunting land has a current low market value of $800 an acre and a high of $1,500 an acre, with $1,000 to $1,200 an acre a common price. That's a one-thousand percent increase in 14.5 years. Recreational use of the land motivates most buyers. "They want a mixture of land uses," says Harvey. "Some open land for planting game feed. Some woods, some slough."

I bought fifty acres of wooded river frontage property ten years ago in August 1993 for $30,000, or $600 an acre. In contrast, 53.75 acres in Section 16, Orton Township on the Crow Wing River sold by Eugene and Shirley Ertel brought $97,000. in March 2003. That's $1,805 an acre, a three-hundred percent appreciation in 9.5 years.

Gary Kern of Wadena Realty has listings along Highway 227 and west of Oylen. "My buyers aren't speculators," says Gary. "Many are looking for hunting land." Wadena Realty has a listing on County 18, Orton Township. It's a forty-acre parcel, no improvements, no river frontage, and the asking price is $1,000 an acre.

A trip through Certificates of Real Estate Value in the County Assessor's office shows sale after sale of bare land in Lyons, Orton, and Huntersville Townships from Potlatch to BWCA. BWCA is a partnership in Sauk Center, Minnesota. None of the Board of Directors or major stockholders of Potlatch have ownership in BWCA, according to Chuck Anderson, the "CA" in BWCA. Potlatch sold seven parcels of bare land to BWCA in Huntersville Township in 2002 and at least one in Orton. River frontage land hovers around $1,200 an acre; non-river frontage, $300 an acre. When asked if he considered these sales "arms length," Anderson said, "Yes." When asked if I could purchase the land from Potlatch for an equivalent price, he deferred to Potlatch.

The Potlatch/BWCA sales are impacting the market, especially the secondary sales from BWCA to developers or private parties. BWCA purchased a 188-acre parcel that straddled the Crow Wing River in Section 8 of Huntersville Township from Potlatch for $137,000. They sold it as a developed parcel—survey, roads, and utilities—for $380,000, which is about $2,000 an acre. That supports the Ertel sale of $1,805 an acre.

So what's the message? Land right now is performing infinitely better than the stock market. With more and more farmers and ranchers reluctant to allow hunting on private land, purchasing hunting land will be more common. To accommodate this new hunters' market, Potlatch has announced a new lease program. Hunting rights on a 192-acre parcel across the river from me in Lyons Township are available for $1,298 per year. That's likely to spur land sales.

Today, we say, "I remember when you could buy that land for $100 an acre." Ten years from now, our kids will say, "I remember when you could buy that land for $1,000 an acre."

TAKE ME OUT TO THE BALL GAME

JACQUES MARTIN BARZUN, American philosopher and educator wrote: "Whoever wants to know the heart and mind of America had better learn baseball." Extending that adage, whoever wants to know the heart and mind of Nimrod had better learn the Nimrod Gnats baseball team.

The Gnats played their first home game of the 2001 season on Sunday. The weatherman, not a baseball fan, provided rain showers, clouds, 100 percent humidity. But, just like show business, the game went on. From the chatter and high spirits in the dugout, the sun could have been shining.

Nimrod drew a bye in the April 22 opening weekend, and lost to the Menahga Red Sox in the bottom of the ninth last weekend. This weekend, it was the Red Eye Country Boys. They learned humility last weekend in an 18 to 1 loss to Midway.

Stigman Field looked picture perfect. Infield and outfield grass was green and freshly mowed for the third time. Agri-lime was raked along the baselines. Pitcher's mound was soggy from the rain.

"Play ball" sounded at 2:00 P.M. Hard core fans braved the mist to showers to rain to cheer on the home team. Jon Lillquist eased in a few practice pitches to Aaron Funk, and the game was underway. Three Country Boys up; three Country Boys down. Jon throws with an economy of motion, looks like he could last nine full innings, if he had to.

The home team took the offensive. Batting order was Lillquist, Stromland, Funk. Then the chatter started. "C'mon, Lilly." "Jump on it, Strommer." "Good eye, Hank." A couple of walks, and we had two men on base. Mike Hepola stepped to the plate. "C'mon, Hep. Spank it!" And spank it he did, with a stand up double. Then the Cannonball, Mike Cannon, took a leisurely walk to first, and RT, Ryan Tuorila, banged out a single before the side was retired. Score, 2 to 0.

Jon faced three more batters in the second inning. Decided that he could stay dryer if he retired them one, two, three, which he did. The home team got downright offensive in the second half. Before the inning was over, the entire batting order had showed their stuff. Score, 10 to 0. Had all the makings of the longest day in baseball history for the Red Eyes.

And the chatter continued. Lots of "C'mon babe's," "Take care of it, Turbo," "Set the table for the big boys." Good communication between the players, analyzing the pitcher's stuff, commenting on the condition of the baseline, identifying weak spots in the outfield. That, plus good natured ribbing.

The rain started, stopped, started. Umbrellas and a blue tarp went up in the stands. Some fans watched from a pickup with wiper blades on. The pitcher's mound turned soupy. The rain was cold. The outfield grass was slick. No one said a word, just played ball. The pitcher squinted through driving rain to pick up the signal. The batter gripped a wet bat, squinted right back to see where that ball was coming. It could have been eighty degrees and sunny, the way they played. The magic number was five full innings, if this were to be counted as a game.

Somewhere, someone started a collection plate from the fans in the stands. The nominal admission cost is $2.00. Sunday's take was undetermined, but it has to fund equipment, uniforms, traveling costs, field maintenance. In typical Nimrod style, much of this is donated.

There was a healthy feeling of competition between teams, but there was a feeling of kinship too. Small wonder, when some of the players on competing teams are brothers, cousins. But the attitude of the players is what struck me. Almost military-like, they played in the rain without questioning Eddie Hepola's sanity as home plate umpire. When the Country Boys screwed up on a couple plays, there was no ridicule from the dugout. And when the home team was at bat, there was constant encouragement from team mates.

How did they look to Charlie Tuorila, coach/manager? "Good! They started hitting. And the defense was good."

So Nimrod did itself proud again Sunday. A heads-up baseball team. An enviable ballpark. A loud and lively cheering section in the stands. Next Sunday, Nimrod plays host to Sebeka. Be there!

Incidentally, Nimrod won when the game was called in the seventh, 14 to 5.

TAKE ME OUT TO THE BALL GAME . . . AGAIN

TAKE A CHILLY MAY AFTERNOON, add a driving rain squall, a few hail stones, a fifteen-mile-an-hour wind out of the north, and what do you have? The baseball season opener, that's what. Sunday, the champion Nimrod Gnats played host to Laporte and taught them the requisite lesson in humility.

"We have a strong team again this year," says Coach/Manager Charlie Tourila. "We lost outfielder Matt Erickson, but we picked up leftie pitcher Dave Anderson." Dave played for Nimrod a couple years ago and came close to playing for the Gophers this year. He started on Sunday for Nimrod and is credited with the win.

Like the weather, the game was a typical opener. A few bobbled balls, overthrows, collisions, pitches in the dirt. But, all in all, the team looked good. Some tight pitching, error-free catching, attentive fielding, fleet-footed base running. And some hard hit balls.

Which brings up the subject of bats. Due to a rule change this year, aluminum is out; hickory is in. And what a thrill to hear that baseball smack wood! No more metal pings. "Aluminum took over in the '70s," says Charlie. "Most of the guys have never batted with wood." The rationale behind the rule change is safety. The ball doesn't snap off a wood bat as fast as off aluminum, thus sparing an occasional pitcher. "Don't expect as many home runs as last year," says Hank Aaron Funk.

Also making its debut Sunday was the new covered bleacher section. Thanks to volunteers Jeff Pederson on construction and Doug Hart on welding, the fans sit comfortably out of the wind and rain and, someday, out of the sun, we hope. Three rows of seats were ready for Sunday's opener, which included only the hardest of hard core fans. Thanks to Ruth's secret recipe hot chocolate, the fans stayed warm. Tingly warm.

The next Nimrod Gnat project is a ball field sprinkler system. Lights for night games are still in the talking stage. A domed stadium is even further out, along with the skyway over Main Street to Hillig's Mercantile.

As for the game itself, Laporte got off to a good start with two runs in the first inning. Nimrod found its stride in the second and retaliated with six runs. They never gave up the lead after that.

There are two new teams in the conference this year—Verndale in the South Division, and Wolf Lake in the North. Nimrod plays one game against each team in the North Division, and two games against each team in the South. There's a good selection of home games.

So, the home town team did itself proud Sunday, even without some of last year's stars who are still attending college. Big cheers go to Jeff and Doug for their work on the covered bleachers, plus the team members who pitched in and the merchants who donated materials. If Minneapolis has its Target Center and Saint Paul has its Excel Energy Center, then Nimrod can have its Jeffco Hart Center. And all that construction without a bond issue. Looks like those bingo games and spaghetti dinners last winter paid off.

We're off and running for the 2002 baseball season. A sharp team on the field, comfortable fans in the stands. And the old-fashioned smack of baseballs against wooden bats. Now, if we could get Jeanne at Riverside Grocery to sell double dip ice cream cones . . .

Incidentally, Nimrod won over Laporte on Sunday, 14 to 4. The next home game is with Huntersville on May 19. See you there. Hopefully, it will be warm enough to do without the hot chocolate.

RUNNING THE BARRELS

SHE'S RIDING TALL IN THE SADDLE OUTSIDE THE ARENA, running tight circles, jack rabbit starts, freeze frame stops. It's a brilliant May morning, all sun, no clouds. Just clouds of dust below. She hears the announcer call her name inside the arena. He reads a short bio—a hometown, the horsy clubs presidentships, the silver buckles won. She's psyched. So is her horse. On cue, she bolts through the double doors into the darkness of the arena. There's a white barrel to the right. She circles it, banking her horse into a turn until her stirrup drags dirt. She clears that barrel and heads across the arena to the second. Same routine. Then she heads for the barrel at the far end of the ring. She's lookin' good! She approaches the third barrel, gives it a wide berth—maybe an inch or two—to keep the barrel upright. She clears that one, leans into the wind, and heads for daylight. She trips the electronic timer at 14.187 seconds. Years of practice; thousands of dollars of horse flesh, tack, and training; and a weekend in the bunkhouse end of a horse trailer, and it's all over in fourteen seconds. That's if she's lucky.

Welcome to the world of barrel horse racing. Los Gauchos Ranch, north of Dad's Elwell Corners on Highway 64, hosted the Minnesota NBHA 2002 State Championship this past weekend, May 17, 18, and 19. Jane and Ryan Melby, proprietors of Los Gauchos, are no strangers to competition. Jane won the National Barrel Horse championship twice. Ryan won the title of All Around Cowboy. Jane will compete as well as host this event. So will her kids, Cayla, the youngest competitor at four, and Colton, who wins the youth competition.

This is weighty stuff for barrel horse people. Curry comb the flanks, loosen the belly strap, circle the exercise ring. The small talk among the contestants reminds me of deer hunting opener—this year's running times, last year's competitions, the buckle instead of the buck that got away.

Nimrod area is well represented at the Barrel Horse Championship. Jane, Colton, and Cayla Melby; Betsy, Lonnie, and Lacey Kuschel; and Avis Bell are among 178 contestants in Open Competition, twenty-four contestants in Seniors, and eighty-four contestants in Youth Competitions. They compete for $33,000 in prize money and awards, including eight Pro Rider trophy saddles, forty Red Bluff buckles, and NBHA mirrors, equivalent to the gold, silver, and bronze medals of the Olympics.

Lonnie Kuschel is our token male in a competition dominated by Jan, Julie, Rhonda, Kelli, Darcie, Becky, Michelle. Lonnie holds his own with the distaff set and rides off with best time, 13.931 seconds, in the Seniors Short Go.

Barrel racing is a participation sport, not a spectator sport. There are no reserved box seats like a rodeo. No clowns to amuse people or drag out the day. No attendants hawking cokes, popcorn, programs. The announcer makes a perfunctory introduction, the rider rides in and rides out, the time is announced. Next!

The cheering section is site specific. It's the family of the next rider. Mom films the event on video. Dad leads the cheering section. "C'mon Kelly, or Krystal, or Katie! Lean, girl, lean! Give him some rein! Atta girl. Now bring him home."

For these few seconds in the arena, people have dragged horse trailers around for months, spent more for tack and training than they've spent on house payments, given up golf or card club. She rides well. She knows how to compete. She feels good about her performance, about herself. Suddenly, it's all over. She smiles. Suddenly, it's all worth it.

TREES

DRIVING NORTH OF TOWN ON COUNTY 14, I see a field of tree seedlings—Norway pines. Acres of seedlings in straight rows, evenly spaced, standing tall. I project backwards to the days when this land was all treed, like the stands of second- and third-growth timber that surround this field. And I imagine the back-breaking, gut-wrenching job it was to cut timber, grub stumps, and clear brush and branches before plowing virgin prairie. I imagine the joy of seeing land cleared, crops planted and harvested, cattle fed. Now, a century later, the land is being planted back to trees, intentionally. Life is a cycle.

And riding that cycle comfortably are the tree planting crews of the DNR's Nimrod Station. This year, two crews will plant 658 acres of privately owned land with 395,000 seedlings. On top of that, they will plant 131 acres of state land with 93,000 seedlings. All of that within four weeks ending May 26.

Those little green seedlings begin life at Badoura Nursery, north on State Highway 64, ten miles south of Akeley. Along with the General Andrews Nursery, the nurseries have a combined seedbed acreage of 270 acres and production capability of forty million seedlings a year. Nimrod DNR will process orders for about a half million of those. Coniferous species grown and distributed are Norway pine, jackpine, Scotch pine, white pine, white spruce, black spruce, Norway spruce, Colorado spruce, and Black Hills spruce. Deciduous species include black walnut, green ash, red oak, and silver maple. Shrubs are caragana and wild plum. All are native Minnesota trees and are intended for a variety of uses, not all of them timber production.

On this damp late April morning, the crew at Badoura is removing three-year-old jackpines from seedbeds with a mechanical blade and bulk packing them in crates to be hauled to a packing shed. There they are sorted, culled, and counted by crews and placed on a conveyor belt to a packer. He places them in plastic lined boxed, twenty-five to a bundle, 1,000 to a box.

Glenn Pederson is one of two contractor planter/vendors for the Nimrod DNR. He is in Badoura to pick up 56,000 seedlings to be planted on the Rife farm north of town. We check on the planting currently in progress at the Pulju farm, across the highway from Rife's.

Ryan Eastlund unpacks boxes of seedlings, separating and untangling roots for ease of planting. Ardell Horton drives the tractor. Denny Wilcox rides the planter. Trees are planted in rows nine feet apart; trees are spaced eight feet apart. In twenty years, alternate trees will be removed to allow about a twenty foot growing diameter.

"Yield is a factor of weather," says Lonnie Lilly, District Forester. "In good years, like this year with adequate moisture, we expect ninety percent survival. In a dry summer like last year, we're lucky to get seventy-five percent."

Another problem with seedling survival is gophers. "Especially on farmed ground," says Lonnie. A third problem is disease. The current threat is gall rust, a disease of jackpine. No jackpines are being planted on private land this year.

Glenn has planted trees for the DNR for twenty-three years. He estimates that he and his crews have planted over three million trees. Currently he has one crew planting. Back in his heyday, when reforestation was the buzz word after the Nimrod to Badoura forest fire in 1976, Glenn had eight crews planting, making him unquestionably the biggest employer in all of Nimrod. Of course, it helped that he was the sole contractor planter/vendor at the time—the only game in town.

So, as I'm driving around and see those ruler-straight rows plowed by Ardell, and the seedlings, well grounded and standing tall, planted by Denny, I take a minute to consider Nimrod's contribution to replenishment of the planet's supply of oxygen. What would they do without us?

PULITZER POETRY

PULITZER PRIZE WINNERS WERE RECENTLY ANNOUNCED, and not one winner from Nimrod. Not even a nomination. My ghetto friends tease, “So much for your bragging about the high level of culture up there!”

Well, April being poetry month, let’s get a head start on next year. Poetry is the easiest category because it’s the shortest form and, by definition, is totally obscure. Heaven help the reader who understands what is being said on the first reading. Or the second. Or the third.

Poetry is either rhyme or free verse. In Minnesota, the dividing line between rhyme and free verse is St. Cloud. Nothing below St. Cloud rhymes. The line is inching north.

To get started, I offer some poetry I wrote for a creative writing class last fall. The first one rhymes.

NIMROD, MN

The limo eased between the trucks at our cafe
A sentimental journey on their wedding day.
They met here on a college outing, you’ll remember
Canoeing down the Crow Wing River last September.

Now they return. The bride, a cherry tree in bloom
Eclipsing the gray tuxedoed groom.
Attendants genuflecting in her wake
Like sugar blossoms on a wedding cake.
Enter bride and groom. They stop. They start
Toward the table where he carved a heart.

Nimrod Chronicles

"See. Here it is!" Attendants scurry. Then they pause
To watch them kiss. Applause. Applause.

Laughter. Excitement. Loud and joyous racket
The groomsman slips a bottle from his jacket.
With high bravado, he proffers a toast
To endless love of friends he loves the most.

They see us, plain folk of a lower class
Talking crops and weather, the price of gas.
Condescension vibrates from their booth.
We're rubes. We're rustic and uncouth.

They watch us grinning, and they mock
The way we laugh, the way we sit, the way we talk.
Contrasting styles of life, extremes of which
Are richly simple; the other, simply rich.

The groomsman's tux. What color is that? Mauve?
So young, urbane, sophisticated, suave.
"Waitress, will the chef prepare a quiche?
He laughs the laugh of adolescent nouveau riche.

He sips a drink, aims an imaginary gun and shoots
To our table. "You must be cowboys. You're all wearing boots
And seed corn hats and flannel shirts and jeans."
The uniform of men of independent means.

"What do you do in this hick town? What keeps you here?"
"Oh, horseshoe tournaments, sheepshead games. And beer."
Grinning, he reports our answers to his set
And gets a laugh. But nothing like the one we get.

"What's the charge?" The party's heading for the door.
"Ten bucks," she says. He flips a twenty on the floor.
The rich folks' concept of noblesse oblige—
Tossing cans along the road for poor folks to retrieve.

They're gone. We laugh. The waitress tucks a ten
And pours a round. "Where were we then?"
"My pasture ponds are drying up. Looks like an early freeze."
"Third crop hay looks good this year. And pass the sugar, please."

The second poem is free verse. A person doesn't have to know me very well to recognize who inspired this one.

THE SAWYER

His hands. Blue veins bulge from knuckles to his gray haired wrist
Where he wears a watch. I don't know why.
He measures time in work hours until dark.

His other wrist, a copper band.
Keeps the rheumatism down, he says.
At sixty-six, you have to play the angles.

His shirt. Buttoned at the neck and sleeves
Despite the heat of late July. Beneath the shirt, white
Neck ribbing shows. Two other ribbings at the wrist.

His overalls. Faded, worn, and patched
By a seamstress who considers sewing not an art.
Sometimes fabrics match. Stitches ramble on the edges.

His stature. Abbreviated,
Bent from bending, flexible.
A Willow whipped by wind.

His saw. Maintained better than his truck,
Or house, or health.
Gleaming teeth that gnaw at trees.

> He pulls the starter cord. The saw bolts
> And screams until the trigger lock's released.
> He sets the choke and thumbs the oiler knob.
>
> He sets the saw, surveys the popple one last time
> Before the felling cut. Four lengths here. Four eight-foot lengths.
> I'll fell it to my right. Right on that stump.

The man. Drops the tree on target. Grins.
Blue veined hand tilts the visored cap
And wipes the sweat and dust.

The last poem is part of a trilogy entitled "Thoughts While Shaving." More free verse, but lighter.

BOOTS

I like boots
    lace ups
    Wellingtons
    westerns

They pamper my feet
    lift my arches
    hug my ankles
    touch my legs

I really like the new boots
    Thinsalite insulation
    Gore-tex lining
    carbon rubber outsoles
It's not a fetish
    fetish feels driven
    non-functional
    closet behavior
But then, I do have several pairs
    One for each hour of the day
    One for each day of the week
    One for each corner of the closets

So, there. I'm not offering these as Pulitzer candidates, but rather to get everyone's creative juices flowing. Right now, everyone should be saying, "Damn, I can do better than that!" The Pulitzer Prize for Poetry citation says "For a distinguished volume of original verse by an American author, $7,500." Happy writing.

NIELSON GARDENS

TWO INCHES OF SNOW FRIDAY NIGHT. Maybe another ten or twelve last night. Highway 10 closed between Staples and Wadena. Blizzard warnings out. Visibility near zero. No travel advised.

Winter got you down, Bucky? Past the point of getting a rush from the Gurney and Burpee seed catalogs with their promises of New! Pumpkin, Rock Star; New! Bush Bean, Tenderlake; New! Cherry Tomato, Favorita? Time for a spring tonic. Smell some warm dirt. Touch some baby green plants. Breathe some warm, humid air. Follow me to Nielson's Greenhouse, south of town, west of the Nimrod tar.

Before I begin on Jean and Pete's operation, I have to comment on the number of home businesses in the neighborhood. "What commerce do you have in Nimrod?" people ask. A grocery store, bar and grill, service station, and bus garage. Across Main Street, a blacksmith shop and the flagship store of the Hillig Mercantile chain. But head in any direction, and a person will find mechanics, a sign painter, building contractors, an Avon distributor, truckers, canoe outfitters, an electrician, wood workers, welders, snow plowers, an artist, and the list goes on.

And that doesn't include the ranchers and farmers. Cattle must outnumber people a hundred to one. And cattle are outnumbered only by horses. There's a home business on nearly every tract. And I'm one of the few locals who doesn't have his own saw mill.

Back to the greenhouse. Jean and Pete started the business in 1979, after trying U-Pick strawberries and vegetables. Their best customers seemed to be the local deer population, so they moved the business inside. The first greenhouse was a twelve-by-twelve structure for starting tomato and cabbage plants. And following that, a thirty-by-sixty greenhouse and expanded plant populations.

Meanwhile, Pete was milking cows and doing farm chores with the help of three boys. Jean was keeping house and running the greenhouse with the help of five girls. Jean accepted her role (and still does) as the woman who raises the garden, cooks the meals, cans the beans, bakes the bread. And the cookies. And the peach pie. As the greenhouse business grew, they looked reality in the face, sold the dairy cattle, and switched to beef, which freed Pete to mix planting soil, design heating systems, and build more greenhouses.

Now, twenty-two years later, Jean and Pete have over twelve thousand square feet of greenhouse space. Last year, they sold over four thousand geraniums; this year, they have about five thousand. Wave petunias, begonias, and fuchsia baskets number in the hundreds. Not to mention flats of tomatoes, cabbages, and peppers, marigolds, alyssum, and snapdragons, almost as far as the eye can see.

The grand opening is Mother's Day. The whole Nielson family returns. Coffee and homemade cookies are served in the garage. It's like a family reunion of neighbors and friends, feeling good, buying big. Hugs all around.

I can say, I think, that Jean has the local market sewed up. But her regular customers include long-distance buyers from the Twin Cities, out-state Minnesota, North and South Dakota.

The greenhouse business begins each year during the first week of January, when Jean selects her seeds. Years of experience tell her what sells; intuition predicts which new varieties will thrive and appeal to her market. She orders seeds and plugs. A semi delivers five pallets of supplies.

February 1. Pete lights the heaters, and in five days, the greenhouse is up to temperature for germinating and transplanting. Seeds and plugs arrive by Federal Express. On February 10, they start seeds in the germination trays; geranium and fuchsia plugs in pots. Jean is commanding officer. Pete mixes the potting medium—compost, peat moss, Perlite, a shot of lime and fertilizer. Son Lyle is the materials handling specialist—pails of dirt to the planters, trays of planted pots to the next greenhouse. Two neighbors volunteer their services in the planting operation.

A friendly conflict erupts! Pete, after years of calling the shots on the farm, forgets and starts directing traffic. Jean reminds him of the chain of command inside the greenhouse, and seats him on the other side of the furnace. She can't see him; he can't see her. They laugh about it. And suddenly, I see a love story here. Married forty-six years, raised eight kids, had their share of health problems, and still moving forward heart to heart. He tosses a teasing comment at her, sips his coffee, grins. She comments right back, touches his shoulder, smiles. Both are hitched to the same cart, and that cart is full of the best flowers and vegetables I've seen in fifty years of gardening. And I thought those healthy plants were the result of good soil!

HUNTERSVILLE SPRING TRAIL RIDE

AT 1:45 LAST SUNDAY AFTERNOON, Al Krupke saddled up Buddy, a seven-year-old appaloosa stallion. Buddy was a stranger to Al, but Al was no stranger to horses. Al adjusted the belly strap, slid on the bridle, and attached his canteen. Almost two o'clock. Time for the Huntersville Spring Trail Ride, and Al was the trail master. Al has missed only five spring trail rides since 1966, and has been trail master for fifteen years. He knows the trails.

Trail riders can usually count on rain, or even snow, for the spring ride. But this year was warm and sunny, with temperatures in the seventies. The woods were picture postcard perfect, with May flowers, violets, and marsh marigolds abloom; popple, birch, and oak in light lacy foliage; robins, finches, and wrens providing background music.

At two o'clock, I expected the lineup that we see on the fall trail rides. Horseback riders, wagons pulled by draft horse teams, kids on ponies, dogs barking, colts running beside mares—a string of riders and animals worthy of a John Ford western movie. But when Al raised his arm and called, "Let's go!" about a dozen riders formed the procession, followed soon by another eight, another four, another ten.

The ride is about fifteen miles, according to Al, and this year, it took about three hours. That's a lot of riding for Sunday cowboys, but there are plenty of stops along the way. And the pace is leisurely, slow.

Trail riders arrived Friday night in a variety of contrivances, from mobile Taj Mahals to modest pickup camper toppers. Everybody pulled a horse trailer.

Meals are served on the grounds and at the Huntersville Outpost bar and grill. But the best food, at least the best smelling food, is prepared over campfires.

Saturday night, a dance band played in the campground's dining/dance hall. All ages bounced around the floor. Kids danced with mothers, dads, and each other. Outside the dance hall, campers circled campfires, providing a moody, frontier light. I looked for my Nimrod neighbors, but they were celebrating a wedding in Las Vegas, recovering from a horse fall in a St. Cloud hospital, or clearing brush from their new lot on the Crow Wing River. Even without the Nimrod hard core, the event was well attended—almost one thousand registered, according to Norma Finn, president of the Bushwacker Saddle Club, the sponsoring group, out of Motley, a fifth-tier suburb of Nimrod.

Huntersville State Forest is located in the northeast corner of Wadena County, about eleven miles north of Nimrod, and encompasses an area of fifty-two square miles. A map of the area looks like a checker board of state and privately owned land, much of the privately owned belonging to Potlatch. The DNR administers 16,448 acres of land in the forest. And a river runs through it, actually two rivers: the Shell and the Crow Wing.

There are about 150 miles of logging trails and a twelve-mile designated horse trail that has two loops and a river crossing. The fall ride usually takes the south logging trails to accommodate wagons; the spring ride took the north horse trail, due to logging trails being underwater.

Sunday morning. Another beautiful day. Another trail ride scheduled for one o'clock. Trucks and trailers are snaking out of the campgrounds at noon. I asked Al if there would be a ride today. "Nope. They took their rides this morning. We're losing our crowd." The campers had other options. After all, it was Mother's Day and fishing season opening weekend. And the Nimrod Gnats were playing Sebeka at two o'clock.

I walked around the camp site—the smell of smoldering jackpine campfires, the sound of horses neighing for something, someplace familiar, the sight of spring—green, green, green.

HERE COMES DAVID COTTONTAIL

EASTER SATURDAY—THE WARMEST, SUNNIEST DAY of Holy Week. It's noon, and toddlers to twelve-year olds arrive in Nimrod carrying Easter baskets, ice cream buckets, plastic shopping bags. One ambitious boy carries a ten-gallon pail. They step up to the table where Margaret Rathcke, with an assist from Roxanne and Bethany Pederson, register them for the annual Nimrod Easter egg hunt.

The Easter egg hunt was a Pat Rathcke idea in 1973, when he squired little Dean Gilster around the field looking for eggs. Today, Dean is back on hand with two of his own hunters.

Meanwhile, in Stigman Field, behind the registration desk, men of the Rathcke clan and their team, are hiding thirty dozen dyed eggs in two ball parks — one park for toddlers to six-year olds; the other for seven- through twelve-year olds.

And where is the Easter Bunny? Well, he's sitting on stage before a decorated trellis, posing for pictures with skeptical children or tittering teen-age Nimrod "royalty." Glenda Gilster sells tickets for the privilege of sitting on the Easter Bunny's lap. The bunny speaks in a rabbit-y voice. Who does he/she sound like?

The "royalty"—Miss Nimrod and Little Miss Nimrod and their courts, have donned tiaras and are selling raffle tickets to the crowds. Prizes are displayed on a table inside—plush rabbits to crocheted doilies.

The whistle will be blown at one o'clock, signaling the beginning of the twenty-seventh (some say twenty-eighth) egg hunt.

The Easter bunny is still inside, posing for the Polaroid, but, more often, seems to be resting, even napping. Tomorrow, Easter Sunday, is his big day. Then on Easter Monday, he will be presiding over the White House Easter Egg Roll, a tradition since 1878 but diminished this year by President Bush's decision to

quash the sale of a commemorative 2001 Easter Egg. (Economy move? Bowing to advocates of separation of church and state? Not a constitutionally authorized function of the federal government? Who knows?) Anyway, the Easter Bunny has a lot of hopping to do, and he's pacing himself. But his/her voice sounds familiar.

It's nearing one o'clock. One hundred and six hunters have registered. Kids from Nimrod, Sebeka, Menahga, Verndale, even the high-rent district of Pequot Lakes. They line up in front of the ball parks for last minute instructions from egg hunt organizers. And last minute coaching from anxious parents and personal trainers. "Carry the pail high in your left hand." "Run to the far, open end of the outfield." "Tie your shoes." It's a perfect day for a hunt—full sun, fifty-nine degrees, even a hint of green in the infield, if one uses imagination.

The gun sounds; the hunt is on. Here's an easy way to measure aggression. Some of these kids take to the chase like California gold rushers. Others, especially toddlers, spurred on by anxious parents, stand over the egg, pause, contemplate, and seem to conclude "Why? I don't even like eggs."

The hunt is over in five minutes, maybe ten. Catch of the day ranges from zero to a dozen. Some of the eggs are numbered, and they are worth money, prizes. Then there are raffle winners to be announced. The "royalty" assembles on stage to draw lucky tickets. JoLynn Weaver and Linda Kuschel pick prizes; Nancy Gilster reads the names of lucky winners; Barb Chapman records. Kelly Rickard of Pequot Lakes wins the grand prize, a night's stay at the AmericInn in Wadena.

By two o'clock, it's all over. Margaret and Nick Metteer still have turquoise dye along their fingernails. They hope some of the eggs will make it into egg-salad sandwiches. Organizers tally up the take from the raffle, about seven hundred dollars, which goes to the Nimrod Jubilee Days queen pageant fund.

Here's another example of big energy in a small town, population seventy-five, according to the new census figures. Lots of volunteer labor and contributions. The hunt is intended to be self-financing, not a money maker. There is a turkey dinner earlier in the year to raise money for the expenses, estimated at 175 dollars. The raffle money goes to a different pot.

Cars exit parking areas, north and south. And at the end, the Easter Bunny is seen climbing into a pickup truck. I just remembered who he/she sounds like—Miss Frieda from the Nimrod Jubilee Days parade.

THE BIG NIMROD GARAGE SALE

PEOPLE WANT TO SHOP, AND THEY WANT a shopping center that handles everything from a cedar-lined sauna, oak firewood, and dog kennel to a computer, fine china, and Acme western boots. Where to go? The Nimrod Community Garage Sale. Eat your heart out, Mall of America!

Saturday, May 19, was the big day. The Nimrod Booster Club sponsored the sale; Jenny and Rick Pederson took the lead. Sale bills were dropped in an area from Leader to Sebeka, from Blue Grass to Huntersville. Calls for pickup came from Verndale and Wadena. Local businesses responded generously—ten yards of gravel from Menahga Concrete, one thousand board feet of tongue-in-groove pine and aspen from Frisbie Mills, potted geraniums from Nielson Gardens.

On Thursday, the massive sorting and pricing effort began. Clothes along the north wall, electronics on the west table, toys on the stage, the inevitable knick-knacks in the center. Glenda and Cheryl agonized over the right price; Rick and Dave winged it. Outside, the parking area looked like Menards.

All of this was intended to raise funds for Nimrod's Jubilee Days, an annual community celebration on Labor Day weekend. The sale bill said, "Help keep Jubilee Days Alive." My take on that is Jubilee Days is every bit alive as freedom of speech.

The sale was scheduled for eight to four on Saturday. At seven, the crowd was already milling. Pre-sale shoppers eyed that one-of-a-kind quilted sampler, ten-piece cocktail set, collector quality McCoy pottery. At seven-thirty, parking was a problem. When the doors opened, it looked like the Oklahoma land rush. Within five minutes, JoLynn was in high gear at the check-out stand, giving totals to cashier Jenny. Interesting that no one haggled over price. But how could anyone, with twelve eager buyers standing behind, waiting?

To provide even more options, the Nimrod Royalty sponsored a coinciding bake sale. Rice Krispies bars and brownies by Ashley and Amber, cookies by Minnie and Jessica, a cake by Tara (or was it Tara's mother?). Nancy Gillster directed that effort. Barb Chapman was money handler.

By eight-fifteen, the line at the cashier's table extended to the middle of the hall, and open car trunks and pickups appeared at the doorway, with Ardell, Jim, and Terry providing the muscle to hoist fence posts, furniture, big appliances. By ten o'clock, the discounting began. Dollar-a-bag clothes dropped to a dollar for two bags. Electronics were severely slashed. Every offer was considered. By noon, it was quiet. By one, it was over.

As evidence of tactical genius, the Booster Club identified a local to remove the unsold stuff—all the unsold stuff, at the close of the sale. By two o'clock, the truck was loaded and on the way down the road.

So how did it go? Over $3,000, according to Rick, with some possible late sales still coming in. The bake sale grossed about $200, according to Nancy. The Jubilee Days budget is about $6,000 for 2001. Big cost items are fireworks, parade awards, and kiddy game prizes. Here's another example of Nimrod pulling together, getting together, having fun together. "The Little Engine That Could" syndrome.

In 2002, Jubilee Days celebrates twenty-five years of continuous celebration. Plans are already in motion for next year's Silver Anniversary extravaganza. We're looking for an artist to paint a thirty-six-inch circular saw blade for a fund raising raffle. With all the talented quilt makers around, how about a Nimrod Historical Quilt, designed and sewn by local talent? Think about it, Ann, Beth, Elsie, Margie, others.

So, when Labor Day rolls around, and the Nimrod Jubilee Days banner billows above Main Street, thanks go to all the donors, helpers, customers. It's everyone's time, effort, and enthusiasm that keeps the banner flying.

NIMROD BUZZ

THANKS TO ALL WHO CONTRIBUTED TIME, money, and prizes to the annual Easter Egg Hunt. Even with marginal weather, the town parking lot (Main Street) was full. Rumors are that Pat Rathcke is still finding eggs in the bleachers.

Poor Jeanne at Riverside Grocery, trying to keep birthday candles in stock. Connie Frederickson must have taken a full box for her Easter birthday. Ruth Downer probably needed three boxes for her April 8 birthday. And Glenn Pederson will need at least two boxes for his birthday on tax day, April 15. Many happy returns, folks.

Wedding bells will soon be ringing. In case anyone was out of the country and hasn't heard, Dave Gilster and Karlene Potratz, an estimable young couple, will take the trip down the aisle of Nimrod Lutheran in September. Wondering about the perfect gift? How about one of Jerry Sweeney's custom-crafted back scratchers? If that doesn't suit, Dave is registered at Ted's True Value in Sebeka.

Welcome to Nimrod, Lucille and Arvin Burton. The Burtons moved from Cloquet into the Chapman house on Easter Sunday. Arvin has already found his way to the men's table at the Nimrod Coffee Klatch. Seems he's a scratch golfer, so, readers, be careful if he asks you to play a round for money.

And welcome home, Amy Schermerhorn, from a brief stay in Rochester. You brought spring back with you! We heard Jerry stayed up all night cleaning the kitchen before you returned.

Speaking of spring, the Crow Wing River unofficially opened on Sunday, April 6. Nothing dramatic, just an ever-widening swath of blue water and a parade of ice flows, accompanied by a chorus of Canadian geese.

The four teams of the Nimrod Pool League enjoyed a Sponsors Dinner and Award Night on Wednesday. Chef Robert whipped up braised wing of chicken and filet of meatloaf. Gordy Parks walked off with first prize. Donny Borg is still grinning, not about winning or the meatloaf, but about beating Mike Roberts.

Mark your calendar for Friday, April 19. The nationally prominent Nimrod Do Gooders will sponsor an all-you-can-eat Spaghetti Supper. R&R Bar & Grill is host again, and service is from 5:00 to 8:00 P.M. Free will offerings will be used for community projects.

Finally, Horn-and-a-Half and MacDuff, Scottish Highland cattle at Brigadoon Farm, announce the arrival of the season's first calf, Rob Roy, a bouncing baby bull. Mother and son are doing fine. Stop by for a beef jerky cigar.

OF MAN AND MACHINES

WHAT STARTED AS A MEMORIAL DAY tribute column to a World War II veteran got bumped in favor of high school graduation and spring roundups. But Fred Graba's story isn't set in a World War II Army training camp in Baltimore or a motor pool in the Marina Islands in the South Pacific. Fred's story is set on the Sebeka road, west of Nimrod, and it is timely any time of year.

Fred was contemplating a Model T Ford when I arrived. The car was stripped to bare essentials—frame, engine, transmission, steering, and electrical system. Fred was cleaning the carburetor, which fouled because a sediment bowl was missing on the makeshift gas tank. Too bad, because we would have taken a ride. Fred built the Model T from parts and assemblies he had accumulated. The wheels are a mix of Model T and Model A. There's no interest in authenticity here. Just a strong urge to make it work.

There's also the gasoline engine Fred built from spare parts. Everything but the fly wheel and frame are scavenged. This engine hasn't been put to work, but two others have—for sawing wood and grinding feed. He tries to demonstrate the engine, but it refuses to fire.

Then, there are the tractors, including one that Fred built. I didn't count his inventory, but we both agree he has fewer than the John Deere king, Maynard Benson. Fred's favorite is a late 1950s Co-op brand, with about thirty-five HP, live power, and hydraulics. He hits the starter button, the engine fires, and all four cylinders purr like the day the tractor was born.

Fred was born in 1919 on the family homestead just west of his present home. To give an idea of how things were back in those days before duct tape, Elvis Presley, and ball-point pens, Woodrow Wilson was president and was brokering treaties with our World War I allies over a defeated Germany. Henry Ford was halfway through his nineteen-year production of fifteen million Model T's. Commercial hybrid seed corn was still in development. And a three-cent postage stamp still cost three cents. The family moved to Washington State, lured by four dollars a day wages in the logging industry. The transplant didn't take, and the family was back in less than a year.

Fred's dad died in 1933, when Fred was fourteen. He and his brother Homer farmed together until Homer married. Fred farmed until 1943. Until then, he had a deferment from military draft. "I was the only man left in the

neighborhood." Fred says. "Everyone else was drafted. I wanted to serve too." They held an auction, sold the dairy cows, and Fred received his 1A classification the next day.

Fred took infantry basic training and spent time in Baltimore guarding U.S. prisoners. When the war in Europe was over, he shipped to Seattle for transport to the Marina Islands, due south of Japan. Fred worked in the motor pool there and saw no combat. But he was in the area when the atomic bombs were dropped on Hiroshima and Nagasaki. Five months later, he was discharged and came home.

Fred married Gladys Ostlund in 1950, and that year they bought the eighty-acre farm where they still live. To that, they added another eighty acres.

Fred is bearish about farming prospects in this part of Wadena County. The one crop he points to with pride is a 1991 crop of sorghum that he planted north of the Cat River. The sorghum grew to twelve feet, an incredible height. Fred plowed it under as a green manure crop with his trusty Co-op tractor and one-bottom plow but not before he photographed the sorghum dwarfing him and his tractor for all the doubting Thomases.

Fred helps son Duane with the farming now, and the responsibility for crops and cattle is not his. That leaves time for tinkering—getting that handmade gasoline engine to run and assembling the body to the Model T chassis.

Fred lights up, like his hand-rolled cigarette, when he talks about his mechanical projects. Every now and then, I see a mischievous grin, and I'm not privileged to know what's behind it. We make one more trip to the gasoline engine to see if it will start. No luck. We walk through the shed where walls and rafters are covered with head gaskets, V belts, specialty tools, and tune up kits. "Duane will have a time getting rid of all this stuff when I'm gone," Fred says.

I wouldn't hold my breath. At eighty-five, Fred still has plenty of projects and a genius for making things run. I'll be back, Fred, when you get the carburetor on that Model T. And maybe the cab. And the seat.

THE ROAR OF THE GREASEPAINT, THE SMELL OF THE CROWD

THE *REVIEW MESSENGER* STORY of the Madhatter's production of *Arsenic and Old Lace* prompted a memory and a call from Nimrod reader John Marshall. "Did you know," John asked," that we produced a play in Nimrod?" No, I didn't know that, but I'm not surprised. Somehow, Nimrod and legitimate theater just go together. We certainly have enough characters in town to cast a dozen plays.

Back in the early 1930s, John and sister Alice (Oehlenschlager) acted in a play that opened in Nimrod, charmed the critics, and played to standing-room-only audiences. Flushed with success, the cast took the play on the road. We don't know the full itinerary, but we do know it closed after lackluster ticket sales in Clarissa. "We barely covered expenses on that one," says Alice.

The play was *What About Betty?* According to Internet sources, Walter Richardson wrote the play in 1926. No synopsis of the plot is available, but Alice describes it as a combination mystery-romance that all comes together in the final scene of Act III. The two leading men get the two leading ladies, evil is defeated, truth and justice prevail, and they all live happily ever after.

In the cast with Alice and John were Ann Nielson, Bill Sales, Evelyn Hughes Borg, Jim Gobel, Magdeline Gilster Coventry, and Bill Nielson. Ann and Evelyn shared leading lady roles. Alice recalls that Ann was dating Ernie Komula during rehearsals and the play, and Ernie might have been a bit jealous during the love scenes.

Esther Nielson Nelson, Bill and Ann's younger sister, recalls the play being produced in the winter of 1934-1935. Esther was a student of Alice Marshall, and too young to be in the cast. She remembers this play and another that starred her brother Bill.

The cast rehearsed at cast members' homes. Lunch followed, of course. Final rehearsals and opening night were at the Nimrod Hall. Admission was twenty-five cents, with a special rate for families. Staging and props were modest, and were simply packed in the back of a truck for the road shows.

Alice remembers the whole theater experience as a lot of fun. "The young people then had nothing to do. Without busses, many could not attend high school. The play was a chance to get together and have fun."

So, we have a tradition of legitimate theater right here in Nimrod. How about reviving it? I can see Dave Pederson as Curly in *Oklahoma!* Ann Stigman, Clara Frame, and Elsie Riley in *Three Sisters*. JoLynn Weaver as Maria Von Trapp in *The Sound of Music*. Dale Hillig as Tevya in *Fiddler on the Roof*. David Gilster as Professor Harold Hill in *The Music Man*. Ray Pederson as King Lear. And we could have three or four casts of *Our Town*.

Where do I order tickets?

FISHING SEASON OPENER

NEWS ITEM: THE TRAVEL COORDINATOR FOR GOVERNOR VENTURA announced that the choice for the Governor's 2003 Fishing Season Opener has been narrowed to Lake Ossawinnamakee or the Crow Wing River. "It should be a slam-dunk," says an aide who spoke on the condition of anonymity. "The governor will find it easier to say 'Crow Wing.'"

What a coup! Nimrod hosting the Governor's Opener on the Crow Wing River next year. Best we do some planning. Not at City Hall. Not at the Community Center. But at the Nimrod seat of power—the men's coffee table at the R&R.

Who should host the event? "Since he's the top political figure in the state, how about Mayor Gilster?" suggests Raymond.

"Hell, no," says Harold. "The Gov's an entertainer, not a politician. Put him with Rick Pederson. Rick was a wrestler, once."

"He's coming up for a fishing trip," says Ardell. "Line him up with our best fisherman, Jeff Pederson."

Nomination seconded and nominations closed. All those in favor of Jeff say "aye." Jeff is elected.

"This is the dumbest idea I've ever heard of," says Jack Graba.

"Okay," says Ray. "Now we need someone to be governor in a dry run on this year's opener. Someone not too savvy. Not too swift. Somebody who talks before he thinks." Just then, I walk into the R&R. "Our prayers are answered," says Ray.

It's all set. Jeff will pick me up at the ersatz governor's mansion (Rick and Jenny's Winnebago), which is parked beside the bus garage on Main Street. The garage will be converted to a security outpost, or a media center. We don't know which yet.

Memo to Todd Wadena Electric Coop and West Central Telephone: We'll need extra power and phone lines for the governor's entourage and hundreds of reporters. You have a budget for public relations? We don't.

In the meantime, I need fishing gear. And a license. And practice of my nordeast Minneapolis diction. It's off to Ted's Hardware for an Eagle Claw rod and reel set (on sale for $17.97), a senior citizen fishing license (a bargain for $6.50), and a book of Minnesota Fishing Regulations. What used to be printed on two sides of a three-by-eight folded piece of paper now runs seventy-two pages. Of course, it's cool to know that the state record for longnose suckers is three pounds, two ounces.

The Nimrod ladies hear about the planned visit and decide to invite the governor's wife, Terry. Since Terry is a horse woman, responsibility for her itinerary goes to the Riders of the Crow Wing.

"Let's do a horse show competition and make her an honorary judge," suggests one past president.

"No, that puts her on the spot. Let's do a driving clinic and give her a chance to meet more people," says another past officer.

"Let's do a trail ride," says a third, "and show her the countryside."

Three motions. No seconds. The agenda is tabled.

"How about hosting the occasion at a local farm. I'll offer mine," says one member.

"Sure, you want to show off your stable," says another. "We'll need space. Let's use the ball park."

"With all the money we've spent on the riding ring, we'd be stupid not to have the event right here," says a third.

Three motions. No seconds. Location is tabled.

"I suggest that we have our regular menu for lunch," says one prior officer.

"And I suppose the first lady will eat Sloppy Joes?" says a second. "Let's show her some down-home Nimrod cooking and make it pot luck."

"You people never fed a dignitary before, have you?" says a third. "Security would go crazy. We better have it catered."

Three motions. No seconds. Menu is tabled. Meeting adjourned.

On Saturday morning, Jeff picks me up at the Winnebago, and we walk to the R&R for breakfast. We know it's a special occasion, because Delores and Donna are both wearing dresses. Delores scrambles some eggs, and Donna delivers hot coffee, with cups rattling in saucers. Jack Graba scowls from the other end of the table. "I still think it's a stupid idea," he says.

Memo to Bob and Ruth: Stick with sweatshirts and jeans. Get rid of the saucers. And get rid of Jack too.

After breakfast, we drive to Anderson Crossing with Jeff's Grumman canoe in the back of the pickup. We slip into the Crow Wing River, wave to the cameras that will be there next year, and we're off.

Memo to Lund Boats, NYM: Since you're practically in the shadow of our water tower (if we had a water tower), you might want to introduce your new twin-plated, marine-grade aluminum, riveted I-beam construction river fishing boat and electric motor here next year. Gratuities cheerfully accepted.

We drift down the Crow Wing, casting at shore, snagging a rock or deadhead now and then. Canadian geese, eagles, and a dozen varieties of ducks swim around us or fly over.

"There's a female hooded merganser (*Lophodytes cucullatus*)," says Jeff, sounding like Ranger Rick.

"Looks like a duck to me," I say, and give him a gubernatorial grin.

Casting with my new spinning reel is erratic, so I work the center of the river, and Jeff works the shore. I eventually snag a little northern snake. The pressure is off. The governor is not skunked. We try a variety of spoons and spinners, lures and leeches, trolling and casting. We try bottom fishing for one of those oversized scavengers that we saw while canoeing last summer.

Memo to DNR: Any chance you could stock this stretch of the river with some five-pound walleyes?

We're near the end of the trip. The Nimrod bridge is on the horizon. Right about at Riske Rapids, I get a hit that nearly pulls the rod out of my hands. Jeff steadies the canoe while I shift right to left. This is one big fish! He's swimming downstream and taking us with him, over the rocks into what is the closest thing to white water that the Crow Wing has. Jeff's paddle hits a boulder and shatters. He holds a broken three-foot handle up, and we start to spin. I can't stay ahead of this fish, and soon he has me tied up in a straight jacket. We're heading for the Nimrod bridge, sideways, backwards. Jeff keeps us afloat; I reach for a jack knife to cut the line.

A pickup passes over the bridge, an indigo blue Chevy 1500 pickup. It stops, and a man walks to the railing, leans over, and watches us twirl toward him. He shakes his head. "I told you it was a dumb idea," says Jack Graba. "Watch out for the dam at Pillager."

I guess Nimrod can't back out of the invitation now. But then, the governor faces re-election before next fishing opener. If that fails, we could coach him on how to say "Ossawinamakee." It's better fishing there anyway.

POST PROM PARTY (P3)

11:00 P.M. SATURDAY. THE ELEVEN P3 chaperones meet the P3 committee at Lori Lea Lanes in Park Rapids to decorate the dining room, set up the registration table, and display the prizes, prizes, prizes. The guests are due at 12:30. In the meantime, there are balloons to be inflated, tables festooned, schedules displayed. Ninety-one guests have pre-registered. I admit to a slight apprehension of this barrage of teenage adrenaline and hormones. Palace revolts have been staged with fewer than ninety. But the spirit is upbeat, optimistic, positive. And the planning is comprehensive. We are advised how to deal with even the slightest breech of conduct.

12:30 A.M. Sunday. All for nothing, it turns out. Prom goers and prom stay-at-homes arrive en masse. Excited, gorgeous, handsome, ready to party, ready to relax, ready to have fun. Registration is a piece of cake. Everybody's inside. We lock the door. Ralph Lauren is shed; Levi Strauss rules. There's a mass exodus to the bowling alley.

1:00 A.M. Sunday. The Pizza Ranch cranks up the ovens and turns out pizzas. In the next hour, we devour fourteen king-sizers. For those not bowling, there's a caricaturist in the lounge who captures the spirit of the posers in a few deft strokes. Others play pool or table hockey. Some just chat. I glance at the clock. It's 2:00 already. Bowling is a good idea. It absorbs teenage energy and it takes time. For every gutter ball, there's a strike. High fives all around.

2:30 A.M. Sunday. The karaoke setup is complete, with enough speakers to accommodate Target Center. A couple brave souls submit their choices and grab

BEERS
ABERCROMB

the microphones. That breaks the ice, and we soon have Boyz Into Men and Spice Girl wannabe's singing songs that I've never heard. No matter; it's not my party. And they're putting on a great show, battling acoustics less than those at Carnegie Hall.

3:00 A.M. Sunday. Time to crown the Post Prom King and Queen. And who wins but a prom couple, and an item since grade school, Grady Kirk and Sarah Femling. They get the spotlight as they dance together, wearing laurel crowns and sashes proclaiming their royalty.

3:30 A.M. Sunday. Back to bowling, and billiards, and caricatures, and card games, and karaoke. The helium balloons are disappearing, and we hear an occasional misplaced soprano voice. (Helium is not on the list of banned chemicals for this chemical-free event.)

4:00 A.M. Sunday. No break in the energy yet. Maybe a few folks sitting in small groups, leaning against whatever is available. Bowling is the big play. Nick Metteer gets a strike. Jenna Puttonen, his date, gets two strikes, back to back.

4:30 A.M. Sunday. Everybody assembles in the dining room for distribution of prizes. It looks like there are two prizes for every attendee, from six packs of Pepsi to the ubiquitous patio chairs from you-know-who to television/VCRs. Davis Whitaker wins a pail of car wash supplies, although he's currently car-less. Amy Ratcliff wins a two-wheeled dolly, although she doesn't have to hustle milk cans anymore. Louie Malone and Bryan Pederson walk off with the TV/VCRs.

5:00 A.M. Sunday. The doors open; the weary crowd pours out. In five minutes, the parking lot is cleared, except for one car with a flat tire. A huge thank you to all businesses and individuals who donated prizes. But the real heroes of the night are the young men and women who were guests. They had a well-behaved, great time. For parents who wondered what their sons and daughters were doing until 5:00 A.M., relax! They were bowling, singing, chatting, chomping pizza, shooting pool, posing, playing cards, collecting loot. Congratulations to all ninety-five attendees on your exemplary behavior. It was a pleasure spending a few hours with you.

Summer

NICE CORNER OF THE WORLD

MIDDLE OF JULY, MIDDLE OF SUMMER. Must be the old-school-year mentality that says summer is June, July, August. Time to review accomplishments, survey the present, plan the remaining weeks.

In a word, summer is good. New farm babies—as of Monday, four Scottish Highland calves, another Arab-Belgian cross colt, thirteen baby chicks. All doing well, thank you. I'm way past capacity for these fifty wooded acres. But I have trouble with herd reduction. Which one of the kids do you get rid of?

The river vacillates this year, up and down, fast and slow, cold and warm. Wild rice is growing in the slow waters of the bay. The sand bar at the bend is inches below water. Canoe traffic is light. Seems strange, because the river is so calm now, so clear, so relaxing.

The bald eagle perches predictably at the bend. Sam, the great blue heron, stands stoic in his assigned spot in afternoon shade. Warblers, finches, and phoebes work the river for mayflies that reflect sun through their wings and float like thistle seed.

Midsummer has its own smells. Fresh cut clover. Bales of new hay. The aroma of blooming basswoods rides in on a breeze from the driveway. Subtle, mysterious, alluring.

Wildflowers switch from pink and purple to yellow and orange. Tiger lily, brown-eyed Susan, goldenrod. Cattails form in road ditches. Wild babies breath blooms in total abandon.

This is my year to take a break from all capital improvements, to cut back on maintenance. No garden, no sidewalk project, no fencing, greenhouse, or sauna. Strangely, I'm getting accustomed to the untrimmed grass, the stalks, brown and seeded, waving in the breeze. And where I did mow, it's brown, brittle.

Chipmunks work the cattle feeder for spilled corn. Red squirrels steal from the unattended dog dish. A fox makes gutsy daytime forays, scouting a chicken dinner.

At noon, it's quiet. The windmill rotates slowly, indicates a breeze from the southwest. Horses stand side by side, head to rump, swish each other's flies. Cattle are up to their bellies in the stock pond. Calves sleep in the shade, alone. Mother hen dusts herself in the shade of the barn, in powdery sand. Baby chicks watch, mimic.

Pasture grass is low. Tonight, the cows and horses will surround the bale feeders. Weatherman says sixty percent chance of rain. Clouds gather, move slowly north. A sudden breeze builds, blows north, billows sheets hanging on the clothesline soaking up river woods air.

During the night, an owl calls. Close to the house. Calls again. One of the joys of talking to animals is deciding what they say. This one says, "Hey, nice corner of the world." I agree, roll over, and sleep.

This morning, I check the pasture. I count Highland calves. Five. I count again. Five. A new calf born last night. Cute little bull calf. He lies under a birch tree while mother eats at the bale feeder, doesn't move until Kelly the collie sidles up, whimpers, sniffs. Proud mother waddles over, licks his coat, looks at me, and says, "Kinda cute, huh?" Proud father, MacDuff, stands by the barn, chews cud with a grin, and says, "That's my boy!" Draft horses watch from their side of the fence and say, "He has his mother's color."

Back to the house for coffee. I'll listen closer to that owl next time.

A LETTER FROM HOME

BRYAN PEDERSON IS TRAINING for the National Guard at Fort Jackson, South Carolina. He completes his ten-week basic training on August 16. Bryan celebrated his eighteenth birthday in June and will be a senior at Sebeka High School this fall. His service in the National Guard qualifies him for four years of college tuition and text book fees.

Dear Bryan,

First off, I'm proud of you for giving up your summer vacation to serve the good old U.S.A. and to make an investment in your future. You're missing a lot of fun, but you'll get payback for the rest of your life.

You're wondering what's going on around Nimrod. Lots! You heard about cousin Tanya and John's wedding. Great day. Full house. Fun folks. Grandfather Raymond delivered the bride in the vis-a-vis carriage, with Percheron stallion Denver under harness. Of course, your little sister tried to upstage the bride after the ceremony by climbing on Denver's back in her bridesmaid's gown. But Tanya took the challenge.

Speaking of weddings, Adeline Avelsgard and Marv Griffith tied the knot. They hosted a dance at the Community Center a week ago Saturday night. Another big crowd. And the food! Buckets of home-fried chicken, ham, salads, breads, cakes. It looked good, smelled better. I can't vouch for the taste. The Taste O'Nimrod potluck picnic did me in a couple of hours earlier.

Nimrod Chronicles

The annual Nimrod Tubing Extravaganza was a hoot. But six hours on the river pushes the limits, don't you agree? We had the biggest crowd ever. Perfect day, warm water. The river is down from two weeks ago, and, as a result, I'm on a first-name basis with some of the rocks in the rapids. There were a few feats of daring-do other than the endurance trial. You're great-uncle Jeff got a standing ovation for his canoe hand-stand.

And how about them Gnats? They finished their regular baseball season: twelve wins, two losses, and won the first two play-off games: twelve-zip over the Red Eyes, and ten-four over Sebeka. Get your order in early for a Go Gnats 2001 T-shirt. Do you think our little town is ready for all the media attention when the Gnats win State?

We celebrated a couple birthdays without you. Family, friends, and neighbors feted Bob Hames on his seventieth with a lawn party. He's a noisy neighbor, but only once or twice a year. Your great-grandmother Irene turned over another year but still looks half her age. I understand she was carded at McDonalds when she asked for a senior discount.

Our neighbors in Sebeka and Menahga celebrated their mid-summer festivals with the usual parades, food, concerts, food, contests, and food. Your band buddies did an outstanding job at Sebeka Ag Appreciation Days. The jazz band played some great old tunes, great arrangements, great performances. Having all those band members come together on a summer Saturday afternoon was impressive.

Of course, you'll be home for our big party, Nimrod Jubilee Days, on Labor Day weekend. Planning sessions are in full gear. Will you be wearing your military uniform on your own U.S. Army Recruitment Office float? I didn't think so.

I understand from your dad that PT is a challenge. Well, Bryan, we wouldn't ask you to do anything we wouldn't do. So, to spur you on in the push-ups department, I'll match you one for one, with a goal of thirty-five by August 6. I snapped off fifteen this morning, and I'll do at least sixteen tomorrow. But I will not compete with you in running.

Other than that, life goes on. Ann Stigman opens the Post Office every morning at nine. Locals gather for coffee at the Bar & Grill. Rich Grotberg doesn't sell much gas to the canoe crowd.

First crop hay looks good, now that we've had two weeks of dry weather. Dean Estabrooks delivered twelve bales this morning and cleared the gas line of my International tractor so that we could unload it. Don't think I don't take guff for not having a John Deere.

I called Amanda and left a message on her answering machine. Thought she might want to add a couple words. She hasn't called back. I expect she's not taking calls from "other guys."

Keep me posted on your push-up progress, buddy.

Funk
family FARM
FUNK

GNAT BATBOY

SO, THE LOCAL BASEBALL TEAM WINS a trip to the State Tournament. The manager is interviewed. The players are photographed. Fans are quoted in the newspaper. Does anyone care what the batboy thinks?

Yes, Paul, we care. Paul Funk, heading for second grade this fall, is batboy for the Nimrod Gnats, who are heading to the State Tournament for the second time in three years, this time as regional champs. Paul is a third-generation ball player, and seems to have combined the savvy, intuition, and agility of all his lineage. "He'll be the best," says Dad Charlie.

Paul says that he gets appropriate attention for his position, but feels the Big Thrill when his name is announced during pre-game team lineup. Especially when he is announced as team manager Charlie Tuorila's right-hand man.

Charlie has a quiet style of management and admits that the players know the game better than he. Management turns out to be a group consensus thing, with Charlie acting as catalyst and spokesman.

Charlie is proud of the overall record of fourteen wins and four losses, and the tourney record of five wins and one loss. He saw the Urbank/Parkers Prairie Bombers as a game where things went right for the opposition, and things went wrong for the home team. The loss hurt, because the team knew they were better than the 20 to 2 score indicated. It may have been the energy that fired the two subsequent Bomber defeats, 13 to 9 and 20 to 6.

Charlie is impressed with the amazing support of the fans. He compares the hometown support, at home or away games, with support other teams get. "Nimrod loves the Gnats, and they know the game," Charlie says. "Their comments are often right on." I wonder what and how much the players and coaches hear from the dugout or playing field. Nimrod can out-decibel any fans I've heard, but with the focus required at bat, or on base, or on the mound, what do they hear? Whatever they hear, it makes a difference, Charlie assures me. And he thanks the fans for it. Then I wonder how it would feel to listen to Mark Schermerhorn's often caustic, color commentary for two hours.

Batboy Paul has his favorite players and, not surprisingly, his two older brothers make the list. However, "Hank" Aaron makes the list with a caveat. "He pops too much!" Steve makes the list because he's the youngest team member to suit up. Paul picks Gregg Crabb and Ron Lillquist as best pitchers, and brother Aaron as best catcher, "Paul knows the strategy of the game as well as a player," says Aaron. "He called for a sacrifice fly ball once, when that was the correct call. How did he know that?"

Paul grins when he talks about Ryan Tuorila's home-run fever during the tournament. Seven homers, which added votes to his Most Valuable Player selection at Regionals. Ryan is a member of a baseball family too, with father Charlie as team manager and brother Delroy as infielder. Teammate Aaron says Ryan is in a home-run zone. And what does Ryan attribute this to? Not a fair question, going into State Tournament, but Ryan smiles and 'fesses up. Two cheeseburgers before the game and Nancy's brownies, with white frosting on the side. That, and a lot of confidence.

Incidentally, Nancy and Ryan have announced plans to marry next summer. At Nimrod. On the ball diamond. During the seventh inning stretch. Could that happen anywhere but Nimrod? No. Will everyone be there? Yes.

Batboy Paul gets respect from the fans, who, like me, admire his hustle. Brother Aaron races him to home plate at the end of an inning to retrieve bats. Sister Sarah catcalls from the bleachers if he makes a miss-step. The bleachers are full of hard-core fans, like Kim and Jeff Pederson, who attend every Gnat game, are impressed with the local support, and call it good Sunday afternoon entertainment. With two young sons who play their own game during the Gnat's game, they will probably have their Sunday afternoons filled for a long time. Kim talks about the families of players who turn out: Harold, Gladys, and Judy Metteer, Joyce and Eddie Hepola, Mark and Mary Beth Brockpahler, Jane and Joe Brockpahler, Jenny and Rick Pederson, and others. Then, there are JoLynn, Kevin, Ruth, Deloris, Cindy. And Mark.

Much of field maintenance is the work of fans. Jeff Pederson will help with construction of covered bleachers this fall. A sprinklered ball park is in the plans. And a lighted field still looms on the horizon. Shall we bid on a domed stadium, wonders Mark.

After three of the home games, the fans struck up grills at Stigman Field and had cookouts. A party for the team is planned after Labor Day at Stigman Mound. Watch for the announcement.

So, Paul, the Nimrod Gnat batboy, has his uniform freshly laundered and is ready for the Lake Henry team at Miesville (west of Redwing) in the State Tournament on Friday. Lake Henry is an unknown to me but shows a population of ninety on the State Highway map. Ryan Tuorila knows of the reputation of their rowdy fans who use bull horns and cow bells. We can top that, right Nimrod? Nobody talks about game two until we've won game one. If the home run heat wave continues, we'll play right into Labor Day. Can we delay the Jubilee Days parade until the team comes home?

We're with you at State, Gnats. You have a town with a great baseball tradition rooting for you. You have your own experience, beginning as batboys yourselves, plus Little League and high school ball. You have a great season behind you. You're good enough to go to State, and you're good enough to win. We'll be cheering for you as you enter the field. And, of course, we'll save a big cheer for the batboy.

FATHER'S DAY

I'VE NEVER BEEN MUCH TO CELEBRATE Father's Day. Or Mother's Day. Or birthdays. Or anniversaries. Seems to me that everyday is father's day, and everyday is an anniversary. Designating a specific day seems like a sales gimmick for Hallmark cards, the flower people at FTD, or the restaurateurs and their elaborate brunches. So Father's Day rolled around this year, like any other Sunday, until . . .

Two friends, recently married, announced the birth of their child, her first, his fourth. The announcement came by e-mail (of course) and was accompanied by two photos: one of father and son nose-to-nose, father looking profoundly responsible; the other, with father pinching son's cheeks together to make a little "O" mouth, to the delight of his older half-sisters. I realized then that I had no pictures of my dad and me. I also realized that I wished I had.

I was the fourth child, first son. I imagine the joy Dad felt at finally having a son, but if there was joy, I didn't feel it. He was a German-American farmer, the son of German farmer immigrants. Something in the genes said, don't pay too much attention to the kids.

My mother died the year after I was born. I have heard that it was dad's persistence that kept our family together until he remarried three years later. I have also heard of the heart-wrenching loneliness of a young father, whose love for my mother was the envy of the township.

Growing up in the shadow of three older sisters had its advantages and its shortcomings. Lots of playing school and playing house; not much tree climbing

or baseball. Dad loved to hunt and fish, for food and sport. I remember getting a new Daisy Air Rifle and going squirrel hunting with my dad. I also remember killing my first (and only) squirrel and putting away the gun.

I'm sure I disappointed him by not enjoying the hunt. And he disappointed me when he gave my baseball and bat to neighbors, because I didn't play with it anyway.

I don't remember his attending our Christmas programs or end-of-the-school-year picnics. I don't remember his interest in my classes or grades. He had left school in fifth grade, and eight years of education seemed adequate for his kids. Without athletic prowess, being small for my age, in the lean years before World War II, my opportunity to excel was in my studies, an area where he had little interest.

My dad was a big man, "Popeye" arms, barrel chest, probably two-hundred and thirty pounds. I remember my sister's advice: You better grow up big and strong like dad so that you can get a job. At one-hundred and nineteen pounds at age sixteen, I knew I wouldn't.

Dad never gave me advice. I joke about his only nod in that direction. As I was leaving home at sixteen, he said, "Well, take it easy." Of course, I didn't. I left the farm, got a job in the Twin Cities, and didn't return to finish my senior high school year.

I disappointed him when I returned home after two years in the Army with a new Buick Special hardtop convertible—three holer, baby-blue exterior, cadet blue leather upholstery.

"How much did you pay for that?"

"Three thousand, five hundred dollars."

That's about what he had paid for the farm.

Again, I disappointed him when I gave up my job as a tool and die maker at Honeywell after graduating from the University of Minnesota and took an "office job." Letting go of those high wages and job security was beyond his comprehension.

I disappointed him again when I told him of my intention to divorce my (first) wife. He was quiet for a while, and then said. "Figure out a way to work it out." Not the acceptance and support I would have liked, that I knew I wouldn't get.

I have scratched my memory for occasions when I pleased my dad, or when he expressed that pleasure. The only occasions that qualify are the birth of my sons, whom he was free to love, with no expectations on his part. And love them he did—my older son, Mark, for the skipped-generation traits of hunting and mechanical aptitude: my younger son, Greg, for his disposition toward medicine. Dad's dream was to be Greg's patient when Greg earned his MD.

Later in our years, it was clear that if anyone was going to break this pattern of mutual disappointments, it was I. I started with letters, one a month, signed "Love, Jerry." The letters were warm-up exercises for me, small talk, family news. I saved his replies and just finished reading them. They are full of talk about the weather, his good health, his garden, and the vegetables he gave to the widows in town. The letters are signed "Love, Dad and Gabby." Finally, the word "love" entered our vocabulary. Not spoken; just written.

Dad died in 1985, at the age of seventy-nine. He wintered alone in south Texas in the latter years. Neighbors found him slumped in his chair, his trusty dog Gabby on his lap. His last letter was written on the day he died.

So, it's Fathers Day 2001. Dad has been dead for sixteen years. I feel that he reveals himself in my brothers and me as we grow older. We inherited his good health, his love of the land, his work ethic. We can aspire to inherit his generosity, his willingness to help others. "Just call Louie" was the by-word for neighbors, friends, and family who needed help We can aspire to inherit his faith, his trust in prayer. The image of his much-abbreviated sign of the cross, burying his face in his hands at the Prayer Before Meals is clear in my memory.

So, Dad, a belated "I love you," and thanks for the good genes and good example you gave me, and for the gifts you made me earn myself. I just wish I had a picture of you holding me, nose-to-nose, looking profoundly responsible, or pinching my cheeks to make a little "O" mouth, to the delight of my sisters.

I DO, I DO

SATURDAY IN NIMROD, THE CHURCH BELL RANG. And rang. And rang. And rang. Finally, it stopped. Pastor Hendrickson raised his hand in blessing, opened his mouth to speak, and the bell rang one final time. Acolyte David Gilster was on a roll.

Welcome to the wedding ceremony of Tonya Marie Rydie and John Allen Grimsbo. Welcome to the Lutheran Church, where it's standing room only on a warm, sunshiny, late June day. And welcome to Nimrod, where we can count on a fresh twist being added to established traditions.

Folks are milling in the parking lot, reluctant to give up the last breath of fresh air, the last puff on the Marlboro, the last opportunity to chat, inform, joke.

"You got any hay down?"

"Only twenty acres. Baled two-hundred bales today. How about you?"

The parking lot is full, and there, beside the lipstick-red sports model, is a coal black Percheron draft horse, harnessed and hitched to a white wedding carriage, but tied, for the duration of the ceremony, to a tree.

"How's your garden doing in all this rain?"

"The strawberries are late, but the peonies are gorgeous."

There's the grandmother of the bride, Patty Mae, and it takes a moment to recognize her all gussied up in a blue ruffled dress. And there's the mother and father of the groom, Joyce and John, meeting and greeting guests, John with the hearty stockman's handshake. There's the great grandmother of the bride. No,

there are two great grandmothers of the bride, Irene and Delpha Almy, both looking resplendent, both trying not to outshine the bride.

There's Deana Skov with one crutch and two little cowboy attendants. Who is that lady in the flowered dress running up the choir loft? That's no lady; that's my neighbor Cindy, the singer formerly known as Lonesome Dove, and today's soloist. That tuxedoed dude, offering his arm to all the female guests. Can that be Ryan Pederson? He certainly does clean up good. What a job he and Gerry Grimsbo are doing, seating the crowd of ladies in special-occasion dresses, men in ruddy cheeks shaved to holiday smoothness.

Now the bride is being ushered to her seat. No, it's not the bride; it's the bride's mom, Roxanne. Is she radiating happiness? Apprehension? Relief? All of the above?

The church hums with small talk; the pews are decorated with smiles. A breeze off the Crow Wing River blows through the woods, picks up the scent of warm pine, and sails through the windows.

Guests are seated, and the ushers, with help from the bride's personal attendant (and aunt), Robin, roll back the white carpet. Mary Beth steps up the pace on the organ, and the procession begins. Can that be Bethany? In a dress? With her hair all teased in an up-do? Wearing eye shadow? And, oh my God, it's Corey Hart! I've never seen her without Levis. Here come the scene stealers — Tayler and Brock, flower girl and ring bearer, she in her petite gown, he in his miniature tux. Tayler is confident; Brock is tentative. Flash bulbs pop. Tayler and Brock march, arm in arm, to the processional. Two hundred voices murmur "Aren't they adorable."

The groom is at the altar, flanked by Joe and Coleman, his best man and groomsman. Mary Beth hits the "sustain" pedal, the guests stand, and a vision appears at the entrance of the church. A radiant bride walks in, on the most beautiful day of her life. She smiles. A floating cloud of white, tethered to earth by the arm of beaming Brad. Then the bell rings. Five minutes of bells. Or was it ten?

Pastor Hendrickson offers a sermonette on love and marriage. Should we get the new standard "During our meetings preparing for this day, I was impressed with the commitment of Tonya and John . . ."? Or the old standby from St. Paul's letter to the Corinthians about what love is not? He opts for the realistic approach. "We're not created perfect. You'll have your good days and your bad days. May the love that you feel for each other today and the love of your family and friends carry you through."

After the ceremony, after Mary Beth rocks the organ with an up tempo "Jesu, Joy of Man's Desire," after the guests kiss the bride and shake hands with the groom, after white-shirted boys escape their mothers' clutches and play tag in the church yard, after neighbors and friends visit in the warm June afternoon, then Raymond Pederson, grandfather of the bride, slips a bridle on Denver, the black Percheron draft horse, and drives the wedding carriage into the middle of the parking lot.

Then, another twist. Bethany, longterm friend of Denver's, accepts a dare to climb on his back and sit sidesaddle in her lavender gown. Photographs all around, and Beth hops down. Corey, not to be outdone, says "I can do that," slips out of her heels, and climbs aboard. More photos. Will the bride allow her attendants to upstage her? Not on your life. Up she goes, her gown billowing in the breeze. Where is that Rex McDonald photographer guy? Where does it end? Not yet, folks. Up goes the groom, straddling a patient, relaxed Denver. The bride, her smile outshining her diamonds, raises her chin and turns to kiss the groom. A Kodak moment.

Down they come and board the carriage for a ceremonial ride through Nimrod. I ask driver/grandfather Raymond if he was concerned about Denver being tied to a tree and possibly backing the carriage into the red sports car. "Only when those damn bells wouldn't stop ringing," he said.

MY FIRST CANOE RIDE

By Kelly, the Collie

LET ME PREFACE THIS BY SAYING THAT IT WASN'T MY IDEA. Not the canoe ride. Not writing the *Chronicle*. But my dad insisted. (We call him Dad because he calls us animals his kids. Weird, huh?) He's taking a writing class and having trouble with "point of view." His instructor chides him: "Everything you write sounds like it's coming from a sixty-eight-year-old, white, male, Republican."

So he pretends he's a Jewish, dwarf, gay, Civil War vet. The results are disastrous. Guess whose point of view he tries next? Mine, a collie dog. Who's surprised?

I've seen him canoe many times. I follow him to the river, then run along the shore, barking like I fear for his life, wading until my belly hits water. I give up when he rounds the point at the north end of the farm, go home, and wait for the sheriff to arrive, hat in hand and a dour expression, giving me the bad news.

Today when I follow him, he lifts me into the canoe. It's an old plastic Coleman seventeen-footer, about as stable as a Banana Republic, Dad says. The canoe is in the river, tethered to shore. I take a step inside. The canoe wobbles, and somehow I know not to go farther. I test shifting my weight. I think I got it. Dad thinks so, too. He steps into the canoe. We're held in place by reeds of wild rice. We wait. He bites the bullet, pushes off. We're in open water.

We head upstream—easier than it sounds—with wind at our backs. I think I have motion response figured out. When I stand on the left, he shifts on his seat to the right. This is okay. Five minutes on the water and I'm sitting, enjoying the ride.

We hug the left shoreline, and, like Euell Gibbons, he points out chokecherries that make tart jelly; arrowhead plants and cattails with edible tubers; plump cattails that look like overcooked corn dogs on a stick. The water is clear. Minnows glide, swim against the current, then glide again. Turtles sleep on rocks in the morning sun. They allow us to glide by without diving. Ahead, a half dozen turtles rest, half on top of the next one, like fallen dominoes. A bald eagle drops from the sky, glides toward us, tilts right, and soars over the woods. When we look again, the turtles are gone.

We're near Frames Landing now. Kids in hot pink bathing suits splash in the river. I smell bacon frying. The bass line of a rock tune sounds inappropriate in the wilderness.

Frames Landing is the spot where we turn, head downstream, float home. Easy, right? Wrong. The wind is in our face now. We're both in back of the canoe.

Next time, Dad says, he'll tie me in the front. Our combined weight forces the canoe sideways and rotates it until the heavy end leads the way.

"Not to worry," says Dad. He turns the canoe around and heads to shore. All is well for a few hundred yards until a breeze rustles trees along the bank, sways the cattails ahead of us, and blows in our faces. The canoe heads for a reedy shore, bounces a couple times. Maybe I panicked, because the next thing I know, we're tilted toward the water. Dad tries to shift his weight, which make the tilt steeper. Now I know how Kate felt on the *Titanic*. And no Leonardo in sight.

Suddenly we're in the river. No big deal for me, right? My ancestors invented the dog paddle. Dad must have planned for this. He's wearing only enough clothes to avoid arrest. He keeps his cool. The water is warm, maybe two feet deep. He tries to right the canoe, empty it. No luck. We walk to the opposite shore, do what has to be done. We board ship again.

"Look," Dad says in his Marlin Perkins voice, "wild life on the river." Two families of Canadian geese, four goslings in one, five in the other. They dive, preen, stand in the water, flap their wings. Unusual for his spot of the river at this time of year.

We're heading for the final bend now. I'm comfortable enough to lie down. The canoe tilts when I rest my head on the gunwales. I stretch and drink. The water is clear, clean. I like canoeing. I give Dad my broadest Julia Roberts smile.

Our small sandy beach is straight ahead. Dad says this is a dry run for a major canoe trip we'll take this fall, fodder for a story that will be a floating version of Steinbeck's *Travels with Charley*. Written from his point of view, I hope.

Never a dull moment on the river.

HAPPY BIRTHDAY, ELSIE

IT MUST BE SOMETHING IN THE LOCAL WATER. Three of our Nimrod matriarchs celebrate ninety years of living in 2002. Clara Frame led off, followed by Elsie Riley and Ann Stigman. Elsie's birthday was June 29. We will celebrate it at an open house on Saturday, July 6.

Elsie's family lived in Bluegrass country where she attended District 33 school north of Bluegrass for eight years. She recalls some of her teachers—John Dorn, Minnie Thorson, and a Miss Johnson. She also recalls that those teachers were responsible for educating up to sixty-two students in eight grades. Since Elsie was a good student, her teacher advanced her from fifth to eight grade, and then held her there until she was sixteen.

Her work life started soon after, doing housework for Nimrod families. Housework was broadly defined as cleaning, cooking, laundry, and child care, plus milking cows and tending garden. She recalls working for the Kerns when she was stricken with diphtheria. "I lost my voice," Elsie says. "I used to be a good singer."

She did housework for the Mervin Perkins family and broadened her job description to driving horses and hauling hay. She worked for the Bill Niska family when Bill had the General Store in Nimrod. Elsie recalls that the three older girls attended high school in Sebeka and stayed in town until the weekend. Then Elsie washed and ironed three sets of clothes, filling ten clotheslines. She cleaned the store but didn't wait on customers. She recalls baking pies from apples that didn't sell. She also worked for the Lyon and Sidenkrantz families.

Elsie met future husband Art when she worked for the Riley's at the current Jackie and Don Fredericksen farm. Art had been married, widowed, and was raising a daughter at the family farm. He and Elsie married in 1937 and bought the eighty-acre farm, essentially woods, in 1938. Art cleared a building site and hauled the logs to Floyd Perkins's mill, where he traded his labor for sawing boards. Art and Elsie used an existing set of old buildings for a barn for their few cows and team of horses. They built the house from their lumber— first two rooms, then a third, and then a fourth. Elsie and Art had one daughter, Sandra. They added seventy-one acres to the farmstead and farmed the land where Elsie still lives. She recalls their neighbors, Paul and Virginia Wobbe, and their runaway turkeys and the domino games that lasted until the wee small hours.

And how does Elsie fill her days now? Well, she asked me to delay my arrival until after her programs—*The Young and the Restless* and *The Bad and the Beautiful*. She also plays cards with Lila Perkins and Violet Krueger. And what do they play? Liverpool, which sounds like an interesting game, but is one that can chew up four hours.

Elsie's passion is quilting. She has boxes of double-knit fabric from Evelyn Gilster, and each of Glenda and Harold's kids and grandkids are getting a nine-patch quilt from Grandma's fabric. Elsie has made quilts for her neighbors, church, and community center, plus one for every grandchild and great grandchild. How many quilts has she made? She doesn't know, but we estimate fifty.

Elsie also has a green thumb. She bought a patio tomato plant last year that bore seventy-nine tomatoes last summer. She brought it inside at frost time and it continued to bear another 250. The plant still grows behind a couch in front of a window. Her outside gardening is confined to container gardening, including a new patio tomato.

To what does Elsie attribute her long and healthy life? Staying active and staying involved. She has enough quilt material for another ninety years and enough squares cut and ready for assembly to blanket all of Lyons Township. She treasures the time she spends with neighbor Lila Perkins. She still drives to town on occasion and is always ready for a game of cards. The original well still stands north of the house. I think the secret to her longevity is in the water.

TAE KWON DO: THE ART OF KICKING AND PUNCHING

"LINE UP FACING THE WALLS."

"Yes, sir."

"We'll do thirty jumping jacks, then twenty push ups, and end with ten crunches. Do you understand?"

A weak "Yes, sir".

"DO YOU UNDERSTAND?"

"YES, SIR!"

U.S. Marine Corps basic training? Wrong. Lolita Myers Tae Kwon Do class at her dojang (Korean for "school") in Wadena. Lolita and husband Tom live just south of town on the Nimrod tar. She started teaching Tae Kwon Do at her home, then graduated to a larger space when her class outgrew the home facility.

Lolita started private classes in October 1993, then convinced another neighbor, Sandy Kurzenberger to join her, which she did that December. Since then, the two of them have stair-stepped up the colored belt ladder, Lolita testing for her orange belt in January 1994; Sandy in March 1994. Lolita tested for her black belt in March 1997; Sandy in June 1997. Today they are both world Tae Kwon Do Federation certified instructors.

A word about belt colors. The novice begins with white, the clean slate. In three months he moves to orange and yellow, representing earth, the foundation of living. Then to green, representing a seed planted in the earth; then blue, representing the seed sprouting and reaching for the sky. Then purple, representing royalty. Then brown, representing ripening of the plant. Then red, representing danger, the danger of having incomplete knowledge. And finally black, representing maturity, striving for perfection, and conquering fear.

Tae Kwon Do has interior and exterior dimensions. The exterior ones: physical ability, self-defense, agility, power, and endurance, become obvious as I watch a class. The inner ones: courage, confidence, respect, courtesy, self control, and integrity, are equally fundamental. Students bow to each other, their instructors, and their judges before each exercise. The instructors return the bows. Students are addressed as Miss Andrea; instructors are addressed as Mr. James. An order is answered "yes, sir" or "no, ma'am." A byproduct of this respect is its carryover in the home and classroom. Teachers comment on the respect they are shown by Tae Kwon Do students. Parents drop their jaws when they give an order to their child and are answered "yes, ma'am."

Lolita is a student of Master Spencer Brandt of Bemidji, a thirty-five-year-old black belt who has been a marshal arts devotee since age sixteen. He encouraged Lolita to consider opening her own school, which she did in a converted mobile home at her homestead in January 1998. She started with sixteen students, and when that grew to twenty-six, she rented the former Wadena bookstore in February 2000.

Lolita continues to be a student herself. In October 2000, she, and Sandy, tested for second-degree black belt. In October 2003, she is eligible to test for third degree.

The satisfaction she gets in operating the school is seeing the students grow. Many are perfect physical specimens rounding out their training regimens. Others are in a physical rehabilitation program, working their way out of an illness or physical disability. Whatever their reasons, the stories of students' regaining control of their bodies are legend.

The stereotypical marshal arts student is quickly dismissed when looking at a Tae Kwon Do class. There is an even mix of male and female. Ages range from five-year-old Andrea Westerberg to eighty-year-old Ruth Miller. Ruth started with aerobic exercise classes at age seventy-eight, working on balance. She graduated to Tae Kwon Do, and although Lolita makes allowances for her physical abilities, she doesn't cut her much slack. Ruth has earned respect, because of her age and because of her ability.

Lolita had to earn respect too. And trust. She was intuitively distrusted as a marshal arts instructor because of her sex, size, and age. Watching her lead a class of high school age students will dispense doubts right now, friend.

What has Tae Kwon Do done for her? She feels better physically. She cares for her body as the temple it is. It has increased her confidence. She respects others at whatever level they are. "I can't" is not in her vocabulary. "Maybe you can't now," she says. "but you will be able later."

I have to admit, watching the class exercise in lyrical dance movements is contagious. Sandy Kurzenberger moves like a ballet dancer with a punch. As usual, when it's done well, it looks easy. What do they have for a sixty-nine-year old beginner? Well, Lolita has a cardio kick boxing class at ten o'clock on Tuesday morning at her home studio. And yes, as I write this, I do feel a tightness in my stomach, an ache in my neck. The physical dimension of the program will be easy. It's bowing to my editor that will take some time.

GOLDEN YEARS

IN PUCCINI'S OPERA, *La Boheme*, Rodolpho takes Mimi's shivering hand and tells her his dreams. Mimi, stricken with tuberculosis, recounts her solitary life, embroidering flowers and waiting for spring.

In the Nimrod version, both the hero and heroine are tuberculosis victims. Jerry takes the shivering girl's hand and tells her his dreams. Amy, never content with embroidery and certainly not waiting for spring, bravely shares her dreams. Love finds a way. In the Nimrod version, the way is successful drug treatment for tuberculosis, and the young couple lives happily ever after. Well, at least for fifty years. On May 24, Amy and Jerry Schermerhorn observed their fiftieth anniversary. On Saturday, July 6, they celebrated it with a Community Center full of family, friends, and neighbors.

Amy is the oldest of twelve Hepola family kids from Menahga. Jerry is one of four Schermerhorn kids that farmed with their parents north of town. Amy and Jerry's story together begins at Fair Oaks Sanitarium, now Shady Lane, in Wadena. The year is 1949. Amy has been a patient at Fair Oaks for two years. She is one of twenty female patients on the first floor. Jerry has been discharged from active duty with the Army's 11th Airborne Division in Occupied Japan and has been diagnosed as tubercular. Jerry is one of sixteen men on the second floor.

In pre-drug therapy days, tuberculosis was treated with bed rest, fresh air, and mild exercise. Patients were isolated to reduce infection of others. Weekly pneumo treatments were administered on the second floor, so Amy had the

opportunity to meet this veteran dude from upstairs. For his part, Jerry could look forward to this charming, animated girl from downstairs. (Neighbors have mentioned seeing Amy for the first time in the sanitarium, and how incongruous it was for such a wholesome, beautiful girl to be confined. Her pictures taken then confirm that.) In addition to the treatments, weekly movies were projected on the second floor. However, can you imagine a security system effective enough to limit these two energetic, resourceful people to weekly visits?

With the advent of drug therapy, Amy and Jerry were released from treatment in 1952 and married the same year. They bought the 540-acre farm with the 1916 two-story house where they still live. Four sons, Dave, Darwin, Mark, and Alan, arrived between 1954 and 1960. Jerry logged with Raymond Pederson, forming the famed Pederhorn Logging Company, with worldwide corporate headquarters right here in Nimrod. Their adventures in the corporate Diamond T truck are the stuff of legends. When they cashed out, Jerry spent a brief four-month stint building ABM silos in North Dakota, along with half the local able-bodied male work force. He began his turkey raising career in 1960 with 1,700 birds.

Amy was raising four sons but found time to work for Clara Frame at the Nimrod Co-op. Then, in 1966, she joined the smoke watchers at Nimrod Ranger Station. Her service included duty on the tower during the Big Fire of 1976. She retired in 1984, the same year that she was elected to the Todd Wadena Electric Co-op board of directors, the first (and only) woman to serve on the board. She also represented Todd Wadena on the Cooperative Power board.

Jerry represented the Nimrod area on West Central Telephone's board of directors for thirty years, and retired in 2001. Everyone's heard his story, I'm sure, about their first board meeting in Florida. Amy and Jerry settled into their luxury hotel suite. Swaying palms, wine, guitars, moonlight.

"Did you ever think that you'd be in a beautiful Florida hotel with me, even in your wildest dreams?" Jerry asked.

"In my wildest dreams," Amy answered, "you don't even appear."

And, so it goes. Today, the turkey farm has grown to 6,000 birds, and management has transferred to son Alan. Amy and Jerry hosted a Fourth of July weekend Hepola family reunion at the farm and took the occasion to celebrate their golden wedding anniversary. Eight of the Hepola siblings from around the nation and three of the Schermerhorn siblings joined the party.

Maybe it's not the parallel story of Amy and Jerry that reminds me of the Puccini opera. Maybe it's the musical lilt of their laughter, the enduring and endearing qualities of their life and love. Whatever it is, those of us who know them are better people for it.

GOLDEN GIRLS

1912 WAS A BANNER YEAR. Not because William H. Taft beat William J. Bryan for the United States presidency or because of the Bosnian invasion that led to World War I. Not because Mack Sennett was filming silent movies with the Keystone Cops, or because the Boston Red Sox beat the New York Yankees, four to three, in the World Series. Not because Henry Ford had produced the Model "T," the Tin Lizzie, for four years. It was a banner year because three of the Grande Dames of Nimrod were born—Clara Frame, Elsie Riley, and Ann Stigman.

Sitting with these ladies for a couple hours is a lesson in history, psychology, and sociology. We talked about family, education, employment, transportation, recreation, global politics, Nimrod commerce. Memories of each is fodder for a book. Put them together, and their memories feed off each other, creating volumes.

We met in Elsie's new home—neat, roomy, and, best of all on this hot August afternoon, air conditioned. Conversation was easy. The common memories of these three began in the 1930s. Elsie and Ann both worked for Pete and Suzie Kern, doing housework, helping with farm chores, tending kids. The mischievous eight kids, especially the five boys, were the cause of most of their problems then, their laughs now. There's the story of Markie, "the little shaver," lighting the clothes line on fire, costing Elsie two dresses. Father Pete was stern, and the kids minded. Suzie had her times in the hospital, but she celebrated her one hundredth birthday last year in a Wadena nursing home, still "sharp as a tack."

Elsie talks of the time she had undiagnosed diphtheria during potato harvest but picked potatoes until near collapse.

During World War I in 1917, Elsie's family moved from Boyd, Minnesota, to Bluegrass. Groceries were scarce. White flour was not available. The family ate cornbread and oatmeal and ground toasted barley for coffee. Ann's brother enlisted in the army at Mayhew Lake, Minnesota. Ann remembered his departure. Clara's cousin, Ted Rice (Stella Pickar's brother) also served.

Elsie became animated when she talked of 4-H. She was a leader in the local club, the Gophers, with about forty members. The big events were the plays in Sebeka Hall and the County Fair. For one play, Jeanine Carpenter and Catherine Frame sang a duet. For the County Fair, Helen Frame sewed and modeled a skirt and blouse. Elsie recalled one County Fair when six 4-H members won berths to the State Fair. Alfred Kleinke recently thanked Elsie for her role in getting him to State with his Ag project. Elsie still has her 4-H scrapbook.

Ann and Clara talked about their times together as a mutual support team when husbands Jack and Lauri were on the AlCan Highway or in World War II. One day, they loaded their combined eight kids in Ann's car and headed for the County Fair. On a street in Wadena, Clara spotted a dollar bill tumbling toward them. She convinced Ann to stop, retrieved the bill, found it was a twenty. Free rides, drinks, sno-cones for everybody at the fair.

Clara talked about the role the Crow Wing River played in their lives, and the lives of their kids. It was the center of fun—swimming in the summer, skating in the winter. And the traffic across the river between Stigmann's and Frame's, by boat. Clara didn't see families taking advantage of the Nimrod beach, although she admitted to heavy canoe and tube traffic and camping down river at Frames Landing.

Elsie talked about the house that she and Art built in 1938. Well constructed, she said, and tough to tear down, which they did last year to make room for her present home. It started as a two-room, single-story house, then expanded to three rooms with a bedroom for mom and dad, and finally expanded to four rooms with a bedroom for daughter Sandra. Hired man and nephew Henry Butzin slept in the living room or on the floor. Elsie took up wood cutting with her swede saw and paid off the mortgage with pulp wood sales.

Ann's dad bought a Model "A" in 1927, and endeared himself to the neighborhood by ignoring traffic signs and driving kids to Edna Schermerhorn's store north of town for ice cream cones. Ann remembers Edna's generosity, and the more you praised her, the more ice cream she scooped on, all for five cents.

Elsie started driving a Model "T" at age sixteen. Driver's licenses cost thirty-five cents then, no test required. Her driving was limited to taking Mother to church in North Germany Township. She recalled the trick of the crank start on the Model "T." For her part, she walked five miles to catechism, back when girls wore dresses, but needed four-buckle overshoes to negotiate the snow and mud.

Clara's early memories were car-less. She recalled hitching up old Pauly and Charlie and driving three miles to deliver cream to the Nimrod Creamery and

eggs to the grocery store. Once a summer, the kids were invited to make the trip, the Big Event. She recalls her mother sending her and her sister walking to town with an eight-quart pail of eggs and a grocery list. It was a hot day. Mother agreed to allow the girls to spend five cents on a candy bar. Clara bought an O'Henry and ate melting chocolate on the walk home, which nauseated her. To this day, she can't look O'Henry in the eye.

Ann walked three miles to District 8 Oak Grove school as a girl and swore that she got her bad feet from walking in bad shoes. She and her siblings were directed by their mother not to take rides from a certain slick car salesman. (Nothing changes.) During the winter, she and other rural students rented rooms in town, where they did their own cooking and probably stretched a few of the family rules.

Clara was a student at Orton #1, on the site of the Bill Weisbrod farm. She recalled her first grade teacher Charlotte Hirsch, and chuckled at memories of Cliff Sweeney getting whacked with a ruler for not paying attention.

Elsie attended District #23, a mile and a half north of Bluegrass. The building still stands and is converted to a residence. All eight grades were taught, with a total of sixty-two students. Elsie remembered Minnie Thorsen as a teacher who earned thirty-five dollars a month, which assumed the young lady would teach plus clean the school house. Students hauled wood, fired the wood stove and carried water for the cooler. At that time, one year of Normal School attendance (usually at Staples) qualified a teacher. Ann, Clara, and Elsie remembered their teachers as competent, caring. Well, there *is* the story of the errant Mrs. O'Neill at Orton #2, which may be a "Chronicle" of its own.

The conversations went on and on, one memory triggering two others. It was good to be in the company of these ladies, listening to their reminiscences, most of them with happy endings. Good, also, to realize that at age ninety, all three maintain their own home, two drive a car daily, and one still works eighteen hours a week as Nimrod postal clerk.

You are an inspiration, ladies. Happy ninetieth birthday, and many happy birthdays after this one.

FISH STORY

EDGAR TAPPE MAY NOT BE A NIMRODITE (Nimrodian? Nimroder? Nimroid?), but he has Nimrod connections, and he has the qualification of a full-fledged citizen. Mother and Father were born and raised in Rockwood and North Germany Townships of Wadena County. Edgar was born and raised on a dairy farm in Rockwood Township and moved to North Germany in 1952. Fifty years, a marriage, and ten kids later, he still lives on the 268-acre farm on the Bluegrass Road.

The Nimrod qualification is not geographic as much as it is attitude. Edgar has a ready smile, sees the bright side of life and always has time for the chat. He also brews a hearty cup of coffee.

Edgar is a family man and a fisherman. I have visited him when his sons and daughters are home. Love and affection are a two-way street. They care for him without being solicitous. He accepts their care but not without a hint of discomfort at being waited on, after years of caring for himself. And the fishing paraphernalia! A boat-shaped bookcase, wall hangings of fishing scenes and equipment, a jigsaw puzzle in the form of a thirty-six-inch walleye. Even Christmas tree lights shaped like fish. But his trips to rivers and lakes are limited now to the availability of fisherman friends. He maintains two trucks, one for personal travel and one for fishing. But he hesitates to fish alone.

In 1999, Edgar's daughter built a house a few feet east of the original homestead. The old house still stands, awaiting destruction when the basement of the new house is finished, and the accumulation of fifty years and three generations of living is sorted through and moved in. Edgar has moved parts of his collection of memories—Red Wing crockery on top of the cupboards. A huge sauerkraut crock serves as a table. A pickle crock serves as a magazine holder.

From his east window, Edgar has a good view of the woods. Bird feeders hang from the deck, and birds and squirrels provide entertainment. Three deer (or government sheep, as Edgar refers to them) feed at the deck or at pans of shelled corn in the yard. A gander announces a person's arrival in the drive. Edgar sold his cattle in 1998. A dairyman to the end, he fed Jersey steers until feeding and watering them became a problem. Now, he rents his land as pasture and is pleased that his tenant maintains the land and fences well.

Edgar remembers fishing the Crow Wing River and Spider Lake. Remembers fishing after chores, late at night and early the next morning, catching a two-day limit of bass and crappies. His dad, Otto, and uncle kept a boat on Spider Lake until the lake froze out in 1936.

He recalls dark house fishing on the Crow Wing River along the high banks east of Margie and Maynard Benson's farm. They speared northern pike and roughies, and the mysterious snow fish. (You don't want to know about snow fish, except that they are remotely related to snow snakes.)

Edgar remembers blueberry picking north of Nimrod, anywhere among the jackpines. Buckets full of blueberries and wild strawberries. He recalls rides to a blueberry picking site in an old Volkswagen with his grandparents, picking an enameled bathtub full of berries.

He recalls baseball games in Nimrod where his brother Bill played with the Burgau brothers.

He remembers his early school years, grade one through eight, at District 18 country school, and the names of his teachers—Mrs. Lundberg, Miss Engebretsen, and Mrs. Walker. He had perfect attendance for the first three years. He recalls the abundance of prairie chickens and pheasants then, when every farmer left corn shocks for wild animal food and straw stacks for cover and protection.

Edgar worked at Aldrich Milk Products from 1957 to 1973, and at the Sebeka Cheese plant from 1973 to 1982. Wife Mary and the ten kids tended the farm and did chores. Edgar was a cheese maker and boiler operator. We talked about the creameries and cheese factories around the country then. Creameries in Nimrod, Bluegrass, Sebeka, Menahga, and Butler, plus the cheese factory in Oylen.

After his cheese factory employment, Edgar served as stationary engineer at the Faribault School for the Deaf and the Park Rapids power plant.

Edgar still drives his red Dodge pickup truck and, until recently, was a regular at the Nimrod Pinochle Parlor on Friday nights. His fishing is limited to the availability of a fishing partner. And he did get three days of deer hunting in last season. A few shots, but no deer.

Now, he pours coffee daily for visiting neighbors, family, and friends. He has a library of western novels. He cooks in a spacious, efficient kitchen, and has more food than he can eat. He has the wildlife outside to distract him. Now if he could only find a fishing partner.

OF BOGS AND BATTLES

HERE I SIT, ON THE BANKS OF THE CROW WING RIVER, intimately aware of its scenic beauty, only slightly aware of its biology and historical significance. Time for a trip to Old Wadena Park, a 230-acre tract of land on both sides of the Crow Wing in Thomastown Township. Purpose: to accompany Mary Harrison and Dick Oehlenschlager as they map a trail through a bog area of the park, which will become the Bog Walk.

Mary is executive director of Wah-de-Nah Historic and Environmental Learning Program (WHELP); Dick is assistant curator for the Minnesota Science Museum and son of Nimrod native Alice Oehlenschlager. WHELP is an independent volunteer organization dedicated to preserving and protecting the environmental and historic aspects of Old Wadena for everyone's enjoyment and education. Dick is the consummate biology student. No animal, vegetable, or mineral escapes his scrutiny without his reciting its common name, its Latin name, its genus, its specie.

The bog is about an acre of wetland, walkable this time of year in waterproof boots. Dick identified plant zones and species of willow, bog birch, cattails, swamp milkweed, and more sedges than I care to know about. He watched for holes that house water shrews and pigmy shrews. He talked of the one hundred bird species he has observed in the park, out of a total of probably two hundred and fifty. We saw evidence of deer, raccoons, squirrels—part of the estimated twenty-five species of large park mammals.

The walk will be designed to view wild life without destroying it. Mary and members of the Soil and Water Conservation District office toured four Minnesota bog walks this summer to take advantage of what has been learned. "No straight line walkways through the bog," says Mary. "A bend and observation platform at each point of interest." Mary envisions a walk of about seven hundred and fifty feet.

The project is on schedule. Research into other wetland walks is complete. Mapping the bog, identifying plant zones, and locating the path are in progress. Design of the walkway is undetermined, and may be fund-dependent.

I am familiar with bog walks from the University of Minnesota's Landscape Arboretum in my previous hometown, Victoria, Minnesota. What seems commonplace gets exciting—seeing miniature plant colonies; smelling methane or "marsh gas" oozing from the earth; feeling tough, flexible leaves of leatherwood; hearing croaks and chirps of frogs and crickets. This is the planet as it was created. No improvements, no clearing, no draining, no cultivation. And therein lies its beauty.

Beyond the bog, and connected by wood-chipped trails, are the prairie and woodland portions of the park, the picnic and camping areas, the canoe landings, and the historic site. According to information published by William W. Warren, Old Wadena "was first visited by the white man in 1783 when a party of fur traders established a fur trading post at the mouth of the Partridge River. On the south bank of the Partridge . . . is the 'Little Round Hill.' On top of this hill are found several earthworks, the ruins of the 1783 fur trading post. This was the scene of a battle between the Sioux and the traders."

Standing on the hill, the choice of a post location is obvious. The view is expansive; the site, defensible. Mary relates the history of the post, the battle that ensued, the platting of the town, the relocation of the railroad, and the relocation of the town of Wadena to its present site.

Much of this comes to life at the Old Wah-de-Nah Rendezvous, the biggest event in Wadena Parks. This year, the Crow Wing Muzzleloaders were hosts, re-enacting fur-trading days of the pre-1840s. WHELP presented an historic program at the battle site and sponsored a Native American powwow dance.

Is this sounding like a lot of activity for a county that maintains ten parks, all of which abut the Crow Wing River, on an annual budget of $11,505, the amount proposed for 2002? It is a lot of activity, and it would be impossible without the characteristic generosity of the local population. My Oylen neighbor (and the only man on the part-time payroll), Glenn Motzko, gets high praise from my Nimrod neighbor, Deana Skov, County Director of Planning and Zoning, for his aggressive and conscientious park maintenance and patrol. The Boy Scouts get a round of applause for their trail maintenance and brush clearing. The Senior Seminar out of Staples gets a big thanks for their park development and maintenance efforts. And Charlie's Angels, the Sentence to Serve (STS) adults and youth, get a standing ovation for larger construction projects, brush clearing, and garbage removal. Let me add a thanks to Greg Kempf, retired Planning and Zoning director, for his foresight in procuring the land and establishing a philosophy of keeping the parks natural.

Incidentally, camping fees for last year totaled $8,710, nearly making the parks pay for themselves. At seven dollars a campsite per night, and presuming three campers per site, that's over 3,700 happy campers. That doesn't include people like me, who use the parks for day hiking and canoeing, at no charge.

Much has been written of the history of Old Wah-de-Nah, and it is a fascinating story. Mary tells it well, relying on the research and publications of Doug Burke, John Crandall, Dr. Lund, and others. Soon there will be interpretive signs in the park, providing snapshots of history, geography, and biology. Soon there will be a bog walk to join the prairie and woodland walks, and the historic walk. It's just a matter of time. And money. Want to have a Bog Walk named after you?

DOWN THE LAZY RIVER

PEOPLE HEADING NORTH OUT OF NIMROD Saturday morning saw a convoy of trucks transporting assorted floatation devices—inner tubes, inflatable chairs, rafts, canoes—and assorted people, six to sixty-something, looking like a scene out of *The Grapes of Wrath*. The convoy is heading for—not Anderson's Crossing, the logical embarking spot—but High Banks, further, a lot further, up the Crow Wing River. It's the eighth annual Nimrod Tubing Experience, to be followed by Taste O'Nimrod.

Nimrodites and their friends congregate at David Pederson's at ten o'clock, hit the road at eleven, and start the long float down the river at twelve. This year's group is the largest ever: sixty-nine. Tubes and rafts are lashed together to make flotillas of six, eight, ten. Extra tubes hold snacks and refreshments. The sun shines warm. Water and air temperatures are the same. That old jingle from Hamn's beer comes to mind, "From the land of sky blue waters . . ." Dense green foliage hugs the shore. Earth tones of nature compete with glow-in-the-dark swimsuits, rafts, and "ugly" water shoes. Nature wins.

The first minutes afloat are given to acclimation. "Where are my sunglasses?" "Honey, you keep an eye on the kids." "Anybody want a Bahama Mama?" "Whose idea was it to drop in way up here?"

The next few hours would be easier to describe if this were the *National Enquirer* or *Gray's Anatomy* or *Master's and Johnson's Report on Human Sexuality*. But if you leave your hang-ups at home and bring only your sense of humor, you're in for a good time.

5401

Maybe the best way to describe this event is as a floating sociology lesson. Relationships, both conceptual and actual, get big play. I learn about the mores of the X-Gen, Y-Gen, and maybe even some Z.

After three hours on the river, we approach Anderson's Crossing, where reasonable people would have begun the float. Another three hours to Nimrod. So much for the quick ride, wind at your back, high and fast water. This is an exercise in acceptance, folks. Settle back. Watch eagles glide. Listen to red-winged blackbirds squawk. Smell river air. Slap on another coat of sun screen. Pop a Pepsi. Enjoy the ride.

Five hours later, we approach familiar territory—Gloege's Canoe Outfitters, Riske Rapids. An hour, more or less, to go. Stomachs are growling for real food, not the stuff we've been munching that's condemned by the American Council on Nutrition. It doesn't help when Jackie recites her recipe for baked beans (with four kinds of beans), hamburgers fried in sweet onions, big chunks of maple-cured bacon, finished with salsa and brown sugar.

Then the Nimrod bridge appears. It's six o'clock; six hours on the river. Yet, it's bittersweet to surrender the beauty of the river, the serenity of the float, the camaraderie of good friends. Bittersweet until you smell deep-fried turkey and hamburgers, hot dogs on the grill. Helen and Bob Wagner, the turkey team, greet you with a platter of sliced turkey infused with secret, exotic flavor enhancers. Bob Hames is grilling Pederson beef patties and barely keeping the platter full. That, plus a table of salads, hot dishes, and desserts. Oh, yes, and Jackie's baked beans. We must look like boat people crawling up the shores of Miami Beach.

Another thirty-plus neighbors arrive just for the feast, making a grand total of one hundred. The floaters are easy to identify, with skin tones from pin-cherry pink to chokecherry red. How to top a day like this? I have only one suggestion. Let's pay attention to our intuition next year, and start at Anderson's Crossing. My stomach hurts when I laugh for six hours.

BLUEBERRY SMITHS

BLUEBERRY SMITHS. The name has a *Little House on the Prairie* resonance to it. It conjures up images of a family—mom, dad, and the kids—hiking in the woods, syrup pails in hand, descending upon a patch of wild blueberries and picking enough for a couple pies and a batch of jam, plus some more to sell. Well, that's less than half the story.

The patriarch of the Blueberry Smiths was William E. Smith. He was born in 1848 and traveled by wagon from Villard, Minnesota, to homestead the family farm in Bullard and Lyons Townships in 1892. Mr. Smith declared the local water to his liking and credited it with curing his kidney trouble "without a drop of medicine." William and Alice Smith had six children: Nina, Mason, Pearl, Belle, Edward, and Burt. With all that available manpower, the Smiths amassed 1,100 acres and ran a herd of 200 milking shorthorns. Mina married and left the farm. Pearl and Belle didn't, and they herded cattle until pastures were fenced. Later, they taught school locally.

In addition to the milking shorthorns, the Smiths raised sheep, goats, turkeys, ducks, pheasants, and chickens. Mr. Smith crowed about the quality of clover hay he raised. He was an avid hunter and, from the looks of the family photograph album, a successful trapper.

Beside his agricultural and sports endeavors, Mr. Smith was an advocate of harnessing energy from the Crow Wing River to power industry in northern Minnesota. He predicted a government dam to conserve water and prevent floods.

And he still had time to pick blueberries!

Blueberry picking was a hot industry around here at the turn of the twentieth century. Newspaper accounts relate that a ton of berries was loaded at Sebeka and Menahga railroad depots each morning causing delays in the Great Northern passenger train schedule. Another report cites 400 crates of blueberries being shipped from Menahga each day to all parts of the United States. In 1920, the Great Northern southbound train carried 1,800 crates of wild-grown blueberries. The reporter speculated that this represents half of the crop, the balance being transported by auto by the pickers themselves. These crates weigh about forty pounds and sold for $3.15 each. Wouldn't you like to have the Doane's Liniment franchise then?

An article in a July 1919 Sebeka paper relates complaints of many farmers that transient workers are leaving fence gates open and tearing down fences to drive their cars through the pines in search of berries.

Blueberries were delivered by horse-drawn wagons to railroad sidings until the advent of the automobile. Blueberry production waned as the twentieth century developed and stopped by mid-century.

Youngest Smith son, Burt, and wife, Alice, had two children, Bill and Betty, who still live on the original homestead. Betty lives in the family house, which was built in the 1920s, next to the old ice house which still stands. Bill and wife, Sandy, live next door. Do they still pick blueberries? No, but the legend lives on. Betty says she is still reminded of her family's reputation as the Blueberry Smiths.

I noticed on a walk down the driveway that berries are setting on the plants now. The old timers says it could be a good year—cool spring and plenty of late rainfall. A bowl of fresh blueberries would taste good now. At $3.15, I'll take an entire crate.

ANOTHER MAN'S TREASURE . . .

AUCTIONEER'S NOTE: ". . . This list is only a small portion of the equipment and miscellaneous items that will be sold. There is merchandise in piles that we could not see to list." This note appeared on the full-page auction bill for the July 26, 2002, auction of Lee and Charlotte Wetzel. In other words, this was a sale for auction junkies. Well, North Country Auction promised, and the Wetzels delivered. Starting at 10:00 A.M., and running until 5:00 P.M., it was non-stop bargain hunting.

The auction goods were tractors, machinery, horse-drawn equipment, wagons and buggies, trucks, buses, vans, and a mobile home. Tools, parts, furniture, home furnishings, and yard and garden implements. And antiques. Prices were mixed. A white antique cutter sleigh with red-velvet upholstery fetched 400 dollars. A horse-drawn buggy, black with gold pinstripes, brought 925 dollars. A framed license to grow opium (dated early 1900s) sold for forty-five dollars. In contrast, a McCormick Deering threshing machine (Tyrannosaurus Rex) brought thirty-five dollars. The big surprise was a four-can milk cart that sold for 455 dollars. Who said there isn't money in farming?

Charlotte and Lee bought the Johnson Farm in 1975 and moved their family, livestock, and machinery from a farm in Urbank, south Otter Tail County. They began farming here with eight beef cows and seventeen horses. Lee had some financial obligations on purchased machinery to honor, and the income from the farm wasn't streaming. So he took a construction job in Alaska. That began a series of moves that included a family move to Lemoore, California, in 1978, where they bought another farm; to Kodiak, Alaska, in 1980 for another construction job; to San Francisco in 1981; back to the farm in Lemoore in 1982; and back to Minnesota in 1993. Lee formed his own construction company and specialized in federal government projects.

Between the time they bought the farm in 1975 and their return to Minnesota in 1993, the house and farm were rented to several tenants. Some of

the equipment auctioned was remnants of those rental days; most of it was remnants of Lee's collector days—machinery, equipment, cars, and trucks bought at auctions, garage sales, or private parties from Detroit Lakes to Fresno, California.

Saturday, the accumulation of twenty-some years hit the auction block. Parking was dicey in rain-sopped hay fields. Pickup trucks lined a half-mile of driveway. Neighbors stood in line for bidding numbers (330 were issued, plus the assigned numbers), and for coffee and a donut at the Lunch Box. The P.A. system gave the five-minute warning, and the auction began at ten o'clock. Tarps covered with pails of hardware and piles of harnesses gave way to wagons brimming with automotive, electrical, plumbing, fencing, garden, and woodcutting gear—all the paraphernalia that defines farming. From there, the auction progressed to furniture, furnishings, appliances, books, and records—the softer side of farm life. And from there, it progressed to trailers, the cutter, buggies, and tractors. By 5:00 P.M., Lee and Charlotte heard the final, "Going, going, gone."

The total take exceeded the estimates of both the Wetzels and Erlin Schultz of North Country Auction. "Prices were good on everything, especially horse-drawn equipment and tractors. We got a lot of calls on the D-17 Allis Chalmers and the TO-20 Ferguson," said Schultz. Buyers were local, out-state, and out-of-state, thanks to auction bills, newspaper ads, and the Internet.

The Wetzels were satisfied with the auction, happy with the turnout, and ecstatic with the weather—a day of full sun tucked into a week of rain. Lee expressed surprise at the prices some items brought. Items that were tucked into boxes that the Wetzels hadn't sorted, despite days of preparation and a team of helpers. But the unsorted boxes made it an adventure for the buyers. I bought a box of stuff from a successful bidder (the secondary market?) for a buck that included a Redwing pottery swan planter that has an E-Bay value between five and ten dollars. It's for sale.

It was a good day all around. Good to chat with neighbors. Good for the Wetzels to divest themselves of some worldly possessions and lighten their load to California. Good for some buyer to find that rare New Holland #46 bale loader to round out his collection.

LETTER FROM HOME, II

PFC BRYAN PEDERSON IS COMPLETING his final two weeks of U.S. Army Advanced Intelligence Training (AIT) at Ft. Lee, Virginia. Last summer, Bryan enlisted in the National Guard and took eight weeks of basic training at Ft. Jackson, South Carolina. He came home to finish his senior year and graduate from Sebeka High School in June. Bryan will attend one weekend of training per month at the Wadena Armory or Camp Ripley, and two weeks of training each summer. For all of this, Bryan receives a four-year college scholarship.

Dear Bryan,

Again this year, you're missing an exciting summer. Lots of birthday parties and weddings. Lots of river action. Lots of baseball. But the good news is that the town is exactly as you left it. That's the beauty of Nimrod. It doesn't change. Here are a few highlights from the 2002 summer social calendar.

Birthdays! Do we have birthdays! Three nonagenarians this year—Clara Frame, Elsie Reilly, and Ann Stigman. All are looking good, thank you. All are still driving. Ann still sorts mails and sells stamps six days a week. Ann has the latest birthday of the three. Big party on August 4th. Be there.

We won't have a problem remembering Deloris Shore's age. She reached the legal speed limit on July 16.

A couple weekends ago, we floated the Crow Wing River and feted ourselves at the Taste O'Nimrod at great uncle David's. Great weather. Great turnout. Great tubing. This year, we put in at Anderson's Crossing instead of Leech Lake, resulting in about a three-hour ride. We had about seventy-five on the river, according to official census taker, Aunt Roxie. The big rains had just blown through, so the river was high and fast. Much easier on the posterior than last year, 2001, the Year of the Sharp Protruding Object and the six-hour ride. One bummer event, however. My camera took a dive, so no photographs of tubers stretching the limits of propriety, or your mother sharing her Thermos of Bahama Mamas.

Speaking of tubing, those Nimrod entrepreneurs, Linda and Dale Hillig, have added tube rentals to their repertoire of services at Hillig Mercantile. Two dollars gets you a tube for a day. Linda says that she has fifty tubes, and on a good day, you better have reservations.

You'll never guess the latest addition to the men's Round Table at the R&R coffee hour. David Gilster. Seems the Gilsters sold the milking cows but kept some young stock. David and Karlene tie the knot on September 14. Makes you wonder if there's a connection between selling the cows and saying the vows.

Speaking of weddings, Susie Meech and Larry Krull made it legal in a garden wedding on Saturday, July 20. Mae Stennes, resplendent in black and white, hosted the event in her front yard. Attendants were Susie's kids and their husband/wife/SO. You wouldn't recognize Ryan, Todd, and Troy in tuxes. And how did the bride arrive? In your grandfather's wedding carriage, with Denver under harness. Quite a sight.

You're wondering about Grandpa Raymond's buffalos? They're doing fine. Tame enough to approach on a four wheeler, Raymond says they look great grazing in the pasture as he drives by. They are not your Grandmother Pat's favorite animals, however. I heard that she named the calves T. Bone and Phil A.

And how about them Nimrod Gnats? They looked good Saturday when they beat Sebeka, 9 to 4 to win the chance to play Huntersville next Sunday at Nimrod for the South Lake & River Championship. From there, they go to the Regions at Wadena and Mills beginning August 2. Greg Crabb was on a role at the pitcher's mound Saturday and went the distance. It's not too early to make reservations for State Tournament in Cold Spring and St. Cloud this year. Coach/Manager Charlie Tuorila says the team is playing good, and they're ready to play for big trophies.

Despite all the activity, life is predictable around here. On any given morning, Robin pumps gas at GB's, Donna pours coffee at the R&R, Ann sorts mail at the post office, and Jeanie sells milk and bread at Riverside Grocery. That's the beauty of it. We'll try to keep it that way for you. See you in a couple weeks.

Best regards, Jerry

Bryan has passed the daunting Physical Training (POT) test and his twelve written tests. He writes his final exam today. With each passing test, he and his buddies received more freedom—the chance to go off base, visit the Quartermaster Museum, see a movie, or shoot some hoops. He reports that it has been a good summer.

4-H AT THE COUNTY FAIR

KIDS AND DOGS STAND IN THE ROPED EXHIBIT RING of the arena at the Wadena County 4-H dog show. It's the Grad Beginner class of dog obedience. Zach Nevala of the Red Eye Rollers commands Sheena, his two-year-old collie mix, to sit, stay, with the wave of a hand. He walks to the opposite side of the ring, and faces her. She sits like a robot, one minute, two. Her stillness seems unnatural, not dog-like. You want her to obey, but you want her to be a dog too. Suddenly, she swings her head, snaps a fly. Good! Three minutes pass. Owner/trainers return to their dogs. "Exercise complete," says the judge. "Praise your dog."

Zach ties for first, enters the run-off, walks off with a Reserve Champion trophy. Sheena also wins a blue ribbon in showmanship and places fourth in agility. She wins an invitation to the Regional Dog Show in Park Rapids in September.

Josh Nevela, Zachs's young brother, enters Scrappy, a lovable golden lab. This is Josh's first year, so he enters as a Cloverbud. The judge scrutinizes her response to commands of heel, faster, normal, turn, sit, stay. Josh and Scrappy win a participation award—a green ribbon, and a big round of applause from the crowd.

Kids, dogs, and parents have been training since April in weekly half-hour sessions, plus a recommended fifteen minutes a day. It shows. The kids and dogs put on a great show. And, in the process, learn lessons in persistence, discipline, and competition.

In the sheep department, Chelsea Vasey of East Jolly Jets 4-H, shows Sabrina, a six-month-old Suffolk-Rambouillet. Sabrina competes against older, bigger sheep,

Joshua Seibert
East Jolly Jets 4-H Club
Holstein - grade

and the judges favor size, length, and posture. Chelsea is also showing Lulubelle, a one-and-a-half-year-old ewe. She wins a blue ribbon for both.

Chelsea doesn't spend much time prepping for the show. Her daily schedule allows time with the animals, so they know her, trust her. The sheep are sheared in the spring, bathed before the show.

On Saturday, following the competition, blue ribbon winners enter their animals in the 4-H Pride Auction. Here is a chance for members of the community to bid on animals as they are shown in the ring by their 4-H member owners. The winning bidder doesn't get the animal; he gets the opportunity to reward the exhibitor and provide premium money. Chelsea and Sabrina hit the bid ceiling—seventy-five dollars.

Meanwhile, in the dairy department, Lucas and Caleb Kreklau, also of the East Jolly Jets, spiff up Holstein cows and a yearling calf. Lucas, age seventeen, enters Duke, a three-year-old cow, and Tessa, a fall calf. The judge eyes them for straight spines, deep bellies, full udders, clean grooming. Lucas takes two blue ribbons, wins a invitation to the State Fair with Tessa.

Caleb Kreklau enters a three-year-old Holstein, also wins a blue ribbon. Both win maximum premium bids in the 4-H Livestock Pride Auction.

Josh Seibert, twelve-year-old member of the East Jolly Jets, goes all out for the fair and enters a yearling Holstein in the dairy competition; his dog Cosmo in obedience and showmanship; a butterfly collection in Entomology; a motor in Electricity; and a report on the Polyphemus Moth (he carefully spells it for me.) for Wild Life. Josh also wins a berth in the Regional Dog Show in Park Rapids. Big smiles all around. Josh's proudest moment? His butterfly collection. It must be a knockout.

The County Fair was a success. Plenty to see, a variety of exhibits that reflect Wadena County, with emphasis on 4-H. The grounds were clean, the exhibits informative and well-manned, the ice cream refreshing. Many old friends to chat with, and new friends to meet. That, plus the beaming smiles of kids, and of parents and grandparents who watched their progeny compete and win. Thanks for a great show, kids. Good luck at Park Rapids and the State Fair.

ELECT
BOB
SWENSON
VOTE

NIMROD: MY KIND OF TOWN

BETHANY PEDERSON GAVE THIS SPEECH at the Miss Nimrod pageant during 2002 Jubilee Days. It must have resonated with the judges, because Beth won the crown the next day. It resonated with me. It's one thing to have old-timers crow about the merits of small-town living; it's another thing to hear it from the younger generation.

Bethany's speech:

> Everyone has his own special talent in life. Some people sing beautifully. Some have a gift for writing poetry. Others play an awesome instrument. But when it came to my talent, I couldn't think of anything, so I looked to the people of Nimrod for inspiration.
>
> Can you think of a better place to live than Nimrod?
>
> I have lived in this town all my life and have many happy childhood memories. I'd go to coffee every morning with Grandpa Raymond and shake dice at the men's table with him. I loved to participate in the Nimrod Horse Shows where Katie Johnson and I got bucked off more times than I can count. One year we celebrated my fifth birthday uptown, and Linda Hillig gave me my very own Happy Birthday banner to wear. It made me feel like a princess all day. Even at a young age, I learned the fine art of bargaining by selling a kitten I'd found to Harold Metteer for ten cents. He reminds me to this day about how I sold him a cat, and how it's still alive.

But time goes by, and we all grow older and start assuming responsibilities that come with age, like it or not. This past summer I began my first hourly wage job working at GB's Auto Glass and Service here in Nimrod. It's always fun to see smiling faces and waving hands from the locals when I'm pumping gas. But what I get a kick out of most are the tourists that stop by. They always ask me the same questions: So, what is there to do in this town? Is there any place to eat around here? I tell them to head over to the R&R Bar & Grill for the biggest hamburgers in town.

If you like adventure, you can walk to Hillig Mercantile where they rent you a tube to float the scenic and ferocious Crow Wing River.

If you want a memorable experience, you can have your picture taken in front of the ever-popular Nimrod Post Office. The reason for its popularity is because there's always a crowd waiting to get mail from Postmistress Ann Stigman. Ann has been there for over thirty years and just celebrated her ninetieth birthday. I've seen people getting their picture taken by our Nimrod sign at the south end of town. Currently, we boast a population of seventy-five, but for some strange reason, the locals here tell people that it's sixty-nine. It hasn't been that since 1980.

By the way, if you happen to be in the area around the Fourth of July, you can join the annual Nimrod Community Tubing Party. We start at Anderson's Crossing and float to Uncle David's house where the Taste O'Nimrod tantalizes our tongues. Dave and Jeanne Tellock got things started for us in the mid-1980s, and it's been going strong ever since. This year, we had approximately seventy-five people floating on the river. But of course, someone said that it was only sixty-nine.

Another interesting sight is our Nimrod Forestry Fire Tower. This tower is used to spot fires and is ninety-four feet tall and was built in 1928. Just ask Nancy Gilster how long it takes to climb that during fire season. Nancy is one of our local spotters.

If you're into baseball, buzz over to Stigman Field where you can check out our local team, the Nimrod Gnats, who are three-time State Tournament participants. The Gnats sure liven things up around here on Sunday afternoons. And I got to tell you: that new grandstand is something to see. What's a Gnat, you ask? It's one of those pesky little bugs that fly around. That's why you see us walking around all summer with one arm up in the air just to keep them out of our face!

For sure, you won't want to miss the grand finale of summer. That's right. You guessed it—Nimrod Jubilee Days. A fun-filled family celebration held every year on Labor Day weekend. With events like the pageant, parade, softball tournament, and mud run, there's guaranteed fun for everyone. Next year, our town will celebrate its twenty-fifth annual Jubilee Days, which we hope will be the biggest and best celebration yet. A big "hats off" to all the hard-working locals who have kept it going all these years. Without you, I wouldn't be standing here today.

With all these things going on, I don't know how anyone could ever think of a better place to live than Nimrod.

I love this town! When people ask me where I'm from, I'm proud to say Nimrod. It's a place where you can grow up and feel safe knowing that if there's ever a crisis, there's always someone around ready to lend a helping hand. The Nimrod folks are friendly and fun, and I've learned a lot from them over the years. (Especially Delores and Donna. You know what I'm talking about.) I like to think of the locals as my second family. A family friend, Milt Richardson, once told me, "You can go anywhere to find good people, but you can only go to Nimrod to find the best people."

Well said, Bethany. Thanks for telling the world about some of the good people and events that we might take for granted.

Fall

AUTUMN OF MY LIFE

I WALK TO THE RIVER. A carpet of leaves crunches at my feet. In the distance, a corn chopper drones, slow and monotonous, through a field along the drive. A neighbor's cows call for separated calves. Overhead, Canadian geese fly down river, quiet except for the whir of wings. Chickadees announce that the bird feeder is full. These are the sounds of autumn. Then, a volley of high-power gun shots. A hunter zeroes in his rifle.

I walk in the woods. Most trees are naked. A few tan leaves hang from white birch. The white oaks, ash, and popple are bare. Maple trees that were ablaze last week look stark. Red oak leaves are deep burgundy, heading for brown. Horses nibble on acorns under the oaks. Gray squirrels chat and scamper. Three white-tailed deer appear and disappear over the perimeter fence.

I walk along the river. The water is low, slow, clear. Wild rice stalks stand like sticks out of the flow. A birch tree hangs over the water, its few leaves reflecting. The afternoon sun scatters diamonds on the river. Ferns that stood waist deep in August have fallen flat, brown. Six mallards beat the water with their wings and fly south.

I walk down the drive for the mail. Bring a hammer next time. Calves have stretched fence wire, popped staples. Wild asters bloom, despite last week's frost. There's a smell of ripe hazelnuts, then the smell of chopped corn—sweet, ripe, earthy. A garter snake slithers away from his sunning spot in the gravel. Deer tracks pock the roadway.

Back in the barnyard, cattle lie beside full bale feeders, storing sunshine beneath long coats for the months ahead. Horses return for water, look expectantly for a treat of ground corn. The first hatch of chickens is grown and wanders together. The second hatch is a week old. Mother hen clucks and scratches through old hay. Nine multi-hued babies follow her, peck at anything. Overhead, two swans fly, long white necks pointing east. I glance at the river as an eagle makes the bend, heads downstream.

It's a bittersweet time of year. Each warm day may be the last. Each green stem, each red flower, each yellow leaf may fade tomorrow. This morning, there's a rose hue in the sky. Rain is forecast. The air is ominous. Cool, fresh, sweet, but there's a hint of foreboding. Tomorrow may be cold. Snow.

This weekend, we will make wood—firewood. Summer winds downed trees that were vulnerable from cleared fence lines. It's a good time of year for wood cutting. Heavy work; light sweat. Good to smell fresh-sawed oak, haul it to the house, see the wood pile building. Good to feel the blaze in the fireplace at the end of day.

Early the next day, I walk back to the river. Morning dew dampens the rustle of leaves. I see my breath, see steam rising from my coffee, see mist rising from the river. Blue jays squawk, compete with crows up river. Nuthatches flit from feeder to tree, cracking sunflower seeds. The river seems still, flows imperceptibly. A rooster crows. Cattle are down, looking fat, at ease. Canadian geese congregate downstream, honk incessantly. Red squirrels load birdseed, tuck it away for winter.

Time to get to work. Time to remember the lush, warm, green promise of summer. Time to consider the stark, white beauty of winter. Time to appreciate the rust and gold, the harvest colors of autumn. The best time of year. The best time of life.

JUBILEE DAYS

HOW DOES THE TOWN OF NIMROD, population seventy-five, prepare for a party of five thousand? Casually. Two weeks before the event, I asked First Lady Nancy Gilster, the mayor's wife, if there were meetings. "None," she responded. "Everyone knows what to do."

The answer must be experience. And energy. And imagination. And hard work. It may look like a sleepy little hamlet, but in the Nimrod Community Center, queen candidates are rehearsing their responses to questions like "How do today's teens differ from their parents?" In the ball park, Nimrod Gnats players and fans sprinkle the infield, rake the base lines, reshape the pitcher's mound. In the church basement, the best cooks in the New World peel gunny sacks of potatoes and season beef for the roasting oven.

This is the twenty-third annual Nimrod Jubilee Days celebration. The theme this year is "Slide on Home to Nimrod," in deference to the Regional Tournament-winning Nimrod Gnats baseball team. But it is also a slide on home for hundreds of expatriates who return every year on Labor Day weekend. Minnesota Department of Transportation (MinDOT) saw fit to resurface Main Street for the event. But don't expect curb and gutter, sidewalks, or potted petunias hanging from quaint light posts. We're not that kind of people.

Jubilee Days opens Friday at 7:00 P.M. with a Queen Pageant in the Community Center. It should be a blast. Six candidates, each one a bundle of energy, talent, and charm, vying for the crown. And how will they solve world hunger if selected? Come and find out.

Saturday, the first pitch of the softball tournament is tossed at 8:00 A.M., with sixteen teams registered, according to Charlie Tuorila. The 2000 tournament winners, the Perham Rat Pack, are back. The Nimrod area has fielded a couple local teams. The Nimrod Gnats are selling T-shirts and caps behind the dugout. Here's your chance to fill in your collection of current and previous designs, at some pretty good prices.

At 8:30, the 5K and 10K Run (or Walk) begins at the picnic shelter at Stigman Mound and makes a loop north, according to race coordinator Glenda Gilster. Register early; there were fifty-four racers last year.

At noon, the Jubilee Days parade winds out of the church parking lot and heads north, up Main Street. Look for about sixty units, with prizes in six categories, says parade honcho Margaret Rathcke. Grand Marshal this year is ninety-one-year-old John Marshall, pioneer citizen and great guy. We'll miss his chicken-drawn chariot in the parade this year. A small town parade is a predictable thing. A uniformed VFW unit leading off with the American flag. Marching bands. Crepe-paper floats. Waving queens. Mounted horse patrols. Screwball clowns. Hard candy tossed from fire trucks. But it has a magic, and it works year after year. Kids, bring Mom and Dad early. Parking gets downright nasty toward parade time.

After the parade, there's an Open Horse Show in the Riders of the Crow Wing arena across from the church. PeeWee, Junior, and Senior classes compete in the usual games—barrels, hangman, poles. Don't eat before the senior rescue race. You'll lose your lunch laughing.

In the afternoon, there are kid games in the park, square dancing in the Nimrod Hall, and a concert by the Sebeka High School Jazz Band near the post office. I've heard the jazz band on a couple occasions. Great music, great arrangements, great performances. Worth the trip.

Then, Saturday evening, the Leaf River Hornets play for dancing in the Nimrod Hall. They have a mixed repertoire, but the crowd favors the old-time stuff—polkas, two-steps, waltzes, all of which might be classified as aerobic.

Get a good start on Sunday with the nondenominational church service at 9:00 A.M. The big events of the day are the Sanctioned North Country Mud Run at noon, a street dance at 8:00 A.M., interrupted by fireworks at dusk. The Mud Run is one of the newer events, but grows each year. Motorized hotrods are not my passion, but this is a hoot. Driving a megabuck sling shot, four-wheel-drive dragster through a mud puddle is the ultimate absurdity But it's fun to watch. Check out the crowd, and watch for the Nimrod Hard Core mobile grandstand. Wild!

The Velvet Touch, out of Fargo, I think, makes a reprise at the Sunday night street dance. They did a great job last year, especially the way they worked the crowd. Wear dancing shoes that work in sand.

The fireworks finale rates a ten on the "oooh's and aaah's" scale. Nothing new this year, but those colorful pyrotechnics bursting in the night sky are always a thrill. And it's a great way to wind down the kids before heading home.

There's all of that, plus a treasure hunt, steer weight guessing, mud volleyball, double elimination horseshoe tournament, Ricky's Trivia game, flea market, and Bingo. Hungry? Stop at the Nimrod Hall stand, the Bluegrass Catholic Church stand (good apple pie last year), the R&R Bar & Grill for the world's best cheeseburger, Sunday dinner at the Nimrod Lutheran Church from 11:00 A.M. to 2:00 P.M., or the Pancake Breakfast, cooked and served by the nationally renowned Nimrod Do Gooders on Saturday, Sunday, and Monday, from 7:00 A.M. to 11:00 A.M.

I get tired just thinking about all that. So, I repeat the question. Where does a town of seventy-five population get all the energy?

VIEW FROM THE TOWER

REMEMBER THE OLD *RANGER RICK* MAGAZINES? Forest Ranger Rick taught us to identify pileated woodpeckers, urged us to plant Norway pines, warned us to tend our campfires. Rick was the definitive Forest Ranger—friendly, knowledgeable, and male. Move over, Ranger Rick, and let me introduce Ranger Rita. Rangers Lillian Baker and Lonnie Lilly, dispatchers Grace Horton and Linda Lilly, tower observers Amy Schermerhorn, Evelyn Gilster, Ardee Amundson, and Nancy Gilster. All female employees, past and present, of the Nimrod District Forestry Office, known as the DNR.

Joe Alexander, who served as DNR Commissioner from 1978 to 1991 in both the Perpich and Quie administrations, is credited with advocating women in DNR positions. Again, Nimrod beat the trend. Amy Schermerhorn began as tower observer in 1960. And she replaced Evelyn Gilster.

The DNR was created seventy years ago, in 1931, as the Minnesota Department of Conservation. The Nimrod office predates that by three years. The tower, on Huntersville Road north of town, was built in 1928. It's a ninety-four-foot structure constructed by Aeromotor (of windmill fame), with a seven-by-seven crow's nest atop. Access is by ladder, one step at a time. At treetop level, one is one third of the way up. Locals say this is the last ladder-access tower in the state.

The view is worth the climb. Horses on Deana and Tinker Skov's River Ranch graze in the pasture below. The Crow Wing River meanders, nearly invisible, though dense foliage. Huntersville Road winds north. Nimrod rooftops reflect through the trees. The Foot Hills State Forest, on the east horizon, is the only evidence of hills in this level part of the country.

From the tower, observers scan the world below for smoke, from snow melt in March-April to green up in May-June. Occasionally, there are tower watches in late fall, before snow cover. Historically, observers have been women. Why? Nancy, Amy, and Ardee talk about the primary virtue of patience. Maybe so. On a good day, nothing happens.

Today, the Forestry Office is staffed by Ranger Lonnie Lilly (who grew up in the shadow of the tower); Joel Holden, Technician; and Steve Schwab, Lead Smoke Chaser. Terry Simon, out of Brainerd Area Wildlife, also works the Nimrod area. Firefighters and detection aircraft are contracted on an as-required basis.

The Nimrod office manages state forests, assists in private forest management, and maintains state recreation areas. Huntersville, Lyons, and part of Foot Hills State Forest are in the Nimrod office domain. Management consists of tree planting, trail development, and timber sales. Private forest management is much the same, except the DNR acts as consultant. Three recreation areas are Huntersville and Shell City campgrounds and the Shell City horse camp.

There are thirteen State Management Wildlife Areas in Wadena County encompassing 5,000 acres, under the purview of Terry Simon. Locally, the area includes Strike, Dry Sand, and, the largest, Burgen Lake at 2,200 acres.

The DNR gets an assist from the Minnesota Conservation Corps (MCC) and Charlie Tuorila's Sentence to Serve (STS) "volunteers" in recreation areas—clearing trails, building campsites, general maintenance.

Back to the tower observers, those fearless women of patience, who climb a ninety-four-foot ladder for the privilege of sitting alone for six hours. Nancy Gilster has been an observer for twenty-six years. Climbing the ladder? "No problem," says Nancy. Not nearly as tough as grooming queen candidates for the Miss Nimrod pageant, her perennial task. Nancy knows the landmarks—Sebeka, eleven miles west; Park Rapids and Menahga water towers. She has spotted fires at Itasca State Park and Fort Ripley, fifty miles distant. Any problems up there? Only one; Nancy missed deer hunting season one year, and although she spotted some trophies below, she wasn't allowed to bring her 30-06 up the tower.

Ardee Amundson has been an observer since 1983. She talks about the necessity of patience during the six-hour shift, the beauty of the countryside as trees leaf out in spring. Once smoke is detected, an azimuth indicator in the tower pinpoints direction. Estimating distance is the observer's call. It's difficult, admits Ardee, but it helps to know that the communication tower is five miles away, and that's half way to the fire. Ardee remembers a Mother's Day when she was on duty in the tower. Son Duane brought roses and a balloon. The balloon escaped as he climbed the ladder, but she got the roses.

Amy Schermerhorn was an observer from about 1960 to 1978. She remembers the Big Fires of 1976, when husband Jerry was on the fire line and she was in the tower. She remembers her fear, recalls a lot of scrambling of firefighters on the ground. The 1976 fires come up in every conversation about tower observation.

The DNR is a good neighbor, and much of the credit goes to fieldmen Joel Holden and Steve Schwab. Both are good at what they do, and friendly. In my visits to the office, and Joel's visit to my farm, they take time to listen, take the opportunity to share knowledge. Allen Garber, Jesse Ventura's appointed DNR commissioner, said, "I just want to heighten responsiveness on everyone's priority list." You've done a good job of that.

Post Script: As I edit this, I listen to radio reports of terrorist attacks in New York City and Washington, D.C. It's distracting, frightening, alarming. My prayers go to the victims. My fear is the response, the aftermath. My hope is for a rational course of action.

THAT'S ENTERTAINMENT

IT'S THURSDAY NIGHT IN THE LATE 1940S or early 1950s. People want some entertainment, but there's no television yet. At least, not around here. Maybe a set or two at some rich people's houses in Park Rapids, and one in the appliance store window in Wadena, where townspeople congregate outside the plate glass window to watch Uncle Miltie on the Admiral seven-inch screen. So what's to do? Head for the Nimrod Community Hall and watch a movie, a service of the Stanich Amusement Circuit.

Gene Stanich was discharged from the U.S. Air Force in 1945 and started the movie circuit in 1946. Brainerd was his base of operation, and client towns included Leader on Wednesday, Nimrod on Thursday, Wolf Lake on Friday, Nevis on Saturday, and Akeley on Sunday. Then home to Marcy and the kids.

The Nimrod Community Hall was the theater. Gene would arrive early, and get help from the Stigman boys setting up the screen and wood folding chairs and church pew benches; displaying little bags of popcorn and five-cent candy bars; lighting the stove in winter, or closing shutters in summer. After set up and before the movie, Gene recalls trips behind the hall catching Dick Stigman's fast ball. Dick provided the ball and gloves. "Even then," Gene recalls, "Dick had a lot of stuff on the ball."

Gene also recalls movie patrons arriving early, before the eight o'clock movie. He had a PA system and a phonograph. People visited in the hall while Lloyd Nolan sang "Cool, Cool Water" with the Sons of the Pioneers. Gene used a voice-over microphone for announcements.

The favorite movies were action westerns—John Wayne and Joanne Dru in *She Wore a Yellow Ribbon*; Tex Ritter, Johnny "Mack" Brown, and Fuzzie Knight in *Tenting on the Old Camp Ground*; Hopalong Cassidy in *Sunset Trail*. Abbott and Costello were big. Gene also ran a weekly serial—*Oregon Trail* with Johnny "Mack" Brown, and *Lost City in the Jungle*. Sounds like it might have starred Jon Hall, Maria Montez, and Sabu.

Gene says he advertised in the *Sebeka Review*, and, sure enough, I found his ads from early 1948 in the archives. Remember *Trail of the Vigilantes* with Broderick Crawford? How about *Merry Monahan's* with Donald O'Connor? How about *East Side of Heaven* with Bing Crosby? Neither do I.

Gene advertised local businesses. He color-filmed townspeople shopping local merchants, kids and babies in hand. He coached them to act natural; don't look at the camera! Then he charged the merchants fifty-cents per screening on Thursday nights. Ordinary townspeople, suddenly movie stars, brought their extended families to see their ten seconds of glory on the silver screen.

For feature films, Gene had two sixteen-mm projectors with automatic changeover, so the movies were continuous. Sometime after 1946, a projection booth was built in the hall to the right and above the main entrance. The oversized screen sat on the stage. Gene selected movies himself from a Twin City supplier. He claims his circuit was the only one of its kind in the country. Cost of admission varies with people's memories—ten or fifteen cents for kids, twenty-five or thirty-five cents for adults.

Donna Metteer remembers seeing her first movie in the Nimrod Community Center—Walt Disney's *Bambi*. (I hope it wasn't shown during hunting season.) Deloris Shore remembers her first romance in the semi-darkness of the hall while Marjorie Main and Percy Kilbride played *Ma and Pa Kettle Down on the Farm*. Raymond Pederson remembers the ride into town with brothers Roger, David, Gary, and Glenn in the back of a 1936 red Ford pickup to see Roy Rogers and Gabby Hayes.

Gene sold the business in 1952, six years after he started it. A couple brothers from Akeley bought it but couldn't keep it going. But Gene kept his Nimrod contacts and memories—playing whist with Eva and Kenny Blow, and duck hunting with Lauri Frame and Jack Stigman.

I had lunch with Marcy and Gene Stanich last week. They are retired and live on Serpent Lake in Crosby. My parting shot as I left was to extract a promise from them to return to Nimrod sometime next summer. We could have an old-timers' reunion. Or we could have a film festival at the Community Center. Anybody have copies of *Oregon Trail*?

THINGS IN THREES

SEEMS LIKE TRAGEDIES OCCUR IN SETS OF THREE. First, on a national level, the terrorist highjackings. The repercussion of that will take years to unravel. Second, my only living aunt died, and we, my brothers, sisters, and cousins, are now the oldest generation. Finally, I endured a divorce trial on Wednesday. Not an easy day, I assure you. Not an easy week.

The good news is that we had scheduled our annual Mevissen brothers' fishing trip for last weekend. The timing was brilliant. Not to detract from the enormity of world and personal events, the opportunity to spend time with family was a welcome distraction.

There are six brothers, and all six broke away for our twenty-first trip, this year in Turtle Lake, Wisconsin. Location of the weekend extravaganzas varies between Minnesota, Wisconsin, and Manitoba.

After twenty-one years, procedures become routine. Jim and Frank, arguably the best fishermen, catch and clean fish. Phil and I cook. Mike and Bill wash dishes and clean the cabin.

Also, after twenty-one years, the fishing part of the trip becomes incidental. This year, for example, fishing was limited by weather to one-half day. Did it ruin our weekend? No sir. The attraction for me is catching up on family news, breaking away from routine, isolating myself from current events. Good thing, because the sunfish I caught cost me three dollars apiece, when amortized over a fifteen-dollar, non-resident fishing license.

In twenty-one years, incidents become legends. One year's misfortune becomes next year's laughing stock. The first year, we tented and watched rain float across the tent floor. Then the rain floated eggs in the fry pan. One year, sister Kathy baked brownies for the trip. And baked them, and baked them until they were as cutable as quarry tile, in retaliation for her not being invited. One year, Mike forgot his rod and reel and fishing tackle. We won't forget the trips across the bog in Lake of the Woods, sinking to our shoulders in primordial muck, hanging to the gunwales for safety, wondering what creatures were eyeing our thrashing legs, laughing until we lost our strength.

By the time we catch up on family history, eat three knock-out meals, and rehash memories of earlier trips, not much of the day remains for fishing. That's fine. We always catch enough for one good fry.

As I review the trip, I'm amazed at the distance I placed between the week and the weekend. I've heard reports and read articles about the importance of coming together with family and friends at a time of crisis. What is the therapy? Maybe it's the return to bedrock values, in our experiences, our lives. Despite how national and personal tragedies may impact us, there are constants. One of those is the support of family.

If tragedies come in threes, then good news should also come in threes. I'm heartened at how America has come together since September 11. I'm pleased at how the national dialog has shifted from responding to acts of war to acts of crime.

I'm heartened by the thought of my aunt reuniting with her parents, her husband, her son. And her sister, my mother, after sixty-six years.

I'm heartened by the completion of the divorce trial. I won't know the results until December/January, but I hope for equity, justice.

Add to those, the love and support of family and friends, good health, a positive attitude, and the beauty of late September. Life is good.

THE LITTLE TOWN THAT COULD

THE TOWN IS BUZZING. Ground crews irrigate the ball fields. Pit crews grade the mud run. Do-Gooders scrub pancake grills. Riders of the Crow Wing drag the horse arena. Signs, posters, and T-shirts proclaim the events. In the Community Center, the Nimrod Pageant committee tries desperately to harness the energy of seven little boys who vie for the title of Little Master Nimrod. Good luck!

How does a town of seventy-five people prepare for a party of 5,000 visitors? With experience and planning. This Labor Day weekend is the twenty-fourth annual Nimrod Jubilee Days. The celebration begins Friday night with the Queen, Little Miss, and Little Master pageants. It wraps up on Monday with a pancake breakfast and the final games of the softball tournament. Between Friday and Monday is a 5K and 10K Walk and Run, a parade, open horse show, street dance, and mud run, plus kids' games, treasure hunt, horseshoe competition, bingo, karaoke, and food, food, food.

Margaret Rathcke, parade coordinator, expects seventy-five entries in the parade in seven categories. The theme of the celebration is "Red, White, and Blue in 2002." In response to that, Margaret expects nine color guards. The Grand Marshall this year is a group of area veterans from several wars. Watch for the Sebeka-Menahga marching band. There are cash prizes for the top three entries in each category. Contestants are asked to begin lineup at ten o'clock for a noon parade. There are no entry fees. Watch, also, for the fetching, if not aging, perennial Miss Nimrod contestant. We may quibble about her appeal, but you gotta love her car.

RED, WHITE & BLUE
IN 2002
NIMROD JUBILEE DAYS
NIMROD, MN - POPULATION 69

The twentieth annual Nimrod Jubilee Run leaves Stigman's Mound Park at 8:30 A.M. Saturday morning. Glenda Gilster and Anne Graham offer ribbons to the top three contestants in each of seven age categories, plus medals to the top finishers in the men's and women's divisions, and a T-shirt to all participants. The courses are 5K and 10K, and if someone doesn't feel like running, walk.

Charlie Tuorila coordinates the softball tournament, which begins at 8:00 A.M. Saturday. Twenty-two teams have registered this year, including two teams with local talent—the Philthies and a Sebeka high school team. This is a fund raiser for the Nimrod Gnats, who provide umpire services, the balls, and ground maintenance. Cash prizes of $300, $200, and $100 plus a trophy go to the top three contenders. Watch for teams who dress for effect, not for success. And don't expect to hear any talk about strikes, players' salaries, or luxury tax splits. We're talking entertainment, not big business. No charge for admission.

Noon Sunday is the Sanctioned North Country Mud Run. There are nine categories with first, second, and third place trophies for the winners. Terry McAllister, mud run coordinator, expects about 170 entrants, making the Nimrod show the event with the most registered trucks in the North Country circuit for four consecutive years. There are also non-sanctioned runs for local drivers. Our sole, local sanctioned driver to date is Goober Weaver who is sure to get a thunderous applause from the grandstand. The grandstand has a life of its own and doesn't rely on mud runners for stimulus. It helps to have grilled Rickburgers and deep-fried Wagner turkey, plus Jenny's own recipe for high-octane Kool-Aid. Watch the Big Boys out of Wisconsin in the open and cut tire classes. They make a lot of noise, but they're no competition for the grandstand clatter.

For the 2002 Royalty Pageant, the committee extended the competition to little boys for the title Little Master Nimrod. Unbelievably, there are seven candidates. If they don't steal the show, I'll be surprised. Six-year-old boys are not designed to follow the rules. We'll see. Five little girls competing for Little Miss Nimrod are predictably sweet, well-behaved, and all smiles. The six candidates for Miss Nimrod offer a wide range of talent, all of it interesting, entertaining, and commendable. Perennial emcee Deana Skov will have her hands full keeping this show moving. It begins at 7:00 P.M. on Friday. With the introductions, speeches, boardwalks, dance number, talent presentations, and questions and answers, we hope there's time for a couple cowboy poems.

N
NIMROD

Race Course

Starting Friday, the spotlight will be on the participants of Jubilee Days. Today we offer a resounding round of applause to the committees, the sponsors, and the donors that make this event possible. They've outdone yourselves again.

HALLELUJAH! IT'S OVER!

THE TWENTY-FOURTH ANNUAL Nimrod Jubilee Days is history. And what a party it was! Lots of highlights. Here are a few.

Parade: Red, white, and blue prevailed. Eleven color guards, and the grand marshal was several grand marshals—all veterans. Speaking of grand marshals, last year's designee, John Marshall, returned for this year's parade and watched from the sidelines with daughters Shawnee and Sally and grandkids.

Pageant: The candidates for Little Miss and Little Master Nimrod stole the show. A close second was Queen Bethany's energetic and sincere speech extolling the virtues of life in small-town America. It's gratifying to hear words of praise about our way of life from the younger generation. Congratulations to all the queen candidates: Bethany Pederson, Beth Kuschel, Heather Evavold, Katie Johnson, Cody Bell, and Naomi Whitaker. You're all winners for the experience.

Mud Run: Cars were queuing into town at eleven on Sunday morning heading for Gilster Amphitheater. Terry Rathcke McAlister gave up ticket taking this year and raced. And won! The Nimrod Bahama Mama stand, with the Queen Mum presiding, lived up to its advanced billing. If my photographs are fuzzy, well, there's a reason. Lots of fun, food, and friends.

The Horseshoe Tournament: Won by a local, Eddie Hepola, in the singles, and by Eddie and Pete Nielson in the doubles. Two double ringers for Eddie as he was being photographed. Talk about a pressure player!

Soft Ball Tournament: Twenty-one teams played Saturday and Sunday, with a Tuorila/Hepola team winning first place. The prom queen team was especially graphic in their ballroom gowns and leotards. Expenses may have exceeded budget, what with all the homerun balls that cleared the centerfield fence.

Guess the Weight of the Bull: Would you believe 2,414 pounds? And that's down from his spring weight.

Food. Food. Food: How could anyone resist the dessert table at the Lutheran Church? Or Jean Nielson's potato salad at the Senior Center? Or the barbequed beef at the Do-Gooders stand? Or the pancakes and sausage at the other Do-Gooders food stand? Or the world-famous cheeseburgers at the R&R? T'was not a weekend for dieting.

Horse Show: Another good turnout, with high point trophy going to Nimrod local Rachael Richards. Congratulations to Rachael and all the contestants.

Mud Volleyball: Excellent mud this year, and lots of it. Volleyball players came to win, and they came to get dirty. Their uniforms are beyond Tide; they're candidates for the burn barrel.

Flea Market: How about a sweatshirt? A set of salt and pepper shakers? A complete collection of bodice-ripping romance novels? A hydraulic cylinder? It was all there , and more. Sorry, we didn't have live chickens for sale this year.

Kids games: Thanks to Pat Rathcke and gang for including the tots in the Jubilee. It was great to see all those kids hopping toward the finish line in gunny sacks or scrambling in the three-legged race or shuffling through straw, looking for quarters.

The 5K and 10K Run: Another pair of locals, Janice and Ray Hiedeman, won first prize in their respective age groups. One 5K contestant missed the turnoff, and ran 10K, and still placed.

Street Dance: Another good show by the Fantastic Convertibles. It was fun to see kids dancing with their neon glow necklaces. Mid-town Nimrod looked like Times Square on New Years Eve. Where do all these people come from?

All that and more at the Twenty-fourth Annual Nimrod Jubilee Days. We had great fireworks, a treasure hunt, church service, square dancing, bingo, karaoke, and queen coronation. And we had great weather. The breeze on Saturday was a godsend. The rain passed before the action began on Sunday. And the rolls of thunder on Labor Day morning were a round of applause for a great weekend.

SEPTEMBER SONG

ASH TREES ALONG THE RIVER are tinged with yellow-gold. Floes of foam ride the current. Wild rice stems stand tall and still, hiding a pair of mallards. A breeze flutters the popples. There's a post-summer quiet in the air. It's September.

After Labor Day, we shift gears. Morning comes later; evening comes earlier. A primordial instinct urges an inspection of chain saws, the marking of trees to be cut, the stacking of the wood pile.

Acorns fall on the patio table in a drummer's paradiddle. The ground below oak trees is a bed of marbles, a haunt for squirrels. Cattle stand under the trees and nibble on acorns, grazing in place. The draft horse bumps an oak hard, and showers the ground with more nuts.

Wild asters in purple fluff line the lane. Crowsfoot grass waves along the drive. Clumps of hazelnuts fall from husks.

In the garden, tomatoes hang from vines like great Christmas decorations. Green beans dry in their pods. Unpicked lettuce goes to seed. Zucchini vines set out to conquer the world.

The only sound is the wind. Then a kingbird calls. An owl hoots. A crow caws. The wind blows again, and the ground is pelleted with more acorns.

The corn we worried about on the Fourth of July is higher than the proverbial elephant's eye. One round cut on the edge of the field shows that the chopper has been tested. Round bales of hay lay aligned in farm yards, the white man's testimony to a long winter ahead.

What did we do to deserve this beautiful end of summer? Days are warm; nights are cool. The sumac is red. The clouds are white. The sky is blue.

It's a beautiful country. God bless America.

ORANGE

6:30 A.M., TUESDAY. LIGHT FOG AT TREE LEVEL. Three-quarter moon high in center sky. Trees are silhouetted, black and blank, against a pink yawning sky. Silence. Darkness lifts, and now the trees are textured. No breeze. The sky is clear. Chickadee weather. I see my breath, but the chill is temporary. Pasture grass is green. Woods are carpeted in browns. Popple are black scars over gray. It's Tuesday of deer hunting week, and I'm in the stand with grandson Mike.

The Nimrod deer hunting season begins Thursday or Friday. Not the shooting season, but the arrivals. Armored personnel carriers jam Highway 10, head north on Highway 26 for Nimrod, or Highway 71 for Sebeka and beyond. Orange-clad hunters, intent, sit on the edge of their seats, look impatient, anxious, prepared for battle. Behind them, in the pickup box or trailer, a pair of four wheelers. And inside the truck, 30-30 Remingtons, GPSs, advanced digital communications systems. Is our little peaceful hamlet being invaded? Yes, but by friendly forces. Suddenly the threat of a foreign ground invasion loses its sting.

My son Mark, grandson Mike, and two friends are hunting on my farm this year. Last year, Mike hunted with them for his first season. No luck. And last year, Henry Butzin hunted with them for his last season. One of the friends hunts from the Henry Memorial Deer Stand. Saturday morning, they get a young buck. Nothing on Sunday. Then, Monday, after the weekend hunters have returned to the city, my four hunters returned to the woods.

Seven A.M., Tuesday. Sun is still under the horizon. I can see fence lines at the north and south ends of the pasture. No sign of deer. A couple ducks fly over. A red squirrel scampers in the jackpines. A crow caws. I see potential firewood strewn through the woods, enough to last several lifetimes.

We're closing in on the optimum deer harvesting time of day. Yesterday, I heard my son's high-power rifle, one shot, at eight o'clock, followed by two other shots. Then, quiet. An hour later, a pair of grins walked into the yard. Proud grandson, prouder dad. Mark shot one; grandson Mike shot two, one bullet apiece.

Deer hunting weekend ranks up there with opening of fishing season, Fourth of July, and Labor Day for Nimrod traffic. Two hundred and nine hunters registered for the biggest buck and biggest doe contest. By close of business Monday, a 220-pound buck was the leading contender for a 270 Savage bolt-action rifle. A 155 pound doe was leading for a .22-caliber Marlin Magnum. By Monday night, over 400 deer were registered, according to Rich Grotberg at Nimrod Service.

The R&R Bar & Grill bounced this weekend, like a boxcar of Sunkist oranges. Feels strange to walk in and not know everyone. Lots of oft-told stories of chances had, shots missed, bad angles. Didn't I hear these last year? And the year before? Adding to the confusion was the karaoke entertainment. No offense, gentlemen, but your songs were some of the longest three minutes in show business.

Hungry hunters filled up on roast beef at the Senior Center on Saturday night. Lila Perkins, Mildred Bickford, and Marcy Shore were all smiles, happy with the turnout, about one hundred and ten meals served when I checked in.

Seven thirty A.M., Tuesday. The sun peeks through the trees and ignites the tops of red oaks to the west. Shots are fired off to the north, louder than a .22, quieter than a 30-30. Geese honk from the river. A gray squirrel hustles under the fence. The air is brisk, smells like fall. No deer.

My grandson had made the big announcement Monday morning. Not one, but two deer. With only two bullets from his 30-06 Winchester bolt action. The ten-power scope put him on top of the animals. I notice a change. His voice is a bit lower. There's a new confidence in his gait. He's maybe an inch taller. This is how legends are born. This is coming of age, Nimrod style. He tells his story, "My First Deer," and retells it around the fireplace Monday night. And on the telephone to Mother and sister back home. He will tell it countless times during his life.

I'm proud of him, and pleased to get some immortality out of the story too. Mike got his first two deer at Grampa's farm.

LAST HURRAH

WE MADE IT! The twenty-third Nimrod Jubilee days celebration was the biggest and best yet. Every event, from the queen pageant to the final pancake breakfast, was well planned, well executed, well attended. The town, and the townspeople stayed in party dress for three days. No small accomplishment.

It's tough to single out specific events to highlight, but here are a few.

Beth Pederson and Beth Kuschel, pinch-hitting with a song at the queen pageant, on thirty seconds notice. So what if it wasn't perfect. That takes guts, and they pulled it off.

John Marshall, parade Grand Marshal, riding (not driving) in a vis-a-vis, looking regal, proud at ninety-one. Good choice, parade committee.

The Well Oiled softball team, blasting back-to-back-to-back homeruns in the softball tourney. Eighteen teams competed. Two days of entertainment on two ball fields.

Little Sam Bell, defying fear, running the gunny sack race with dad, Roy, in the Riders of the Crow Wing horse show. We start our cowboys young here.

The cooks and hosts at the Nimrod Hard Core picnic table and temporary bleachers at the Mud Run. It took dizzying speed and deafening noise from the stock and street-open machines to distract from the partying in the bleachers. Lots of local contestants, lots of energy, lots of fun.

The pickup teams in the mud volleyball games. Throw those clothes away, folks. No amount of soaking will wash out Nimrod mud.

The queen candidates, who entertained us with their talent, staggered us with their poise and wit, charmed us with their beauty. Congratulations, Queen Amber Nelson and all the contestants. And a hearty thanks to emcee Deana Skov for keeping the show moving, and interesting.

The Wet Spots softball team, who won the Beer Trophy, obviously designed by Anheuser Busch. The trophy looked good doing the wave at the dance Sunday night.

The impromptu local talent at the street dance, singing along with the Velvet Touch. Great talent and a great show. And great acoustics. A special thanks to Bob and Ruth Stahl of the R&R for footing the bill for the band.

The dedication of the horseshoe pitchers, an escape from the hubbub of the party. The concentration, the slow arc of the pitch, the clang of horseshoe on stake. Like an old-fashioned Sunday afternoon.

All the tasty meals and snacks at the Hall, the church, the stands. It was good to see lines of hungry folks, and tables of neighbors, friends, visitors enjoying the food, the company, the party.

The sounds of the Sebeka High School Jazz Band. It's always a pleasure to see young people turn out for a non-school event and do a great job. You were fun to hear, to watch.

A non-cattle man outperforming the professionals in the bull weight guessing contest. Rich Grotberg nailed the weigh at 1,700 pounds and walked away with the prize.

I missed the 5K and 10K runs, the Leaf River Hornets Dance, the Sunday dinner at the Nimrod Lutheran Church. But my plate was full. There are a couple more stories that deserve mention. Jeff Pederson won the Defecating Horse contest. (For the uninitiated, the idea is to guess which square on a grid of 100 squares that a horse will select to honor with his waste.) Back to the story: Jeff donated his prize money to the Nimrod Gnats baseball team. Another local, a cook at Taste O'Jubilee, Bob Wagner, won the drawing grand prize of a $1,000 savings bond, and donated it to the team. That's great spirit, guys, and part of what makes our town a joy to live in. That, and all the time, energy, funds, to pull off a great party, that this was.

So, the Jubilee is over for another year. Back to shorter days, cooler mornings, hints of yellow on the ash trees along the river. Feels like we've turned the corner on summer. And Jubilee Days is the last hurrah.

NIMROD FAIRY TALE

ONCE UPON A TIME IN THE KINGDOM OF NIMROD, there lived a horseman, Kurt, and his lady, Margaret. They arrived in the late 1980s from Switzerland, looking for a home to continue Old-World traditions. One of those traditions was breeding, training, and riding Lipizzan horses. Another tradition was a fierce independence and dedication to the task at hand. A third was an expectation of the highest order of performance and conduct from themselves and others.

The first tradition endeared them to the people of the kingdom. During the autumn festival, Kurt donned his black riding habit, mounted his white Lipizzan stallion, and pranced in the parade. Lady Margaret dressed in gold and red and blue silks as Scheherezade and rode an Arabian steed. In time, Kurt became disenchanted with the other horsemen in the festival. He could not hide his disdain for their western saddles, their casual riding habits, their lack of attention to the animals. So they retreated, Kurt and Margaret, to their fiefdom east of the village.

That's where I met them Saturday. Kurt Jordi and Margaret Fischer have 240 acres of pasture across the Cass County line, and raise Lipizzans, Arabians, Clydesdales, plus a menagerie of other breeds and animals.

A person couldn't be born with Kurt's respect; he or she had to earn it. He tolerated my inane questions, but his impatience showed. Karl, the standing stud at Jordi's Lipizzan Farm, is groomed, saddled and standing in the barn when we arrive. "Do you ride him western?" evokes a tirade about the folly of cowboy saddles and western riding. Wrong position. Forces the horse to work with his front legs only. Margaret mounts the stallion and exercises him around the ring. His gait is easy, confident, perfectly measured. Kurt explains the gaits, the routines, the "airs above the ground," including the trademark Capriole, where the horse jumps with four legs off the ground. At the height of the jump, he kicks out his

hind legs. A picture of the Capriole performed by Karl's sire is a textbook execution of the leap.

"Does anyone ride Karl other than you and Margaret?"

He knew where I was going with that. "People have mounted him to be photographed," he answered.

I screwed up my courage. "Can I do that?"

The next thing I knew, I was riding around the ring on a fabled Lipizzan stallion, a first, obviously. But also the first time in an English saddle. I was not a convert yet, but I would be more tolerant of English riding from then on.

We walked into the pasture accompanied by the two dogs and Marushka, the miniature jenny. Lipizzan mares grazed beside three Clydesdale draft horses which Kurt employed at Cragun's Resort for hay and sleigh rides.

Kurt gave a brief history of the Lipizzan breed. It was developed by the Hapsburg monarchy as a horse of royalty. The Hapsburg family, which controlled Spain and Austria, began the tradition during the Renaissance. Seven sire lines were established of various colors. White and gray prevail today. The intent was to develop a light, fast horse for use in the military and the Spanish riding school. Four hundred years of selective breeding have made the Lipizzan one of Europe's oldest breed of horses.

We finished the tour of the barn, pasture, and paddocks, and Margaret invited us inside for coffee. When we looked at an aerial photograph of the farm showing the former wood-frame barn, the inevitable subject of the fire three years before comes up. That fire killed eleven horses, including a prized team of Clydesdales, Lipizzan mares and foals. Any fire where animals are destroyed is a tragedy. But this one felt heightened because of the rarity of the breed. And the sensitivity of the owners. I understood then why I had to earn Kurt's respect. And his trust.

Kurt sported a bad hip after two hip replacements. But he still rode the fabled Karl, still rode the Endurance Trials at Pillsbury State Park, a twenty-five to one-hundred-mile ride. He rode an Arabian enduro mare, English saddle, of course.

Before and after his surgery, Fran and Mark Kueker lent a hand with chores—cleaning stalls, feeding, bringing the horses in and out of the barn. Fran admits to a feeling much stronger than that of employer-employee for Kurt and

Margaret. Kurt became her instructor in the art of horsemanship, then later in English style riding. When Fran injured her back in a fall from a horse, they commiserated about their fates but continued to work together, leaning on one another, physically and emotionally. Mark Kueker substituted for Kurt at Cragun's with the hay and sleigh rides, allowing Kurt to honor his contract. Kurt is effusive with praise for Fran and Mark. Fran says the feeling is mutual. Kurt's old world values—hard work, dedication, working for what you want—are aligned with hers.

So this was my introduction to *haute ecole* and to another fabric in the Nimrod quilt. Kurt and Margaret recently built a new house. Their barn and riding ring are large, well equipped, comfortable. The herd is rebuilding, although on a limited scale. My hope is that they live happily ever after.

WE GET LETTERS

LETTERS CONTINUE TO POUR IN to this hapless correspondent from readers who seek truth, an honest man, or happiness ever after. Herewith, an attempt to soothe their jagged nerves.

Dear Nimrod Chronicler:

My daughter sends me your column religiously. After a year's reading, I expected everyone up there to be a talented painter, woodworker, or horse trainer; everyone to be healthy, athletic, and in shape; everyone likely to live to 100 or more. When I visited Nimrod during Jubilee Days, I found the same mix of clods, screwballs, and perverts that we have here in Iowa. What happened to Truth in Advertising?

Signed, Curious in Keokuk

Dear Curious:

For starters, you saw 5,000 people here during Jubilee Days. The population of Nimrod in seventy-five, and the population of Greater Nimrod, which is a five-mile radius from the R&R Bar & Grill, is probably 200. I don't mean to call the people from Sebeka, Leader, and Bluegrass clods. They are good people, and they are all related to Nimrod folks, by marriage if not by blood. If you took pictures, review them. The folks with the twinkle in their eyes, the grins on their faces, the lilt in their gait, those are the Nimroders. I can't speak for the rest of them. It's what happens when we open the gates once a year.

Dear Nimrod Chronicler:

I noticed that Aunt Frieda did not march in this year's Jubilee Days parade. With the man behind the costume now happily married and living away from Nimrod, I wondered about continuing the tradition. I thought I was confident in my sexuality until I slid into the crinoline skirt. I totally lost it when I pulled on the panty hose. How is it that women can wear Levis and flannel shirts and actually look good in them? My wife thinks that I am a closet cross dresser for even thinking about this.

Signed, Pretty in Pink

Dear Pretty:

Don't even try to fill David Gilster's shoes. He has the support of the entire community, and we would love him if he dressed as Attila the Hun. I don't want to discourage you, but rather ask you to be creative. How about poofing your hair, pulling on a sweat shirt, and coming as Deloris Shore? Or growing a beard, slowing your speech, and coming as Dale Hillig? Or getting a western hat —a tall, salty, western hat, cracking a mischievous smile, and coming as Walter Warner? These are people we can relate to.

Dear Nimrod Chronicler:

Have you noticed the number of drugstore cowboys that hang around Nimrod? Feathers hanging from their Stetsons; hot pink rhinestone shirts; designer jeans; and $500 ostrich-leather boots. After chatting with a couple of them, I find that they might own a horse or two, but they don't know a withers from a shank. What gives?

Signed, Unrequited Cowgirl

Dear Unrequited:

You've hit upon a local phenomenon. Up here, the wannabes want to be cowboys, not CEOs, AFL quarterbacks, or movie stars. Do you want to talk to a real cowboy? Some of our biggest cattlemen wear seed corn hats and lace-up boots. But don't write off the Stetson set. They do add color, and some of them are prettier than our ladies.

Dear Nimrod Chronicler:

Do you realize that we are less than two weeks away from deer hunting season? My man hunts, along with every other man for miles around. For those of us of the gentler sex, we have to get out of town if we don't talk Winchesters, or Federal cartridge, or multi-zone buck permits. And I absolutely refuse to wear blaze orange to walk to the mailbox. So where do we go? Lose our minimum wages at the casino, or lose our self-respect at the Chippendales show in St. Cloud? It doesn't seem fair.

Signed, Once-a-Year Widow

Dear Once-a-Year:

You're missing the Big Show if you leave town. Opening weekend in Nimrod is the World's Fair, Mardi Gras, and Winter Olympics combined. Put away your aprons and have Hunters Supper at the Senior Center. Grab a ruler and measure the grins for big buck trophy weigh-ins at GB's Auto Glass. Slip on some shades to protect your eyes from orange glare at the R&R on Saturday night. Practice your Shania Twain and be a karaoke star. Wear steel-toed shoes if you feel like dancing. You don't have to be a great conversationalist. Just ask the closest guy "Did you have any luck?" and be prepared for a two-hour monologue. You'll go home richer and wiser. You may smell like buck scent, but you'll be richer and wiser.

THE GOOD SHEPHERD

I HEARD ABOUT JP (JEAN PIERRE) Arretche years ago in a passing reference to the Basque sheep farmer who lived north of town. Nothing jelled until I met Carolyn Pulju at her auction last spring. "You'd enjoy him," Carolyn said. "And he's an interesting man to write about." He's also Carolyn's brother-in-law.

The events of summer kept me busy, and the subject of JP took a back burner until fall, which is a busy time for sheep farmers. We finally got together, and it was worth the wait.

JP was born in December 1929 in Arneguy, an area of France that rubs shoulders (the Pyrenees mountains) with Spain. The term Basque is not a nationality or religion. It's a culture with its own traditions and language. "Basques have emigrated all over the globe," says JP. They congregate often, with an International Club get-together every five years. JP and Kathy attended a picnic this year in Chino, California, and the International Club celebration last year in Boise, Idaho.

The Basque language is Euskera, and was outlawed in the native land in an attempt to mainstream the Basque people into French and Spanish cultures. It has since re-emerged and is being taught in local schools. Basque cooking favors lamb and shepherd's bread. Basque spirits favor wine—sour red wine like Burgundy, flowing from a leather bag, or *chahaloa*. Basque music relies on the squeeze box. Basque sports include *hai alai* and hand ball. Entertainment includes tug-of-war and wood splitting. All of these are included in the annual celebrations which last three or four days.

MOTOR
OIL

JP emigrated to the United Staes in 1949 at the age of nineteen. He settled in California, was later joined by his brother, and resumed sheep farming. It was there that he met his future wife, Kathy, a Finnish lady from Menahga. They married, had two children and felt the pull back to Minnesota, where they returned in 1974.

JP raises sheep on 400 acres north of town. The flock of mixed Polypays and Suffolks numbers about 325. He raises oats and hay, and feeds 350 to 400 thousand-pound bales per winter. The sheep crop is wool, slaughter lambs, and mutton for the export market. The wool market is largely dependent on subsidies. Like the cattle market, the market for lambs and ewes is soft now. Lambs that brought over a dollar a pound in May/June were selling for forty-two cents in October.

JP enjoys his work, tends his flock like a good steward, and showers praise and affection on his dogs. Three Pyrenees dogs live with the sheep in pasture, protecting them and herding them. JP lost his oldest dog to a timber wolf this summer but is pleased with the replacement, a young pup named Lena.

JP also believes in the power of work and outdoor living to keep mind and body healthy. Raising sheep seems to be as much about therapy as it is about occupation. It will be shearing season soon, then lambing, then summer pasture. The cycle continues.

When we drive to the pasture, the dogs greet the pickup, and the sheep hover close, inquisitive. JP whistles a call, and the sheep congregate around him, like in the New Testament.

So, we have Kathy to thank for another rich ingredient to the cultural stew we call Nimrod. And we have an excellent local source for lamb chops.

SWINGING BRIDGE

EAST OF TOWN, ALONG THE CROW WING RIVER BANK, between Beaver Creek and North Lyons Cemetery, there lies a length of steel cable buried in the underbrush and extending into the river. The cable is a remnant of a footbridge that crossed the Crow Wing in the late 1930s. John Marshall has written about the swinging bridge in his 1994 book, *Tales from a Crow Wing Native*. There's not much that I can add to John's narrative, but it's an interesting piece of history and deserves retelling every decade or so.

The bridge, so the story goes, was built by the Watab Paper Company to serve their pulpwood cutter camp on the west side of the river. In summer, river crossing was by boat; in winter, by ice. That left early spring and late fall. The camp kids attended school at District 55 North, on the east side of the river. Ergo, a bridge, alternately called the swinging bridge, cable bridge, or footbridge.

The east terminus of the bridge was the Marshall homestead. (A small, rectangular, white blur on the photograph may be the Marshall house.) The bridge consisted of two steel cables, about one-inch in diameter, secured to tree trunks on eight-foot banks on either side of the river. Fastened to the cables were four-by-four spacers to which decking and handrail supports were attached. At this location, the river is an estimated 200 feet wide, and the arc of the cable nearly kissed the water on high river days. Imagine the thrill of crossing on a windy day on your way to school. Your right hand grasps the railing; your left hand clutches homework and a lunch pail. A dog runs after you, causing a vibration that resonates and amplifies under your feet, to the other side of the bridge. Who needs Stephen King?

The bridge, as related by the old timers who remember it, was built around 1937 and lasted only a couple years. Its fate is uncertain, but common speculation is that it was destroyed in a spring ice floe.

John Lyman remembers crossing the bridge and playing with pulpwood cutter camp kids—Dorothy, Margaret, and Joseph Ament—along with his twin sisters, Doris and Dorothy. Alice Oehlenschlager remembers teaching the Aments and other camp kids at District 55 North. Her memory is that Mr. Ament was the camp supervisor who contracted for timber for Watab. She recalls the kids' stories of howling coyotes as they walked to school through the woods, across the river, in pre-dawn darkness.

About a hundred feet upstream of the swinging bridge location is a shallow river area with gentle sloping banks on either side which served as a ford. Important, says John Marshall, because crossing the river with a team of horses and wagon was a challenge at best, life threatening at worst. John recalls a truck loaded with dogs in pens that crossed the river at the ford. He also recalls the difficulty of coaxing draft horses to pull a wagonload of hay up the bank.

The bridge was not only transportation. The figure on the far end of the bridge in the photograph is a man fishing. John remembers the big boys diving off the bridge, not a recommended sport considering the shallow water and rocky bottom.

Today, a clearing on the west bank suggests where the ford ended. A rotted tree trunk on the east bank suggests where the swinging bridge began. The cable may still be visible in the riverbed. Watch for it when canoeing three miles out of Nimrod, where the river turns east, right before the big island.

HORSE POWER

"GIDDYUP, OTIS. WAKE UP, JETHRO. Let's go. Let's go." LeRoy Peterick is rounding the barn with a team of eight Belgian draft horses, harnessed and ready for the Big Event. He drives past Bradley, the performing mule, and heads for the two-bottom plow. LeRoy is not a giant of a man, but he commands this seven tons of horse flesh with authority. His speech is in the high-decibel range, and carries across 160 acres of the Prancin' Paradise farm.

It's Draft Horse Field Day at the Mary and LeRoy Peterick farm, west of Nimrod, east of Sebeka. The event is sponsored by the Central Minnesota Draft Horse Club, their major public get-together and fund raiser for the year. It's a regional group of forty-four members, plus three new members Sunday. The club promotes draft horse farming but mostly acts as a living historic exposition in a time when working with horses is more sentimental than practical. The median age of the membership suggests that this group is an endangered species.

For today, the Draft Horse Club offers field work demonstrations, horse clinics, wagon rides, live music, games for the kids, crafts sales, door prizes, and lunch. The is the sixth year the Petericks have hosted the event. Mary counts 468 paid admissions, plus about half the membership and kids under twelve who are admitted free, for a grand total of about 600.

LeRoy is proceeding toward the plow with his eight-horse hitch. Club members descend on eveners, neck yokes, tug straps, reins, single trees, log chains—all the paraphernalia to hitch horsepower to the plow. That job done,

LeRoy hustles (his only pace) to the barn and reappears with four more harnessed Belgians, drives them behind the hitched-up eight. Club members tug at lines, move horses side to side, construct a twelve-horse hitch.

Meanwhile, more conventional two- and three-horse teams plow, combine, rake hay, dig potatoes, disc, and haul grain bundles for threshing. It's a warm August day. Warm, not hot. An occasional breeze. Not a cloud in the sky. Walking the field awakens memories. Plowed earth smells dry, fresh. Harnesses squeak, plow wheels creak, horses clop clop on the sod and in the furrow. The earth lifts gently, tips easily, crumbles. I feel the supple leather reins, smell horse sweat, hear the rhythm of the clopping hooves. I remember as a ten-year old carrying a Mason

jar of creamed and sugared coffee, wrapped in a dish towel and tucked in a syrup pail, to my dad as he plowed. I remember as a sixteen-year old, plowing behind a team myself.

Paul Nelson of Battle Lake mans the threshing machine. Lawrence Adensam of Carlos has his team hitched to a 1935 restored Case plow. Both are in their mid-eighties, alert and agile. Paul watches the threshing machine gears, tunes his ears for the first sound of trouble. He climbs the side of the grain wagon, fingers the kernels of wheat pouring from the chute, pronounces them ripe, clean. Lawrence, a twenty-year club member, chats with neighbors, drives his team of Belgians, Mike and Prince, with ease. "They lead an easy life," he says. "Some parades, some field days, some sleigh rides."

LeRoy has the twelve-horse team hitched to his satisfaction, and club members clear the area. LeRoy yells the commands. "Giddyup, Otis. Wake up, Jethro. Come on, Mabel, Winnie, Fritz." The team comes to attention, moves forward. There's a lot that can go wrong here, and LeRoy isn't spared that probability. But after a couple "whoa's" and a few adjustments, the team is on the field plowing like a twelve-horsepower machine. As I watch field repairs, I wonder how farmers survived before the invention of baling wire, bungee cords, and duct tape.

Monday, following the Field Day event, Mary and LeRoy are tired, happy that it's over, gratified with the turnout. LeRoy bemoans the missteps of the day —the prong turned wrong on the horseshoe he forged; the broken shear pin on the baler; the "haw" when he should have "gee'd" in the twelve-horse hitch plowing demo. "Everything I touched turned to shit," he says in true horse farmer talk.

Maybe so, LeRoy. But it was a great day for us spectators, reliving old memories, making new ones.

FOWL PLAY

Memo to File
Subject: Turkey Give-away Contest in Nimrod

THIS OFFICE WAS NOTIFIED BY AN ANONYMOUS CALLER of alleged improprieties in the Thanksgiving turkey giveaway contest conducted at the R&R Bar & Grill. Allegations and findings include reproduction of printed turkey coupons, stuffing of sponsor's drawing box, unmonitored drawing of the winning coupon, and improper destruction of coupons.

Background: The *Review Messenger* conducts an annual Turkey Giveaway one week before Thanksgiving where local sponsors are featured in a two-page ad. A turkey coupon is imprinted with the local sponsor's name, to which the contestant adds his/her name and drops it in the participating sponsor's box. There is no mention in the ad of the legitimacy of mechanically reproduced coupons, the procedures for selecting the winner, or the role of an oversight committee to monitor contest conduct. However, it is the custom that three village elders be present at the contest site. Their duties have traditionally been to monitor procedures, select the winner, and secure the submitted coupons. No mention is made of qualifications of said elders, except that they be able to count to fifty. By ones.

Statement of Fact: Margaret Rathcke, Clerk of the City of Nimrod, did, in fact, fill out a coupon with the R&R Bar & Grill imprimatur and deposit it in the sponsor's drawing box. At the appointed hour, 12:00 noon on November 23, 2002, a representative of the sponsor, one Ruth (Mrs. Robert) Stahl, did, in fact, draw a coupon. Ms Stahl is reported to have announced the winner's name, "Margaret Rathcke." Ms Stahl did not show the winning entry to any employee or customer. Instead, she crumpled the coupon, returned it to the box of entry coupons, and disposed of the box in a bag of used pull tabs.

An employee of the Bar & Grill, one Deloris Marie Shore of Nimrod, Minnesota, inquired about the results of the drawing upon arriving for work the following morning, Sunday, November 24. Patrons of the R&R report a look of shock on the face of said Deloris Shore upon hearing the name of the winner, and a conduct suggesting ennui and delirium, prompting a patron at the men's coffee table to misaddress her as "Delerium."

Later on November 24, this office received an anonymous phone tip of contest irregularities. Upon investigation, the contest coupons were located in the sixth of seven garbage barrels outside the R&R. There was no indication of attempted coupon destruction, alteration, or mutilation. The box contained fifty coupons, a large amount considering the population of Nimrod is seventy-five. (It was later determined that seven of the fifty were first-time customers.) Upon examination, it was revealed that the turkey coupon printed in the newspaper had been mechanically reproduced, and the names "Bill" and "Tony" entered on forty-three of the coupons, along with a telephone number which later proved to be that of the employee, Ms Shore. (Contest rules prohibit employees of participating merchants to enter the contest in their employer's store.)

Conclusion: Mrs. Margaret Rathcke, the name on the coupon drawn, did, in fact, claim her prize and did, in fact, prepare and serve the winning bird to her family and guests on Thanksgiving Day. Guests reported no reluctance, anxiety, or misgivings as Mrs. Rathcke presented the entrée, roasted to a golden brown, stuffed with a chestnut dressing, and served with garlic mashed potatoes and giblet gravy.

Ms Shore declined to be interviewed for this article. After a Thanksgiving dinner of honey baked ham and candied sweet potatoes, she is reported to have discussed her allegations of contest impropriety with the Wadena County chapter of the National Turkey Federation and the ACLU.

Margaret Rathcke's recipe for chestnut dressing and Deloris Shore's recipe for candied sweet potatoes can be found at this office's website:

www.turkeyspoof.com.

FOREIGN POLICY AND THE THERAPY OF HORSEBACK RIDING

FEELINGS AROUND NIMROD likely mirrored those of the nation after the terrorist attacks in New York City and Washington, D.C. Shock, anger, fear, grief, sympathy, anxiety, revenge, resolve, forgiveness. The unthinkable had happened, and the loss of life, the physical destruction, the economic impact will long be measured. This is certain: we are a resilient people, we will survive. Life goes on.

And life did go on, per plan, at the fall Huntersville Trail Ride. For thirty-six years, the Moonlight Trail Riders have planned and hosted a gathering of six-hundred (more or less) horses and riders, teams and drivers, cooks, campers, and campfire philosophers. Folks arrived as early as Thursday to claim their favorite spots in the campground in Huntersville State Forest, behind the Outpost. The gate officially opened Friday.

It's a weekend of total outdoor living—camping in tents and trailers, cooking over fires, random and organized trail riding and driving. If you're looking for peace and quiet and privacy, keep on truckin'. The twenty-five-acre campground houses three hundred trailers, corrals, temporary living quarters, western goods vendors, and a dining/dancing hall. Looking at the crowded campground, you realize how we take freedom of assembly for granted.

The Big Ride begins at 1:00 P.M. on Saturday. The day started with a light rain along the river. By noon, it was dry but cool and overcast. A great day for riding. No bugs, no hot sun, no sweating horses. We declined the four-hour official trail ride and hitched an abbreviated ride on the Pederson wagon train. Leaves are slow to turn color this year. No sun spotlighted the occasional red sumac. But the early rain agitated the humus, dampened the pines, charged the trails with the smell of fall. Mix that with smoke of burning jack pine wafting from campfires. Four military transport aircraft flying in low formation interrupted the moment, recalled world affairs.

The Huntersville State Forest is dissected by miles of gravel roads, minimum maintenance roads, logging trails, and riding/hiking trails. It engenders a feeling of isolation, insulation against harsh reality. It may have been the perfect antidote for troubled souls.

Sunday, the wagon master broke camp early for the ride and drive to Shell River campground, in time for the noon turkey dinner. Doris Burgau, sons Gary and Ron, and the Moonlight Trail Riders roasted twenty-seven turkeys on spits, prepared to serve Sunday dinner for four hundred hungry campers and riders. "We've done this every year, except 1976," Doris said. "That was the year of the big fires." The turkey was tasty, the helpings generous, the conversation spirited. Whoever said, "Food tastes better outside," was right. The ambiance of the camp-

ground, the overall feeling of well-being, the irony of the conflict between last Tuesday (September 11) and this Sunday were not lost on the diners.

So, life goes on. The trail ahead is rough. We will recover. Labeling the terrorist incident a wake-up call seems dismissive. But the attack does remind us of our vulnerability. Despite the sophistication of a Star Wars Defense System, a mean-spirited David armed only with a jackknife can wreck havoc on a well-intentioned Goliath.

What is our reaction? How do we accommodate this new reality? Again, my hope is for a thoughtful, measured response. What is the basis for this hatred against the United States? What profound grievances do people harbor that justify sacrificing their lives and the lives of thousands of innocent people? It's more than a difference in cultural values. Perhaps it's time for a show of strength. Perhaps it's also time for a moral inventory and analysis of Mideast foreign policy.

And perhaps it's time for a weekend respite, sitting on a horse or wagon in Huntersville State Park. This lifestyle, this country is good, worth preserving. Thanks to the Moonlight Trail Riders for the distraction.

NIKE
RED, WHITE & BLUE
IN 2002
NIMROD JUBILEE DAYS
NIMROD, MN - POPULATION 69
Bite Me

FOREIGN EXCHANGE

IMAGINE THAT YOU'RE IN YOUR EARLY THIRTIES. You've traveled four continents. You're multi-lingual and speak the Queen's English with just a hint of French accent. You hold a master's degree in business administration. You've sold your pharmaceutical consulting business in Bombay, and you're en route to Paris to open a branch office. But first, you decide to take a holiday. Where do you go? The Great Barrier Reef? Bali? New York City? How about Nimrod, Minnesota?

That's the story of Dominique Yon. Dominique was a guest of host family Glenda and Harold Gilster in July 1985, part of the North American Cultural Exchange League Program (NACELP). He stayed one month with the Gilsters, and their hospitality and the farm experience made an indelible impression. Seventeen years later, he returned for David and Karlene's wedding.

NACELP introduced students of other countries to host families in the United States, with the student paying an administrative fee and transportation. Dominique spent three summers in the United States—in a Detroit suburb, in Nimrod, and in a Dallas suburb. "The Nimrod experience was the richest," he says. How was it richer? "Just being outdoors," he adds. "Helping Harold and David on the farm. Loading hay bales. Milking cows." That, and the love and care that the Gilsters provided.

Dominique had limited farm experience before his visit. His grandfather owns land in the west of France, mostly forested. Dominique spent summers there, clearing brush and trimming trees. The Gilster farm was his first experience on a dairy farm. He remembers the pleasure of drinking fresh milk. He remembers the rich ice cream.

Looking through the family photo album for that summer, it seems little has changed in seventeen years. The kids are older. Danny is taller than Glenda, a lot taller! The three-wheeled recreational vehicle has been replaced with a four-wheeler. The pictures at Itasca State Park could have been taken yesterday. Like the rest of us, Dominique was surprised to be able to step across the Mississippi River. The tubing and water skiing on Spider Lake, and the canoeing down the Crow Wing River are still summer pleasures.

Through the years, Dominique and the Gilsters have stayed in touch through letters and Christmas cards. Then came an invitation to Karlene and David's wedding. Dominique was preparing to leave Bombay for Paris and decided to take a holiday, half way around the planet. His visit was a surprise to David, one that Glenda had trouble containing. He surfaced in front of a shocked David on Friday night at the groom's dinner.

What has changed in Nimrod in seventeen years? "Surprisingly little," Dominique says. "The farm is the same. Glenda and Harold are the same. I feel I could come back anytime. We didn't spend much time uptown during my visit in 1985, but I didn't notice much change there either."

So, chalk up one more for Nimrod hospitality. And, while you're at it, chalk up one for Karlene and David's wedding ceremony, reception, and dance. Some highlights: Church bells calling on a warm, sunny September afternoon. David walking down the aisle, yellow rose in hand, looking for Grandmother. Karlene reciting her vows with sincerity and resoluteness. The smile on the proud father of the bride in the reception line. The hundreds of family, friends, and neighbors congratulating the bride and groom. Jean Nielson's delicious homemade wedding cake. The gleaming white, horse-drawn wedding carriage. The wedding square dance.

It was a great day, worth traveling half way around the planet for. Nimrod hospitality and celebrations are world class. As they say in the old song, "How you gonna keep them down in Paris, after they've seen the farm?"

FIELD OF DREAMS: 2002

THE 2002 BASEBALL SEASON CAME TO A HALT SUNDAY when the Nimrod Gnats lost to the Milroy Yankees at the State Tournament in St. Cloud. It was the Gnat's third visit to State in four years. Pretty good for a small town team. And who considers it a disgrace to lose to the Yankees?

The game got started on the wrong foot when the announcer introduced the Gnats and ignored the batboy, Paul Funk. Paul was miffed but joined the team on the field anyway. And that was only the beginning. The announcer, clearly not Finnish, butchered "Tuorila," making it sound like "tequila" or "Tijuana." Later, he announced #8, our Steve Funk, as substitute pitcher for the Yankees. So much for Junior Achievement in broadcasting.

The first pitch left the mound at 8:30, one hour later than scheduled, under the lights at Faber Field. It was a great night for baseball. The outfield was groomed like Hazeltine National Golf Course. The Nimrod contingent of fans was on hand, with five times the decibels that Milroy fans could muster. We could have used Mark Schermerhorn to heckle the Yankee pitcher who, unfettered, delivered a fastball at the speed of light.

It was a pitcher's duel for the first few innings, and then Milroy started scoring in the top of the sixth, as I recall. There was professional-grade pitching and catching, powerful hitting, and dramatic fielding by both teams. Greg Crabb defined poise and stamina. The Gnats had the bases loaded at one point; the hometown crowd was on its feet, but, like a good intention, it just got away. The Gnats couldn't muster a rally.

At the ninth inning, with the score 8 to 1 in favor of Milroy, and two outs, we watched the fat lady get to her feet. Nate Erickson took a call strike; the fat lady grabbed the microphone. Strike two; she arranged her music. Strike three; she sang. End of season.

Team manager Charlie Tuorila had good words for the team after it was over. "They went further than I thought they'd go," Charlie said, "especially after the six-game mid-season losing streak. But they came back, like true champs, in the late season. They were at the top of their game in the league and regional tournaments." Charlie commented on the big strike zone that the state tourney umpire defined. He ascribed some of the faulty fielding to inexperience in playing under lights.

Catcher "Hank" Aaron Funk was less sanguine. "You have to swing to get a hit," he said. "You can't watch the ball go by and let the umpire call a strike, and lose the game for you."

So, what's next? In 2002, the Nimrod Gnat fans and players constructed a covered bleacher section. In 2003, we will have a sprinklered ball park. Other capital improvements are incubating—a lighted field, extended bleacher seating over dugouts, nets replacing wire screen in front of the side bleachers. The team and the town owe a big debt of gratitude to the volunteers who donated hours of labor and tons of material to get the park in its present shape.

During Jubilee Days, the Baseball Association will sponsor a softball tourney to keep funds rolling in. I suspect we will be playing bingo and eating spaghetti suppers this winter to give the rest of us a chance to show team support. An Operation Round-Up grant from Todd Wadena Electric would look good, especially if the funds went for a co-op electrically lighted field. How much money do they have?

A few more words about the fans. Charlie is unabashed in his praise for community support of the team. The players admit that, by George, it does make a difference with all that hooting and hollering emanating from the bleachers. Sitting among them, I feel their ownership in the team, their rises and falls as the team does well and doesn't. As we say in Minnesota, wait until next year. Thanks coach, team, and fans for a fun season.

NIMROD'S CCC CAMP

A HUNDRED YARDS DOWNSTREAM FROM FRAME'S LANDING on the Crow Wing River is a building foundation. It measures twenty-four by seventy-two feet, has about three feet of exposed concrete, and is filled with hazelnut brush and a half dozen jackpines. During its life in the 1930s, it was a mess hall for the Civilian Conservation Corps (CCC) camp, Company 2704.

CCC was newly elected President Franklin D. Roosevelt's first program to deal with two Depression problems—unemployment of young men and destruction of natural resources. The bill authorizing CCC was introduced on March 27, 1933, to both the House and the Senate, and was on the president's desk for signature four days later, on March 31, 1933. President Roosevelt promised that, given emergency powers, he would have 250,000 young men in camps by July 31, 1933. The first man was inducted on April 7, thirty-seven days after FDR's inauguration. By June 1933, 80,000 men were established in 400 camps, with 155,000 more in conditioning camps. Inductees arrived at forest camps at the rate of 90,000 a day.

One of those camps was at Nimrod. Company 2704 (Project # PE-136) was occupied by August 23, 1934. Land for the camp was donated by Minnie Frame, after the requisite government land survey. Elmer Olson worked on camp construction.

Details of the Nimrod camp are sketchy, but a typical camp housed 200 young men between ages of eighteen and twenty-four. Administration and supervision was by U.S. Army personnel. A camp consisted of eight barracks, a mess hall, office, combined day room and post exchange (PX), clinic, motor pool, and activity rooms.

CCC was designed to employ young men and, secondarily, to provide training. Wages were thirty dollars a month, of which twenty-five was sent to the enrollee's family. Five dollars a month doesn't sound like an impetus to the local economy, but multiplied by 200 men, it's $1,000. In 1934, that was big bucks.

Unemployment was highest on the East Coast, and the land to be tamed or reclaimed tended to be in the central or western states. There was a stated goal of keeping inductees in their own states, but many young men found their way westward. Typical projects in Minnesota included brush removal, trail clearing and maintenance, and clearing woodlots of dead trees. In other states, camps fought forest fires, built sandbag dikes for flood control and cleaned up after hurricanes.

Jerry Schermerhorn recalls the two-ton trucks with workers riding in the back, heading for job sites. He was a third grader at District 21-2 at the time. He remembers the signature blue denim caps that the workers wore as part of their uniforms.

John Marshall remembers that the local camp cleared a fire lane through the family farm and built a dam on Beaver Creek.

Life in the camp was regimented, like life in the army. The day started with six o'clock reveille when the troops rolled out for morning roll call, marched to the commons, and fell out in a race to the mess hall for breakfast. Work details began at eight o'clock. Dinner was packed and served at the job site. The work day concluded at four o'clock. Retreat sounded at six, followed by supper. Evenings were spent playing ping pong or poker, listening to the Jack Benny show, taking a training class, or getting a pass and heading for town.

Clara Frame remembers camp supervisors coming to the farm to buy milk. One of the supervisors, a big Indian man, made quite an impression on the Frame kids. The inclusion of Indians in CCC was the result of an amendment to the original bill. In 1933, the first extended enlistment resulted in 14,000 Indians inducted in CCC camps. By the time the CCC camps terminated, 80,000 Indians had served.

News from the camps to the home front was welcome, and good. The twenty-five-dollar monthly allotment returned to the families stimulated local economies. Camp personnel learned skills, worked hard, and ate heartily. Millions of trees were planted, roads were built, telephone lines strung, and millions of acres of state and federal lands were improved.

Florence Lewis recalls that her late husband, Lloyd, enrolled in the CCC on July 2, 1936, at age eighteen and was discharged three years later on March 31,

1939. Lloyd served at Camp Paul Bunyan #2708 at Nevis, and Company #2703 in Park Rapids. He has certificates for classes in surveying, telephone line construction, and first aid.

Minnesota was in the Seventh Corps Area, along with Arkansas, Iowa, Kansas, Missouri, Nebraska, and North and South Dakota. There were 30,000 CCC workers and 154 camps in the Seventh Corps. Minnesota had sixty-one camps.

Harold Metteer served two terms in the CCC from 1939 to 1942, not in Minnesota, but in South Dakota. In typical Harold fashion, he fudged his way in at age seventeen. Harold served with companies out of Chamberlain and Fort Meade. At Chamberlain, they rip-rapped the banks of the Missouri River, built stock dams, and reconstructed fences. At Fort Meade, they cleared brush and spread crushed rock for the parking areas at Custer Park and Sylvan Lake. Harold did well with his thirty dollars a month salary. He bought a used 1935 Ford sedan for $425. He was discharged in March 1942 and enlisted in the U.S. Army.

The Civilian Conservation Corps lost congressional support and funding in 1942. By then, the United States had entered World War II, funds for domestic programs were scarce, and unemployment was not an issue. All that remained were trails, cleared and replanted forests, parks, and controlled waterways; young men trained in the discipline of the work world; and an empty concrete foundation along the Crow Wing River, the last remnant of Nimrod's Company #2704.

EDGE OF OCTOBER

EARLY MORNING, LATE OCTOBER. Grass is silver plated. A smoky haze rises from the river, softens the tree line. Yellow morning sun sifts through trees that are black, stark, barren. A sliver of moon smiles a tilted grin. Crows call. The air is crisp, and, breathing it, I breathe the edge of autumn, the leading cusp of winter.

Twenty-five degrees with a forecast of fifty. A good day to cut firewood.

And that's what we do. With an assist from my son and grandson and their friends, we fell, cut, load, and haul firewood.

We cut within one-hundred yards of the farmstead. Oaks died around the horse feeders. Summer winds snapped the tops of jackpines. One tree in a birch clump shed its leaves prematurely. Bolts of ash lay where Henry Butzin felled them, crooked and unusable for lumber. Popple surrendered to the tromping of Highlanders in the corral. We have a smorgasbord of firewood.

There is rhythm to wood cutting when I cut alone. My back lasts as long as a chain saw tank of gas. Then there's the loading and a breather trip to the woodpile. Then unloading, the breather trip back, and I'm ready for another load. Not so with a team of wood cutters. The rhythm comes in teamwork— one felling, two limbing and cutting, and the boys hauling.

As the day wears on, jackets give way to shirts, and shirts give way to T-shirts. The sun is bright. The sky, clear. Wind, the bane of sawyers, keeps its distance.

Horses mosey over to the wood cutting, inquisitive or mourning the loss of a scratching post. This is where they hang out in the summer, in the clearing, standing front to back, swishing flies. This is where they feed in the winter. I think about harnessing one of the draft horses to pull logs. But only for a moment. The four-wheeler and trailer are faster, more efficient. And we have only this weekend.

It's break time, and the saws are quiet. Hot coffee tastes good; so does a cold one. There's a racket in all directions. Hunters calibrate rifle sights, practice a smooth trigger pull, expend last year's ammunition. The sounds of October.

And the smells of October. The fallen oak, "Sweet-scented stuff when the breeze drew across it," Robert Frost wrote. The turpentine smell of jackpine. The musty smell of last year's ash cutting, lying on the forest floor.

I muse for a moment in memories of wood cutting as a boy. It's winter, and my dad is driving a bobsled behind a matched team of draft horses. My dad and I aren't well matched on either side of a crosscut saw. "Pull," he says. "Don't push." We drop trees by hand, cut them into liftable eight-foot lengths, and load them on the bobsled for the ride home. I'm warm, sweaty from work. Now the sweat evaporates and chills me. My feet feel like they're frozen. "Walk awhile," my dad says.

Then, there's the wood-making party, with the saw rig powered by the tractor. The belt slaps as the tractor revs up. The blade hums a low moan, then screams to a higher, higher pitch, and settles at high C. Two, three men lift a log to the gleaming blade, push it forward. The blade moans. One man catches the stove-length chunks, heaves them to the woodpile. Sawdust cascades down a hill beneath the blade. Inside the house, there's the smell of roast beef and mincemeat pie.

For now, I admire the woodpile, ready to split and stack, and I know what my dad felt when the hay barn was full to the rafters, the crib bulging with corn. And my mother's admiration of her rows of canned apple sauce, beans, tomatoes, in Mason jars in the cellar. Ready for winter.

I decide to try my arm at splitting. The six-pound maul makes it child's play. Jackpine opens clean, clear. I stoke the fireplace. The fire looks inviting, smells enticing, burns warm, relaxing. Weatherman talks of snow in Ely. Let it come.

NIMROD: CENTER OF THE UNIVERSE

COULDN'T FIND ANYTHING TO DO this past weekend? Unbelievable. Saturday got into high gear with an eightieth birthday party for a beaming Marcy Shore, surrounded by kids, grandkids, and great-grandkids. There was the Sarah Funk/Miles Kuschel wedding, reception, and dance, forging a new Nimrod dynasty of two fine families. Then, the postponed Gnats baseball game on Sunday, with the Gnats bringing home the Regional Championship trophy! Concurrently, there was the two-day Old Wah-de-nah Rendezvous. For those who felt like partying, second tier suburb Leader invited us to their fourth annual Bear Growl festival. Did anybody make it to work Monday?

The Old Wah-de-nah Rendezvous is sponsored by WHELP (Wadena Historic and Education Learning Program) with a big assist from the Crow Wing Muzzle Loaders. The Muzzle Loaders are a group of about twenty-five old-timers who were born about 150 years too late. They re-enact the lives of mountain men, hunters, and trappers wearing handmade period costumes and brandishing an arsenal of handmade equipment, tools, and weapons. The Rendezvous is one of two activities for the group each year, the other being at Voyagers Village in Crow Wing State Park. They are an engaging bunch of guys—talented, humorous, informative. The craftsmanship of their metal- and wood-working is a treat to an eye accustomed to mass production.

Leroy Peterick was on hand with his four-horse Belgian hitch and stage coach for tours around the park, not at a leisurely walk, but often at a brisk gallop.

Lyle Bradly, a Lewis & Clark historian, told the tale of that famous expedition. He told it from the point of view of one of the exploration team, a carpenter who journaled religiously and was the first to hit publication with his account of the journey when the expedition returned east in 1805. We might have enjoyed a little revisionist history here, with Lewis & Clark heading north when they reached the Mississippi, and west when they hit the Crow Wing, stopping at Nimrod for directions. Instead, Bradly stuck with the facts and made it interesting anyway.

Raven Woman, a.k.a. Helen Lindeman, demonstrated traditional Ojibwe life with her clothing, cooking, shelter, herbal remedies, lore, and old style dances. Part of her exhibit was a rounded rock, the wise, protector, grandfather image. Rock, the oldest element on the planet, symbolizing age and wisdom. giving new meaning to the phrase dumb as a rock.

Northwind Crossing, a five member Celtic band, provided musical entertainment with sixteen instruments, plus voices. Fifteen Oshkii Anishinaabeg Native American dancers moved to the beat of six drummers in a traditional program including the grass dance and a modern program featuring the shawl dance, which welcomed Native American military personnel home from World War II and Vietnam.

There were tours of the settlement, the trading post, and the Indian battlefield; a hands-on basket weaving demonstration; authentic early American food; and (are you ready?) a karaoke singer. Somehow it all come together. Somehow it worked.

The Old Wah-de-nah Rendezvous is an annual celebration at Old Wadena Park on the second weekend of August. A special thanks to our one-man County Park Department, Glen Motzko, for a well-groomed site. And thanks to the volunteers—WHELP personnel, Muzzle Loaders, Mounted Posse, Boy Scout Troop 61, for making it happen. Watch for an increase in interest in this period of our history as we approach the bicentennial of the Lewis & Clark expedition in 2003.

Better have a quiet week, because next weekend is a busy one too, with the County Fair, another eightieth birthday and the beginning of the State Baseball Tournament. Go Gnats!

MISS MINNESOTA FROM NIMROD?

THE BEST PART OF THIS JOB IS THE PEOPLE I meet and the places I go, under the guise of journalism. Like interviewing a Civil War veteran's daughter, climbing the DNR smoke watch tower, or judging a karaoke contest. Today, we take the thrill factor to new heights. I interview the Nimrod candidate for the title of Miss Minnesota, U.S.A., Rachel Richards.

Let me put this in perspective. Rachel is twenty; I am sixty-eight, have a granddaughter almost as old as Rachel. But I still get that ticklish feeling, and for that I'm grateful. Having said that, on with the story.

Rachel was asked by Image One, a model and talent agency in St. Cloud who holds her modeling portfolio, to consider the Miss U.S.A. competition. She had two pageants behind her, one being the Miss Nimrod pageant in 1998. She found herself at ease in front of people. She said yes. She was one of thirty-four contestants who competed in Eagen and Apple Valley on Saturday and Sunday.

In the preliminaries on Saturday, she was interviewed by seven judges. "I nailed a couple questions," says Rachel. "But I blew a big one. One of the judges asked if I would consider moving to New York or Los Angeles. My answer was no; my future is in Minnesota. I thought later that if I made it all the way to Miss U.S.A., I would have to be in New York and Los Angeles." Well, Rachel, your answer may have been wrong in the short run, but it was right in the long run.

Saturday night's program included a quick walk-on, plus swimsuit and evening gown appearances. Any trouble appearing in front of 670 people wearing

a bathing suit, heels, and a million dollar smile? "No," she says. "I was more comfortable in the swimsuit than I was in the evening gown." I didn't see her Saturday night, but I did see her at the Nimrod tubing party this summer, where she looked perfectly comfortable in a bathing suit. But I digress.

Sunday night, the finals. Another walk-on, a short introduction of each contestant by the emcee, accompanied by a warm smile from the contestant. The top ten finalists are named. Rachel misses the cut. Then there's another swim suit and evening gown appearance before Miss Minnesota, U.S.A., is named.

Was it a good experience? "Definitely," says Rachel. "'I learned a lot about posture, the right walk, how to carry myself. I'd be willing to do it again next year." What would you do differently? "I'd spend more time toning my body." (What's left to tone? I think, but I don't go there.) I asked Rachel what town she mentioned as her hometown on the application. "Nimrod," she says, no hesitation. Good! It's time we all stop apologizing for the name. A little uneasiness, yes. But no more apologies.

So, we have a local gal who is still on cloud nine after an exciting weekend in the fast lane beauty business. Now it's back to the working world of training and exercising horses at Los Gauchos ranch, north of Nimrod. Rachel is a second year student at Central Lakes college in Brainerd, with a Dental Hygienist major. She took a break from school and plans to resume next quarter.

Rachel asked me to mention her appreciation to all the sponsors who made it possible for her to compete. And thanks to the sponsors from the rest of us too, for spreading the word that Nimrod U.S.A. has other world-class qualities besides canoeing, deer hunting, and the Nimrod Gnats baseball team. We also have world class beauties.

LITTLE WHITE CHURCH IN THE VALE

MAYNARD BENSON REMEMBERS attending Our Savior's Lutheran Church on what is now County Highway 9. His grandparents, Ann and Mike Benson, had funeral services there in 1949 when Maynard was ten. He remembers the church tucked back in the woods, a quarter mile off the road.

Eighteen charter member families organized the congregation in 1896 and held services in their homes until the church was built in 1902. With a strong Norwegian membership, the church was called Var Friesers Norsk Lutherske Menighed, which translates to Our Savior's.

From the church journal of 1902, the following expenses are recorded:

10,000 shingles	$15.00
Shingle nails	.20
Paint	.35
Dower Lumber Co.	35.00

In 1904, the church purchased a box stove for $8.50 plus freight of sixty-six cents and stove pipe for fifteen cents.

Florence Bounds, daughter of church members Josephine and Nels Thompson, also remembers the church. Her family moved to Bullard Township, where son Willys now resides, and joined Our Savior's in 1901. Nels Thompson was one of the volunteer carpenters who helped build the church. Another brother, Alfred, died at age twelve, and is the first person to be buried in West Lyons Cemetery.

Many of the surnames of founding families are familiar:

J.O. Baklund	Charles F. Larson	Olaff Westberg
Thore P. Dahlvang	John Olson	Iver Otteson
Nils J. Clauson	Elias Sonmor	Ole Iverson
Olaus M. Olson	E.O. Ekelund	Lars J. Clauson
Emil Johnson	Andrew Raise	Jorgan N. Hanson
Paul P. Dahlvang	Ole Johnson	Peder Johnson

The first pastor was Carl Amundson; Pastor Carl Norum served from 1897 to 1900. Florence was baptized by Pastor Amundson and confirmed by the pastor of longest service, Edmund Holland, who served from 1914 to 1939. Florence remembers services every Sunday at 2:30. Pastor Holland, a Sebeka farmer, drove a team to a morning service in Leader, then to Our Savior's for an afternoon service. He served without salary to keep the church operating, and accepted the offering, whatever it was.

All five children of Florence and husband Claude Bounds were baptized by Reverend Holland. Florence remembers the spring picnics on Constitution Day, May 17. She remembers pie and ice cream socials, and embroidered dish towel and apron sales. At Christmas, there was an evening program, where bible pieces were recited and candy and apples were given to the kids. Florence remembers Reverend Holland as a good preacher.

Reverend Holland died suddenly of pneumonia at age fifty-seven in the year 1940. The church continued to operate under Reverend Berg of Sebeka and closed in the late forties, after Nels Thompson died. From then, it served as a part-time church and a location for Ladies Aid meetings until it was dismantled and sold. The furniture went to a church in Thomastown; the building was sold to Charlie and Dorothy Hillig, who salvaged the lumber for use in their house. Sale proceeds went to Augsburg College.

Elsie (Mrs. Art) Riley remembers that her step-daughter Ione was baptized in Our Savior's. Art's first wife died when Ione was nine. Mrs. Riley's funeral was at Our Savior's, and she is buried at West Lyons Cemetery. Ione remembers the church tucked way back in the woods, which she dragged a doubting husband to see. On the day of their visit, the church was open, and Ione played the old pump organ, which still sounded good.

Now, some fifty years later, Marjorie and Maynard Benson memorialized Our Savior's Church with a one-quarter scale model which sits along Highway 26 in West Lyons Cemetery. They commissioned Don Hagerman of Oylen to build the structure, and a hefty structure it is. The interior is yet to be finished and furnished. It also awaits permanent placement, as Maynard negotiates with Potlatch for a few feet on the west boundary of the cemetery plot. Once in place, Marjorie will concern herself with the interior and the landscaping.

Another piece of local history is commemorated and retained by the generosity of the Bensons. It is also commemorated by folks like Florence Bounds, who provided a copy of the *Ministeialbog*, a ledger of sorts, which records, in the original cursive, Our Savior's Lutheran Church activities from 1896 to 1947. That should be a boon to all genealogy aspirants. My copy of the ledger goes to the Wadena County Historical Society.

RENAISSANCE MAN

MENTION GEORGE GLOEGE, and what comes to mind? Canoe outfitter? Former academic? Golfer? Cross-country ski instructor and enthusiast? Runner? Husband and father? Fine arts painter? All of the above? The last choice.

George and Lee Gloege own and operate Gloege's Northern Sun Canoe Outfitters north of town on the Crow Wing River. George's academic career includes teaching political science, history, and geography in high schools and junior colleges in Ortonville, Williams, and Wadena, Minnesota. His golfing interests stretch to designing and building a "Cayman" golf course on his river front property and playing nine rounds at area golf courses this year. His cross-county skiing interests include instruction, equipment rental, ski trail design, competitive racing, and a hundred trips out on the boards last winter. His running includes thirteen marathons, including the Boston and Minneapolis, and four to five thousand miles of practice and exercise. His family includes his wife, Lee, plus a son and daughter. And his painting. . . .

George is a self-taught artist. He started painting in 1965, a few years before he moved to Nimrod. It was an interest and a talent he inherited from his mother. His early works were painted on canvas patches, then sides of tents, using latex house paints. He hung his finished work in the bunk house, back when Gloeges provided overnight, inside lodging for canoeing customers. In 1975, he switched to artist's tube paints and canvases.

He describes himself as a folk artist. His topics tend to reflect his interest in history, and there are primitive portraits of Presidents Washington and Lincoln, General Grant, and other Civil War military personnel. He may paint several blocks on one canvas—a portrait, an historic incident, a symbol, flag, or motto. And it sells.

George's art is internationally displayed. He has exhibited at galleries in Big Stone, Nevis, St. Louis, Montana's Red Lodge, Little Falls, New York Mills,

and New Ulm, and probably dozens more. Thanks to the Internet, his paintings are as likely to end up in Paris as they are in Perham.

George was granted exhibit space at New York Mills Regional Cultural Center in 1996. "It was good exposure," he says. He was encouraged to exhibit by Wadena's Kent Speer, and the show generated interest in his work and resulted in at least one sale. His latest exhibit was in Little Falls in 2001.

There's a fine line between folk art and primitive art. George puts an impressionistic spin on his representation of historic events, with an eye for color and design but not necessarily perspective or dimension. If Abraham Lincoln was tall in life, he is gangly towering in George's painting. George is a student of figures, and horses and the human form appear often on his canvases. He paints farm scenes reminiscent of his youth. I see steam engines, homage to his father who was a steam engine enthusiast. And there is a natural element present. Much of his work is set out of doors, in birch woods or on the river. Not surprising, considering his environment.

The paintings are created in "the warehouse" or studio, a separate building from the house, which was built by local talent in 1998-1999. It is a red pine structure with cedar above the logs, north facing windows, and steel roof. There is no telephone, no television, no intercom. Books, finished paintings, stretched canvases, tubes of paints, easels, and works in progress fill the space. The studio allows him to paint when he feels the urge, and walk away from it when he doesn't. Painting tends to be limited to the off-season for canoe rentals. With 125 canoes, six employees, a fleet of vans to transport canoeists, and a seven-day work week, there isn't much time for putting paint to canvas.

With the canoe season over for this year, George is back in the studio. His current painting is an impressionist interpretation of the North Dakota Badlands. He returned to the Badlands last week to paint on site, and to re-photograph the area. "I had many interested visitors who watched me work, and I got help from the local forest rangers," George said. He works on the painting as his muse dictates.

And what a busy muse he must have. Who's following whom? George following the muse, or his muse following him.

RIVERSIDE
GROCERY

RIVERSIDE GROCERY

SITUATION: THE KIDS CALL TO SAY they're dropping off the grandkids. You check the 'frig. The milk jug is low. You check the cupboard. No corn chips or Pepsi. You don't have time to run to Sebeka. Where do you go? To the Riverside Grocery in Nimrod. Although the inventory is limited, all the basic food groups are represented. If you can't buy it at the Riverside, you probably can get by without it.

Now, the Riverside has changed hands, and owner-operator Jeanne Tellock has tallied her last inventory. After fifteen years of purveying to locals and seasonal trade, she's ready for her next life.

The Riverside is one of our candidates for the National Register of Historic Buildings. It began life as the Bluegrass Creamery. When the Stigman Restaurant burned, the creamery building was moved onto the site and transformed into the Nimrod branch of the Sebeka Co-op Grocery, with Clara Frame at the helm as Assistant Manager and Verle Estabrooks as Gal Friday.

Nimrod was bustling then, with another grocery store owned by Lila and Pal Perkins, a creamery, shoe store, blacksmith shop, gas station, and two restaurants. Clara drove to the parent Co-op in Sebeka every other day to pick up fresh meat. In the backroom, she sold feed and candled eggs supplied by local farmers. The ninety-pound Verle is remembered for hoisting one-hundred-pound bags of feed onto pickup trucks.

Clara handed the managerial reins to Dick Rhodes. Ownership later transferred to Dave Chavez for eight years, then to Donna and Jim Metteer for three years, and finally to Jeanne and Dave Tellock on January 1, 1988.

"The building is essentially the same as when I bought it," says Jeanne, "except for the addition of the twelve-by-twenty-four walk-in cooler on the south side." Donna and Jim Metteer had enclosed the backroom feed sales area and resided the exterior.

With husband Dave Tellock an over-the-road truck driver, the store was Jeanne's baby. It had been her ambition to own and operate a Nimrod business. She looked for her niche and found it in the tourist trade—the canoeists and campers in the summer, and the hunters and snowmobilers in the fall and winter. Her sales ranged from a can of pop to a full grocery cart worth a hundred dollars. Riverside is also the Nimrod outlet for the *Review Messenger*, and Jeanne sells eighteen copies a week (or less if the "Nimrod Chronicles" article falls on its face).

"I've enjoyed running the store," says Jeanne. "I've been blessed with good local help, from Margaret Rathcke and Ardie Amundson in the beginning to LaNay Whitaker and Mary Burkness, the current employees." But it's time to move on. Like the ambition she had for a Nimrod business, Jeanne had another ambition to serve on the City Council. She held off for years because she was satisfied with city government. When Jerry Frame declined re-election, Jeanne filed for and won a seat. She serves with re-elected Mayor Larry Gilster, Secretary-Treasurer Lorraine Loween, Clerk Margaret Rathcke, and Councilmen Pat Rathcke and Lloyd Frederickson. Jeanne takes office at the January 2003 organizational meeting.

In the meantime, Linda and Dale Hillig expand their local holdings, and add the Riverside to their chain of businesses—Hillig Mercantile, Hillig Storage, Hillig Tube Rental, and Hillig Forest Products. Linda accepted the keys to the cash register on November 15.

"I don't intend to step in and change the world," says new Councilwoman Jeanne. And that's good. We like our world the way it is. Friendly businesses up and down Main Street that cash a check, stay open a few minutes after six to accommodate late shoppers, change a headlight while you wait, or hand-cancel your letters with the collectible Nimrod, Minnesota, postal seal. Thanks, Jeanne, for fifteen years of supplying the late gallon of milk for the grandkids, the extra can of kidney beans for the chili, and the big smile that comes with your, "Thank you" and my change.

WELCOME WAGON

IN THE PAST YEAR AND A HALF, three families have moved into the neighborhood on County 26, the Nimrod Tar, south of town. Your Chronicler is derelict in his duty to welcome these folks and introduce them to the community. Well, we rectified that this week with visits to the Erdmanns, the Gaschlers, and the Quirings.

Lorelei and David Erdmann are the proud owners of the former Beth and Joe Schmitt house. Theirs is a lifetime odyssey that began in Mankato, where they attended high school. Careers and marriages found them on opposite sides of the planet, but they kept in touch over the years. Lorelei taught in Mankato, moved to Alaska for a career, then to Texas to earn a master's degree, then returned to Ketchikan as a museum curator. David was in government service overseas and returned to Minnesota for an administrative stint at the Veteran's Administration hospital in Minneapolis. They connected at a forty-year class reunion. The rest, as they say, is history.

Lorelei's interests, travels, and talents are evident throughout the house. She collects art and antiques, paints, draws, and tats. David, maybe in self-defense, took up wood carving. He carves wildlife, flowers, and his current project, a life-size head of Christ in butternut. When not carving, David and Lorelei tend the property, thirty-nine acres bisected by the Cat River which ripples outside their living room window. They both love the wildlife and thrill to the visits of deer and songbirds.

David has a voracious appetite for novels—westerns and science fiction, and estimates about one thousand titles in his collection. If you want a Zane Gray, Louie L'Amour, or Max Brand western, David is likely to have it.

Their talents and interests intersect in the carving. David shapes the wood; Lorelei paints it. "She is tremendously talented," says David. And she cooks! Her current specialty is Chinese. No wonder that their home is taking on the trappings of a Bed and Breakfast.

Velda and Jim Gaschler bought the former Jerry Grewing house further down Highway 26. It has new siding and deck and a fenced front yard. The

Gaschlers moved from Colorado, where Jim was in the Adams County Sheriff's Department. They had vacationed in Perham years ago, and decided that this was where they wanted to settle. "It's a different world here," says Jim. "People are responsible, friendly, and they genuinely care."

Velda and Jim have ten acres, and don't be surprised if they turn it into a menagerie. Both of them love animals. Max and Shadow, the two dogs, are *bone fide* members of the family. Two cats have the run of the house. Jim helps neighbors Nancy and Denny Benson with cattle feeding chores, although he has no background in farming. Like the Erdmanns, Jim and Velda are on constant watch for deer, raccoons, and squirrels. The sight of an eagle soaring above makes the move worthwhile.

Velda and Jim are avid fishermen and have met neighbors on area lakes. They fish summer and winter. Spear fishing with Harry Grewing was a first for Velda.

They had heard, of course, the legends of Minnesota winters that last for years, and mosquitoes the size of sparrows. And their Colorado friends and family still expect them to tire of Minnesota and return. "No so!" they both say.

Velda spends her time refinishing and decorating the house. Jim is a woodworker and built the furnishings. Jim's metabolism matches that of a sheriff more than that of a retiree. He calls himself a marble in a pail, always rolling around. Give him a couple years, and he'll pick up the Nimrod tempo.

Delores and Rodney Quiring are hardly newcomers, with Delores graduating from Sebeka and Rodney from Staples. They have lived in Wadena County for years, with one short detour in Texas, and finally found their hobby farm, the

twenty acre former Linda and Dale Hillig home. Again, attached garage converted to a family room, new siding, and a new deck.

Delores knows many of the neighbors and sees them regularly at Fix's Family Foods in Wadena, where she is a checkout cashier and new employee trainer. Rodney is with Mid-State Insulation in Park Rapids.

When Delores isn't punching pads on her new keyboard cash register, she crafts silk flowers and grows the real thing in summer. Rodney is another fisherman, but also has a more expensive hobby—restoring a 1965 Mustang in his heated (and insulated) garage.

Of their total five children, only Mathew, a sophomore at Sebeka High School, is still at home.

Most of the Hillig outbuilding are uninhabited, but the Quirings do have three geese and seven chickens, purchased at a Wadena flea market. Sounds kind of like Nimrod, don't you think?

So there they are. Three new families offering their own unique flavor to the Nimrod stew. A belated welcome, folks. You must know that the quickest way to integrate into Nimrod is to join the coffee tables at the R&R every morning. But, gentlemen, hone your dice-tossing skills first. The men's table doesn't cotton to greenhorns.

GIVING THANKS

I READ IN THE *SEBEKA REVIEW MESSENGER* early in October that Miles Kuschel was named one of four finalists in the National FFA competition for Beef Production-Entrepreneurship. Well, sir, Miles went on to win the award at the National FFA convention in Louisville, Kentucky, later that month.

Here's another "local boy makes good" story. Miles had a banner year in 2002. He won a national award, and he won the hand of Sarah Funk. They were married in August, an "estimable young couple," as Bernice would report in her "Remembrance of Things Past" column in the paper. Miles won't have to scratch for something to be thankful for this Thanksgiving.

Miles is a third-generation member of the Kuschel family beef dynasty. Grandfather Morris may be a man of Ben Cartwright proportions, and the Kuschel Rocking K Ranch may be the Minnesota equivalent of the Ponderosa, but Miles is not Little Joe. He is as goal-oriented as men twice his age, and his goals are lofty. The FFA award recognized his achievement of those goals.

The Kuschels—Morris and Stella, Tom and Linda, and Miles and Sarah—form a three-way partnership. Together they own and operate 5,000 acres and rent another 240 acres for pasture. Together they own and raise 1,000 head of beef cattle. They raise their own hay; they buy their feed. Morris was a Hereford breeder, but the herd color is darkening to black, as in Black Angus, in response to market demand for Black Angus select beef. The Rocking K calf crop goes to feeder operations in Iowa and Nebraska, with 135 head retained in 2002 for replacement heifers.

The year 2002 was not without its downside for the Rocking K. Calving got off to a nasty start with the cold, wet March, and six percent of the calf crop was lost. Then haymaking was delayed and compromised by a wet spring and a dry June/July. The planned crop of 4,000 bales was limited to just over 3,000. To top off the bad luck this year, Miles and dad, Tom, were thrown from their horses in mid-summer, and suffered bruised bones, as well as bruised egos.

All the while, Miles was on his way to Louisville. He was active in FFA in high school but was ambivalent about continuing the ranching tradition. His FFA advisor (and now father-in-law) Charlie Funk helped Miles keep the ranching option open after an opportunity for a Naval Academy appointment fizzled. Charlie encouraged Miles to keep records of his ranching experience. That included a loan to bankroll his first cattle purchase—twenty-one cows in 1998. Miles was fifteen years old.

For her part, Sarah is the oldest daughter of Cheryl and Charlie Funk of the Funk Family Farm north of Nimrod, where the specialty is also, you guessed it, Black Angus. Sarah's dowry included two purebred cows and a heifer calf.

Miles entered the FFA competition through the Supervised Agricultural Experience program, which is designed to develop business skills. With his bundle of herd records—acquisition, health, breeding, and marketing, he won the 2001 Minnesota State Star honor. In April 2002, he won the Minnesota State Beef Entrepreneur award and the opportunity to compete nationally. As reported in the *Sebeka Review Messenger*, he was one of four finalists. His record keeping, now on computerized spread sheets, wowed the judges; the compulsory interview was perfunctory. He walked away with the award in late October.

The award is frosting on the cake (or gravy on the beef) for Miles. Satisfaction comes from setting goals and achieving them. Sarah and Miles have much to be thankful for in 2002. As do the rest of us, when we acknowledge the energy, dedication, and knowledge that these young people bring to a family and a local tradition.